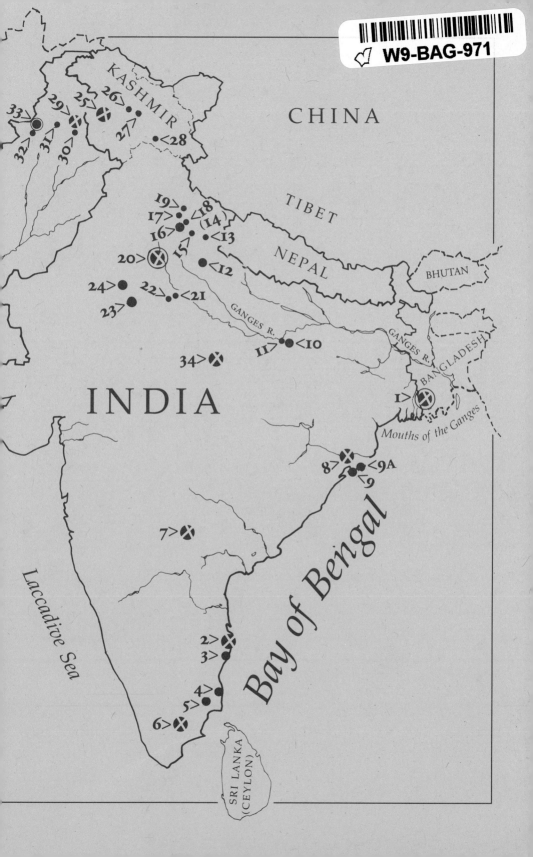

CHINA

KASHMIR

33
29>
32
31>
30>
25>
26>
27>

<28

TIBET

NEPAL

BHUTAN

19>
17>
16>
18
(14)
15>
<13

20>
<12

BANGLADESH

24>
22>
23>
<21

GANGES R.

GANGES R.

11>
<10

34>

INDIA

Mouths of the Ganges

I>

8>
<9A
9

7>

Laccadive Sea

Bay of Bengal

2>
3>
4>
5>
6>

SRI LANKA
(CEYLON)

Journey Back to Peshawar ❧

Enid, Rona's mother, on Dal Lake, *c.* 1930.

Journey Back to Peshawar ❊

RONA MURRAY

Sono Nis Press
VICTORIA, BRITISH COLUMBIA

1993

Canadian Cataloguing in Publication Data

Murray, Rona, 1924-
   Journey back to Peshawar

   Includes bibliographical references and index.
   ISBN 1-55039-034-1

   1. India—Description and travel—1901-1946.   2. India—Description
and travel—1987 and 1989   3. Murray, Rona, 1924-   4. British—India.   I. Title.
PS8526.U77Z53 1993   954.03′5′092   C93-091167-9
PR9199.3.M87Z467 1993

This book was published with the assistance of the
Canada Council Block Grant Program.

First printing October 1993
Second printing January 1994

Designed at Morriss Printing Company Ltd. by
Bev Leech

Published by
SONO NIS PRESS
1745 Blanshard Street
Victoria, British Columbia
Canada v8w 2J8

Printed and bound in Canada by
MORRISS PRINTING COMPANY LTD.
Victoria, British Columbia

FOR MY SON *Jonathan*
AND IN MEMORY OF *Robin, Irene, Lionel*
AND *Agehananda*

Other Books by Rona Murray

POETRY

The Enchanted Adder, 1965
The Power of the Dog, 1968
Ootischenia, 1974
Selected Poems, 1974
Journey, 1981
Adam and Eve in Middle Age, 1984

FICTION

The Indigo Dress and Other Stories, 1986

ANTHOLOGY

The Art of Earth, 1979

Contents

Acknowledgements

I should like to thank numerous people for helping me to obtain the material for this book. Many will remain unacknowledged: those we met while travelling in India and Pakistan: friends, hoteliers, rickshaw *wallahs*, doctors, businessmen, and guides. Others who gave me specific information are gratefully acknowledged: my father, Robin Murray, from whose unpublished memoirs I've drawn extensively, and those whom I interviewed: my mother, Enid Murray, her two sisters, Irene Garrod and Gwen Fraser; Jenny Colbourne, Gillian Hodge, Lionel Brandon, June Brandon and Pamela (Jo) Clay.

I should also like to thank Anthony Jenkins, Dilsher Virk, Gwladys Downes and Agehananda Bharati, all of whom read the manuscript and gave me advice. If there are any appalling errors, Agehananda is not to blame: he was too ill to complete his editing. I particularly want to thank those who travelled with me: my husband, Walter Dexter, Jenny Colbourne and Dale Windrem.

I should also like to thank Cheryl Samuel, who inadvertently started me on this long project, and my editors, George Payerle and Angela Addison. Above all, I am grateful to Theodore Haimberger who spent many hours patiently transcribing this material from one software programme to another in ways completely incomprehensible to me.

PART I

India Then

Chapter One

MY MOTHER'S FATHER,
Charles Gregory, was cremated on a burning *ghat*, in Dehra Dun, close
to the Himalayan foothills. His son, Eric, alone of the white community,
watched the funeral. He sat on his horse at a considerable distance, using
binoculars, while Charles's bearer performed the last rites, normally
executed by the eldest son. One of these took place some time after the
mourners had circled the fire a specific number of times, chanting *pujas*
and sprinkling the body with *ghee*: it consisted of hitting the corpse on
the head when it raised itself. The body does this at a certain stage in the
burning, and the blow on the head is given to break the skull and release
the spirit. It was a blow that devastated Eric, barely out of his teens, who
turned his horse around and rode back to his sisters. They said later that
he was limp and shaking with grief. Three young women, they helped
him from his horse, took him into the house, and gave him several
whiskies.

Charles, a member of four generations on both sides of my family
who lived in India was, like many members of those generations,
influenced by the country's metaphysical beliefs, and had become a
Spiritualist. He had asked to be cremated, but the English in India were
buried, so that there appeared to be no way of complying with his
wishes. Loved by his servants, they offered to look after him, and did. Up
to that time, and possibly still, I've been told that he was the only
Englishman to be released from his life on a Hindu burning *ghat*, replete
with its noise and smoke and casualness. It is no great disaster in India
to die if the death is a natural one; the soul is simply born again
into another body in which it continues its long pilgrimage towards
enlightenment.

Most of my aunts were also Spiritualists. They retained their beliefs,
and in the 1970s Marian, from my father's Murray side of the family,
was one of seventy corpses to go, on a single day, through a cremato-
rium in London. Her disposal was efficient, orderly, and lonely in its
assembly-line box: a stark contrast to that of Charles who in 1925, was

burned surrounded by people in a country where visible flames and smoke released the soul from the body, as they had for thousands and thousands of years.

Eric was the last of my family to leave India, forced out after Independence. Like many other British families, the Murrays and Gregorys had both been there for over a hundred years; most of them were born and some died in the country. All were affected by it.

Those who belonged to these families are now called "the children of the Raj." I am one of them, and after speaking to others I finally returned in order to reconstruct something of the life we lived and to find my own roots. Many others have done the same thing, pulled back by the language, the physical brilliance, the smells, sounds, and textures of childhood, but as a thoughtful Indian pointed out to me, we will be the last. Our children will not be interested, and that moment in history has gone forever.

❧⁂❧

In 1924, three weeks after I was born, my mother crossed London by herself, travelling on public transport, to the Ayahs' Home to find my first ayah, Pranciena Hami, known afterwards as Prancing Nahami because my family was tangled up with horses. I'd just been brought from the nursing home. Even though my mother had gone through a difficult breech birth, it's obvious women were confined far longer in those days than they are today.

I know this is reasonably true because I have a photograph of Prancing holding "her" baby, but of course the event has also become part of the family mythology, a mythology constantly shifting as people grow older, believe what they want to believe, forget, die and re-form into the next generation. This is in part the story of those mythologies, mine and other people's. There is some truth in all of it, and some fiction, and many contradictions. It relies on memories of those who grew up in a world so different from the present in terms of values, class structures, expectations, and even geographies that one can only move into it as Theseus moved into the Minotaur's cave, carrying Ariadne's thread into the darkness, without being excessively concerned over whether the turnings in the labyrinth are fantasy or reality. So, some of the ranks and positions of people I mention may be incorrect; I doubt that my grandfather owned most of Mussoorie, a hill station perched on the approaches to the Himalayas, as my mother claimed, but I don't doubt that my friend Gillian Hodge was regularly taken to the roof of a house by her ayah to make *pujas* to the Moon Momma; I'm confused over a tiger hunt because the photographs I took as a child of the dead tiger are taken in daylight, yet I appear to remember beaters with rushlights carrying it at night into the camp; it seems to me that I was told Indians put saucers of milk out as offerings to cobras, considered deities, and so encouraged them to hang around, but a childhood friend, Lionel Brandon, insists his family's servants were delighted and re- garded his father as a great *sahib* when he shot a pair of these indigenous reptiles. I'm not sure that a young subaltern in my father's regiment was the man my mother claims was involved in the order to fire on men, women and children at the massacre in Amritsar, but the date, the physical details, and the descriptions of his later personality make it probable.

My memories and those of others who enter this mythology all centre around growing up in India or being left at boarding schools in England while parents exercised their talents (or didn't) in that part of the vast pink-red section of the globe indicating the British Empire. Theirs was a Victorian or Edwardian world; even those who were born long after George V had come to the throne grew up in a society that was insular, homogeneous, and about twenty-five years behind the times.

Most of these children, now ageing or old or gone forever, were dragged away from colours and sounds and smells that haunted them throughout their lives. One said, "We didn't really belong there. We didn't belong in England, either. We don't belong anywhere." Some didn't want to return to their childhood home, feeling that everything would be changed, and some wanted to and didn't, and some have gone back, pilgrims looking for fugitive images without knowing what it is they look for. Some, as they grew older, changed with the times. Others didn't, never questioning, for instance, that their daughters should be brought up, as they or their mothers and sisters had been, to manage servants, make innocuous dinner conversation, play tennis, ride horses, speak and dress correctly, and with luck be pretty, although that was not as important as the other attributes. These daughters, they felt, would be hopelessly disadvantaged, would lose caste if they were clever or edu- cated, since they might then become opinionated, or meet the "wrong" kind of husband, or even work. At the same time, their sons' education was so important to them that they would live for years in what seemed to them penury while paying fees to a hierarchy of English public schools.

However, these "India" people agree on some basic matters: growing up, they had little to do with their parents but much to do with animals and servants; they felt secure physically despite earthquakes, snakes, worms between the toes, constant illnesses, and occasional episodes concerning tigers and corpses, and they can't imagine how "latchkey kids" survive; they were aware from a very young age of an accepted chasm between races; most of them remember their parents living highly social lives, in which they were occasionally included; almost all loved their Indian servants—the only Indians they knew—particularly their ayahs, and most hated their English nannies and governesses.

What still impressed my father most when he told the story of Pranciena Hami years later was that my mother had gone alone by public transport. He was not in the least surprised that there had been a dramatic need to find an ayah, although my mother came back from the nursing home to a house filled with women. Today I understand her decision to take the Underground because, typical of so many similar professional families of the time, small extravagances, such as using a taxi, were debated at length and generally discarded, whereas large ones, like keeping a huge house with servants in a then fashionable part of London, as my grandparents did, were accepted without question. I don't know why she went alone, but I do know why an ayah was needed. Although the household included my grandmother (my father's mother) who had birthed six children, and his sister, Marian, who produced another two, and although Irene, my mother's eldest sister was also there, none of them had had anything to do with babies and this particular baby wouldn't stop screaming. There was also a cook and there must have been housemaids, but presumably it was not their business to help out with babies. Hierarchy and duties were firmly established.

I have a photograph of my mother and myself which helps to elucidate the era. She'd brought me home in grand style, dressed in an exquisite white lawn dress and underdresses, hand embroidered in convents in India by young girls who were reputed to go blind because of the fine work; I never heard anyone suggest that perhaps they shouldn't be forced to do this intricate threading: it was simply accepted, like almost everything else, as part of the system. A marvellous new object, I was placed like a doll in the crib of white ruffles with an embroidered awning over its head. In the photograph, obviously taken after Prancing's arrival because the baby is not screaming, my mother is holding its hand and looks, with her bobbed hair, about sixteen. In fact, she was just nineteen, a young girl who'd been brought up, except for short breaks, in a hill station in India.

Prancing had come back with my mother and taken one look at the unsavoury object with which she was presented. She'd cried out in dismay, picked up the baby, and patted its back until it successfully burped up whatever formula it had been given. It must have been formula; apparently nobody in the family could nurse a baby. To do so appears to have been considered slightly obscene.

From that moment on until a couple of months later, when the family went back to India, Prancing took control. She was large, dark, and gentle, one of the many ayahs left in the Ayahs' Home by the last families to employ them to look after a child during the voyage to England. Each child had its own ayah so she wouldn't have been responsible for children in the plural. She would eventually return to India with another family, but could easily have turned up again in that limited coterie of people who travelled back and forth on leave and who passed on information about servants, houses, and the best cabins on the P. & O. Line: "Port Out, Starboard Home" if you wanted to escape the worst of the heat, led to the word "posh." When Prancing walked into the den filled with photographs of her new family, she was delighted to find a picture of another couple she'd worked for and to see the baby she'd once loved had become a little boy in an Eton jacket.

When she was first brought to that house in Nevern Square, part of Earl's Court, the cook was outraged, insisting that she couldn't possibly have a black woman eating in her kitchen. The problem solved itself. Prancing went in to heat a bottle, and they got along famously—no doubt in discussing how inept the professional British were with their babies. Cook defended her former attitude by saying, "But she isn't black. She comes from Ceylon." Racial and class divisions, so much a part of the times that they were unquestioned, were temporarily ironed out.

I found a letter from my father written to me shortly after Prancing's arrival. He'd gone to Scotland, ostensibly to play golf, but probably to get away from a household of women and a screaming baby. Reading between the lines, I'm sure the letter was his way of communicating with my mother in an attempt to justify his absence:

My darling Imp,

   I hope you are sleeping well and don't wake up too often. Also that your black faced nurse is treating you with proper respect and that you approve of your diet. It is better not to drink too much at once otherwise one is very apt to get sick just when somebody picks one up to make a fuss of one. I'm afraid you won't have been having quite so many drives in your new carriage lately, but then remember the egress and ingress is really a bit difficult without a man in the house. If you find that everything is not quite to your taste the best thing to do is to scream heartily. Now is your chance to make your voice heard; but when there is a man in the house it is really only good manners to exercise self-restraint. Remember you're a Sunday lady, and it behooves you to be happy and lucky, and wise and gay! But can one be *wise and gay*, Rona?

   Give Mummy a kiss from your affectionate Daddy,

   Robin.

A generation into the future, Robin—white-haired, self-indulgent, humorous—looked without enthusiasm at my own baby, his grandson, who also screamed and brought up stinking milk. He said gently, "I think it was better in my day, don't you, Darling, when there was someone else to look after that kind of thing?" In my heart, I agreed with him.

❧

My earliest memory is of standing up in a metal bathtub while being washed by comforting brown hands. Of course, these were not Prancing's hands but the memory is indicative of how English children bonded with people who were not their parents. It's almost as if those Anglo-Indians, as they were then called, had, over the generations (theirs was a generational commitment to India) lost the instinct for parenthood. Children were a separate entity from themselves, at least as foreign to them as the people who did bond with these white babies: the ayahs and bearers and grooms (*syces*) and sweepers. Pranciana Hami bonded; she travelled with us as far as Liverpool when my small family returned to India and wept inconsolably when her baby was taken from her.

   No doubt Enid, my mother, also wept during the three weeks' voyage. Robin had already dropped me when showing me off to a friend, and she was terrified she would complete the damage and break me totally. After all, that was the period of realistic German dolls with bisque china heads, and they were undoubtedly the nearest she'd ever come to the real thing. Somewhere out at sea, she banged my skull against the metal of the top bunk while trying to change a nappy and was certain she'd killed me. My father was not much help. He spent the time losing at chess to a man who turned out at the end of the voyage to be a Grand Master. At night, my father studied a book to work out his future moves, and during the day his opponent countered with exactly the right return. It wasn't until the final game that his fellow traveller admitted he'd written the book. Obviously both partners in this recent marital union, already exacerbated by unfulfilled expectations and sexual ignorance, had their own problems and were enormously relieved when they were met in Bombay by a new ayah my grandfather had sent them, more or less by post.

I never felt indifference on the part of my parents, but others in British India did and in some cases still resent it. Their personal histories were intertwined with what is now considered the glamour of the place and period. I'm sure those involved at the time didn't think India glamorous, but in any case children are not aware of adults' conceptions: they live accepting their circumstances as being like those of everybody else. It's only on looking back from a changed world that we realize we, the children of the Raj (a term my father, for example, would never have used) were islanded in a fragment of now completed history. Our memories consist chiefly of images, later clothed with meaning.

One of these images, indelibly printed on my mind although I wasn't present, is of a little boy, about four years old, just tall enough to look out through the window of an élite train which had stopped at a station. Miserably uncomfortable, his painfully broken arm in a sling, his formal clothes suffocating in the heat, and alone because his impatient mother had gone off somewhere, he stared straight into the eyes of an Indian boy of about his own age who was looking back at him with curiosity and awe. The boy was naked except for a cord indicating caste over one shoulder. Sick with envy, the white child gazed at the dark one, wishing he could be free and naked, could change places with the boy in front of him. He claimed nearly sixty years later that he knew, without any doubt, the other child was wishing for the same thing: to be the one travelling somewhere wonderful on a giant train. The little Indian couldn't see the sling or the wretched clothes or know that the mother of the boy he stared at had gone off somewhere, irritated that her social life had been interrupted by a foolish inconvenience. The English child was equally unaware, knowing nothing of caste restrictions, poverty, the trap of illiteracy. The two worlds met for an instant and then passed each other by.

The English child was Lionel Brandon. We'd sat beside each other in our prams. He'd broken his arm while cantering down the drive of his house on a new horse towards his father's bearer, Bhuvan Singh, who was watching him. To show off, he'd let go of the reins, held up his arms, the horse had stopped suddenly, and he'd gone flying over its head.

Image piles on image, each with its own meaning: the unsympathetic governess who pulled him up, ignoring his badly fractured arm, and dragged him into the house; blood everywhere; his mother strapping him to a mattress and driving him off in the car; Bhuvan Singh, not waiting to see what could be done, running clear across the valley to the barracks to get an ambulance; running all the way back; Lionel's sister, June, sitting deserted and frightened on the front steps until her father came home; then her father galloping off on his horse and later returning and putting her to bed: "The only time that happened. He was kind to me. Later that governess boxed my ears because I cried after seeing Lionel alone in a little whitewashed room, looking miserable."

Bhuvan Singh was their favourite person; to Lionel he was a personal father, the one who showed him how to undo his buttons and to pee, the one who was always there as guardian against snakes, wild cats, nightmares. His own father was, like my own, a distant person, generally in uniform: a man who ordered the governess to pin a map of the world on the nursery wall, strode in, and said, "The red is the British Empire and it's for you to look after and protect it."

It was the late twenties. There were some concerns — not, apparently, taken seriously by the military — about Gandhi. The British simply thought they would go on doing what they had done for generations: administer an enormous, complex country and live a decent social life with the perquisites, taken entirely for granted, of the ruling class.

It was also the time of the "fishing fleet." In a country where the white male population far outnumbered the female, and during a period when spinsters were looked upon with pitying scorn as being too plain to get a man, many unattached women went to India to find a husband. If they failed to hook one — like Lionel's older cousin, who then returned to England and married her mother's chauffeur, and like his own governess — they were referred to as "returned empties": a term so derogatory, it's small wonder that those who worked as governesses or nannies became short-tempered as their time ran out. Some certainly would today be considered criminally abusive, but the children in their command were impotent and isolated, occupying the link, along with those in charge of them, in the hierarchical chain of command stretching between parents and servants. The governesses and nannies were all-powerful and were believed; their charges were not, as they discovered very quickly. If children were lucky enough to be left to easy-going ayahs and other servants, these were the people with whom they bonded and whose fading images remained with them to the end of their lives.

We understand each other, those of us who are now scattered across England, Canada, the U.S.: the remnants of a dead empire.

❧

The Brandons lived in Dehra Dun in northeast India, where their father, like my own, was in the 9th Gurkha Rifles. Gillian Hodge lived during the same period in Calcutta, where her father was a *box-wallah*—a businessman. She remembers being always with a tiny, very black ayah, who wore her sari pulled over her face and gave her an enchanted childhood. Together they climbed a turret in her ayah's family house where they would stand in the warm night air above the city chanting *pujas* to the Moon Momma. Together they went to Kalighat, the great temple dedicated to Black Kali, the terrifying goddess of destruction and regeneration, who had formerly been, and sometimes still was, although it was strictly outlawed, supplied with human sacrifices by *Thuggee* adherents. The small child watched the ceremonial stretchers with their burdens being brought in to the burning *ghats* and learned to fear neither corpses nor death.

Her tiny guardian was always there and grounded her life in security, whether she was playing with tiger cubs in the zoo on Sundays when it was supposed to be closed or surviving earthquakes which bent palm trees to the ground and shot open cupboard doors in a deranged house. "The Indians know how to love," she says simply. "It's a gift."

And they know how to laugh. Gillian's goldfish died. Desolate, she persuaded one of the lesser servants, a young boy, to go through their funeral with her. He performed with proper solemnity while they found an appropriate place, scattered flowers, recited *pujas*, and buried the corpses. Then, unable to contain himself, he burst out laughing and couldn't stop, running away and disappearing, it seemed forever. After three days he returned, having regained his self-respect after giving way to his feelings in front of Gillian-baba.

Gillian's ayah taught her the taboos of the country. For example, she learned that the gardener was of the brahman caste and cooked the servants' food. If she let her shadow fall across his preparations, they would be polluted and have to be thrown away: there would not be more — people would go hungry. By extension, she learned to give people their own space and for years was uncomfortable about invading others' private territory. Her instinct, like my own, has been to stand back, considered an aloof quality in the Western world.

The only memory Gillian has of her parents is of being taken down to have afternoon tea with them after her bath, carried out in a tin basin. She remembers no instance of affection from them and was not invited to join them for dinner until she was sixteen. She didn't miss their love, but being dragged away from her ayah to be sent to England to boarding school when she was six years old, was a calamity. Isolated and disciplined, like so many other children, she was desperately unhappy.

Jenny Colbourne, also from Calcutta, left India during the Second World War with her brother and parents. She was close to them, but had been brought up by her ayah, Blanche, who'd also raised her older cousins, one of whom told her he'd thought Blanche was his mother. His real mother was to him the lady who kissed him good night and sometimes asked him to lunch on Sundays. Blanche was part of the family and when all her children were taken from her, she went mad and killed herself. They had not said goodbye because nobody was supposed to know when ships sailed. Jenny had simply been told they were going on a picnic. She had no idea she would never see Blanche again.

That separation was her second encounter with the world we consider real, enhanced as it was by arriving in a dreary railway station in Glasgow. The first encounter, carrying with it the shock that life is not entirely gentle, had taken place in another railway station some time before. Lepers on the platform were besieging passengers for *baksheesh.* A U.S. soldier, laughing loudly with other soldiers at the joke, dropped a coin into the hole where the beggar's nose had once been.

Other things that would shock Westerners today were so common they were taken for granted: people travelling in heat, dust, and soot on the roofs of trains; skinny children with distended bellies (oddly, in photographs, my sister and I also have distended bellies) chanting *Kuch Mama, kuch Papa* (some from you, Mama, some from you, Papa) in railway stations while they did back flips and begged for a few *pice*; the arrogance white children sometimes adopted towards servants—a six- or seven-year-old telling a bearer who brought him a banana to go back and serve it properly on a tray—and their astonishment when transferred to boarding schools at being expected to pick up their own clothes, do their own mending. Jenny, apparently, was so enraged she threw all her clothes out of the window.

We were all surrounded by animals. Pamela Clay, also from Calcutta, was taught by her family's Nepalese and Tibetan servants (she claims she practically never saw her parents or witnessed any affection between them) how to make and fly kites, how to construct reed pipes and play them, but most of all how to manage snakes: she was to pin them down with a forked stick. She remembers being in bed one morning with her door open when a jackal walked in, looked at itself in the mirror, and walked out again. She didn't tell anyone, it seemed such a usual kind of event, and probably was.

Lionel's sister, June Brandon, kept a book on her bed with which to frighten jackals off during the hot weather when we would sleep on our various verandahs: "When I heard one, I'd kick the book off so it would thump on the floor and then I'd crawl out under the mosquito net and retrieve it and wait for the next time. The *chaukidar* [watchman] would go around at night—tap, tap, tap with his stick—but he'd fall asleep and then the jackals would come. The brain fever bird would be calling out, and the humneysota bird with its 'I don't sleep, I don't sleep' over and over again. Flying foxes hung from beams and telephone lines and their fleas would drop off, so we were told not to stand underneath them. And once I found a snake hanging from a beam in the bathroom and got absolutely hysterical, and ran off to find my father who threw it out. He said I was being idiotic and making a fuss over nothing because it wasn't a poisonous one. It was useful; it ate the rats. I felt very humbled. But then a man came to the door on a bicycle to take our Siamese kittens away and said there was a snake in the garden. My father took his #9 golf club out to kill it—he always used his #9 for things like that—and found the snake was a cobra. He told me to keep completely still, and sent his bearer in to get a gun, and he shot it. We knew the mate would be around and weren't allowed to play outside until he'd killed it as well.

"We saw our parents at breakfast after our morning ride. My donkey would come into the dining room and eat toast. It used to wander around the house. Once I was resting in my mother's room—we always had to rest in the afternoon—and the donkey came in and blew into her powder bowl and got powder all over its face. When it put its head up and saw its reflection in the mirror, it brayed, but of course the mirror didn't answer, so it turned around and kicked the glass to pieces. My mother was furious.

"It was absolutely understood by everybody that it was my donkey. One night when my parents were having a dinner party, they brought it in and their guests started riding it around the dining room, going over obstacles. I could hear them from my bed and was outraged, so I marched in and said it was mine and they couldn't do that, and I took it away.

"They were very good parties, and sometimes we were told what went on. One game they played was to hide all the utensils in a covered bowl. The guests had to reach in and take something out and then eat their entire meal with whatever they'd taken. The colonel ended up once with the sugar tongs."

These dinners were long, full-dress affairs. Eight courses were standard. The food was also standard, starting off with sardines on toast and going on to mulligatawny soup, even though all the memsahibs were armed with Mrs. Beeton's 2056-page tome, *Book of Household Management*, which included a chapter on "Indian Cookery" with the advice: "Indian servants are good, many of them: but they cannot be trusted and will cheat if they have a chance, and it is absolutely necessary to look after the cook (*Khansaman*) who will probably be the marketer."[1] I'm sure my own mother must have discussed the marketing, but I know she never went into the kitchen—she said this was not done and would have upset the cook, who was high caste—or had the faintest idea how to make mulligatawny soup, although she probably could have managed sardines on toast if she'd had to.

On her seventh birthday, June was called from her bed to one of these parties and all the guests, in dinner jackets and long dresses, stood up and drank her health. It's probable that my own parents were there since theirs was a small world, twelve officers to a regiment, and possibly June's parents were part of the only dinner party I remember seeing. My frail sister, Dawn, who was two years younger than I, was supposed to have some kind of medicine every night, but that night it had been

[1] This word has nothing to do with "man." Correctly, it's not hyphenated or capitalized, but is *khansaman*.

forgotten. I lay in bed, feeling desperately shy and also nervous about going in to the party—I suppose my ayah had gone for the night—but at the same time thinking she might die, and if she did, it would be my fault. Finally I crawled out from the netting and went to the dining room door and told my mother. After a stunned silence, everyone laughed, and my mother, who was wearing an exquisite sequined dress, came into the nursery and produced the medicine. Dawn remembers the dress and today says this is the only time she recalls seeing our mother in India.

Now, over half a century later, the Brandons and I discovered a connection through a wild cat and the Siamese kittens taken away by the man with his bicycle after the cobra incident. They were coming to us as gifts for Dawn and myself. They were barely with us before they disappeared. By that time, I slept at the end of the verandah in a room slightly separated from the rest of the house, and one night a man, probably a *mali*, came in and demanded that I give him my kitten, which he insisted was in bed with me. I insisted it wasn't, and he stripped the bedclothes off, looking for it. He was no doubt frightened because the kittens were his responsibility and couldn't be found. My mother decided they must have been killed by a mythical and enormous wild cat that lived on the mountain behind the house. This was the only animal, never seen and mysteriously unreal, that I felt nervous about, because it was reputed to be outrageously fierce. Now I know it actually existed.

June's mother, Pauline, decided Bhuvan Singh should kill it as it had also been after their kittens. Having made her decision, she went off to a party. June says: "I was in my room and Lionel was in a little room off it. The idea was that the window should be left open to wait for this cat to come in because it had used that way before. Mother didn't ask how Bhuvan Singh was going to kill it, but she'd promised him something if he did. Away she went, and Bhuvan Singh waited by the window while he told us—we were holding shoetrees or something equally ridiculous to protect ourselves with—to keep back. When the cat came in, I jumped into bed and hid under the bedclothes while he chased it and bludgeoned it to death. Everything came down—the curtains and the furniture and the china washbasin, which was smashed. It seemed to take hours, but at last the cat was dead and its corpse thrown onto the roof. There was blood everywhere. When mother came home, she looked around the room, and said, 'What's been going on here?' She seemed to be astonished."

Pauline Brandon was beautiful and social and obsessed with clothes. After her first husband died, she married into the minor aristocracy. Like many of the British, she was anti-Semitic; it was years before her children worked out that she had Jewish ancestry. Also like many others of the time, she knew nothing about the facts of life and thought when she was seven months pregnant she was swelling because she had appendicitis. We think now that she and my mother, just eighteen when she married and affectionately called "Old Bean" in the regiment, were social rivals.

Pauline had been the youngest of the wives with a small child, but Old Bean, when she arrived back from England with her first baby, was even younger and apparently having a baby gave one some kind of additional status. Their rivalry focused in the Dehra Dun Club, the centre of social life, where precedence was followed as closely as it was in the Officers' Mess. There, Pauline had queened it since her husband had been the ranking officer, but Old Bean's husband, Robin, was his senior, even though at the time they were both majors. Seniority — the system was so well defined — rested on the actual day the man in question had joined the army: April the first, for example, held sway over April the fifth. Until my mother's arrival, Pauline had poured the tea and acted as hostess when the women were involved with the men in tennis parties. My mother still screws up her face when she talks of her: "Of course, that kind of thing doesn't mean anything to me, so I used to say, 'Pauline, would you mind dreadfully pouring the tea today? I'm rather tired after all that tennis,' and so, of course, she did."

Protocol among the memsahibs was quite possibly more pronounced than among the sahibs, and it apparently lasted without the slightest bending until the end. Jenny Colbourne's aunt, who lived in Nainital, was awarded a medal for war work: she was involved in rehabilitating those people who had marched out of Burma. According to the account she gave her niece, she was trying to "chivvy-up co-operation among the memsahibs who were doing nothing and arranged a lunch party to talk to them about it. But in those circles the seating was set according to the rank of the husband, and my aunt put the wrong woman — the captain's wife — next to her, so the major's and colonel's wives were miffed and the whole thing was a disaster. Nothing came of it."

This sense of hierarchy was transmitted to the children. One day when the Brandons were brought over to play with us — and I only remember this happening once — I reacted with dislike towards June, not only because she was older than I was and more aggressive, but also because she had a toy typewriter which I lusted after and which she wouldn't let me touch. When we finally met again, over fifty years later, we both recalled that early contact, and June looked at me in astonishment when I told her how I'd felt. She said she'd been overawed by me and unenthusiastic about the afternoon because I was in some undefined way more "upper" than she was: my father held a rank higher than her father.

As children, we—Gillian, Jenny, Pamela, the Brandons, and myself —all remember the tennis parties. Along with riding, polo, soccer, hiking, hunting, boxing, and shooting, they were part of the intensely physical and social life people lived. All were taken seriously. One woman, Cuckoo Wall, became a myth overnight because the umpire forgot an entire set of tennis she'd played and won, giving her the victory. Undismayed, and aware that one never argued with the umpire in good society, she played the whole set over and won it again. So much was made of this that I've never forgotten it. As for us, we went with our ayahs and were given freedom, since no adults paid us much attention, to climb the huge trees in the Club garden. Occasionally, we would overhear adult conversation. June listened to her father saying caustically to another man, "There are two things that should never run: women and cows." She repeated it, thinking it a good joke, and her father was never forgiven.

Pauline and my mother were also rivals, not only with each other, but also with all the other mothers, when it came to original costumes for children's fancy-dress parties. These were given all over India, and most of the people I've talked to remember them with loathing. They were part of the life of our parents, who were to display their ingenuity through us and our costumes, made by dressmakers (*darzies*) who were always men. They would sit on verandahs for days before the big event, making Robin Hood and Peter Pan and Snow Queen costumes, and we knew that something pretty awful was in store for us. The characters meant little to us; we had no connection with the people or things we were supposed to represent. Also, we were on our best behaviour and among adults who were largely strangers. My particular nightmare, so vivid that when I returned to India over fifty years later I knew exactly where the cloakroom in the Club was located, occurred when I was dressed as an English paperboy.

I was about six and believed I was hopelessly unattractive, possibly because I was continually told how like my father I was. My father was dark and had a military moustache which prickled when he kissed me. He was, in fact, a handsome man, but not to a child who thought in terms of a soft, young, blonde mother, with whom her sister was always compared. In all truthfulness, I have to admit my costume must have been exceptionally original, but to appear in ragged clothes with bare feet and a satchel containing newspapers slung over my shoulder was excruciating, adding as it did to my sense of being ugly to begin with. To make matters worse, my sister was appearing as a dainty blue powder-puff. In any case, I didn't know anything about paperboys, and when a smiling man asked me if he could buy a paper, I hadn't the faintest idea what he meant and felt mortified. Soon it seemed that every adult at the party, many in high heels, was stepping on my naked feet. The pain was appalling. I'd already learned that I should never cry, to do so was utterly shameful, but finally I did. My embarrassed mother carried me out of the room and deposited me alone in the cloakroom to sob in private. On the way out, we passed "Father Christmas" and she asked if I could have a present from his bag ahead of the others since I was obviously leaving the party. He let me choose one off the top, and it turned out to be a rattle. Even at that age, I recognized the irony of being given a baby's toy when I was behaving like a baby, and remember screaming even louder in protest.

Lionel dreaded these parties so much that he has a memory of one which centred on his standing on a bridge over a stream filled with alligators which were snapping and attempting to tear him to pieces. Inside, the party was going on and his shouts for help were ignored. He thinks now this may have been a nightmare; if so, it indicates how he felt about these charged occasions.

We also had private parties. At a Christmas entertainment held at our house, we had a tree lighted with candles in the garage. Dressed up to the nines, we hovered around the tree—children who were largely strangers to each other—while presents were being distributed by Father Christmas. Unfortunately, his beard caught on fire, and he was forced to whip it off, along with his white wool hair and red suit. A tactless little girl shouted: "It isn't Father Christmas, it's Major Murray." I'd known it was my father, but felt ashamed at its being pointed out for all to see: I thought the fiction should have been maintained even if he'd been burnt to a crisp in the process.

In that instance, there were parents present, but generally ayahs or nannies took us to children's parties where we sat around damask tablecloths eating jellies and milk puddings. An ayah stood behind each child's chair, helping her charge to eat and drink without making a mess.

We, the India children, also remember performing at concerts. The adults must have put on shows as well, since my parents, Robin and Enid, met on one of these occasions, but ours must have been separate. We, helped by old snapshots, remember our triumphs. We performed dances as pierrettes and pierrots, as fairies and elves, on the stage in the Dehra Dun Club. We must have taken dancing classes, but I have no memory of them. What I do remember is the wildly enthusiastic applause—I can't believe we were in any way entertaining or accomplished, but that made no difference—and the enormous numbers of flowers we were presented with: bouquet after bouquet, each calling for more clapping. I doubt if many opera divas have received so many. Possibly some of us expected this kind of response to our doubtful talents all our lives and were dismayed to discover we weren't, after all, brilliant virtuosi.

To set the record straight, I should mention that there must have been some tangential social contact between the races. June recalls a party given by her mother which included Indian women and their children. She doesn't know who the women were, but she does know they were so well-mannered that when they were served MacIntosh toffees, which they'd never seen before, they ate them paper and all. In that society, the polite thing would have been to make a guest comfortable through imitation if she did something gauche or unexpected. June doesn't remember if her mother ate her toffee papers.

◈

Thinking about all this now, I recognize something rather extraordinary: these particular "children of the Raj" who were forced out of the country, all, except for my sister Dawn who became a professional horsewoman, grew into artists of one kind or another. Lionel, a successful geologist, is happiest choosing the colours of plants for his garden; Gillian, vibrantly alive, her hair in an untidy bun, her face smudged with clay, is a sculptor; Jenny works with fine porcelain; Pamela is a miniaturist, June a Chinese brush artist: all have shown and sold successfully.

They are not amateurs. My passion became poetry. Were we affected by a vivid physical world which we attempt to recreate, or are we trying to fill an emptiness born from lack of parental ties or from the loss of our original home? Had a political upheaval not occurred, the women among us would no doubt have been part of the fishing fleet and become memsahibs: a dismaying possibility.

Chapter Two

*E*NID GREGORY MET ROBIN Murray at the Dehra Dun Club through his sister, Rona, the beautiful and—according to her future sister-in-law—spoilt youngest child in her family. Rona was my father's delight. He had escorted her around London, taking her to *Chu Chin Chow* and other musicals during a leave after the First World War, still a period when one was in society or out of it. They were meeting people such as Frank Harris, editor, novelist and biographer, who was "in." Robin had been particularly impressed with Harris's courtesy when he met him in the editorial office of a London newspaper, *John Bull*, owned by a family connection, which the writer was thinking of buying. He'd asked my father if they would see each other again at a party that evening, and Robin answered that no, they didn't travel in those circles. Harris said with great charm, "You will, my dear fellow, you will."

I can't believe my father had any wish to travel in those circles, but even so he said each day he and Rona would stick invitations onto their mirrors after the mail came in and then decide which event would be the most entertaining.

They'd gone back from London to Robin's regiment in Dehra Dun and the provincial club where Enid was performing in an amateur concert. She'd returned once more to India from England with her much-travelled family which had already sustained two disastrous voyages. "Voyage" is the appropriate word; today, no matter where travellers go—it can be around the world—they talk of a "trip" because "voyage" sounds pretentious and because wherever their destination, they get there within a few hours. Then, the usual time it took to travel between England and India was three and a half weeks, but any number of incidents could interfere with this schedule, particularly during the war. In 1916, the Gregorys had been torpedoed and deposited in lifeboats while sailing to England on the last ship to be allowed through the Suez Canal. The ship did not go down, however, and finally limped into port. Soon after arrival, Charles Gregory decided he was not going to leave his girl children, whose education was of little importance, in England with a war on, and after being held up for close to a year by difficulties in obtaining tickets and by bouts of measles which one child after another contracted (at the final bout he broke down and wept), he got passages on a troopship going to Canada. They were further held up in Liverpool because of submarines and the deaths, considered very unlucky, of sailors who drank methylated spirits. Luck was reversed when a passenger produced twins and they were off to sea again, spending much time on deck in life-jackets. In Halifax the great explosion of 1917 had taken place so the ship docked at Saint John. After crossing the continent to Vancouver, they took the *Empress of Russia* to Hong Kong, where they had to remain for a month: the boat on which they were to sail to India had been infected with the plague. There the family with its three young children (their brother had been left at school in England) was at a football match when a ghastly accident occurred in the bleachers; a raging fire took off, started by one of the people who were under the wooden structure cooking delicacies for the crowd. Afterwards, Enid and her sisters saw mounds of dead surrounded by relatives who were roasting pigs for the departed to eat in the next world. Finally on board again, they discovered their ship carried 375 mules in the hold. Irene, the eldest child, appalled at their conditions, carried little bowls of water down for them during the long voyage through the South China Sea and Indian Ocean and was much commended for being so tender-hearted.

Those journeys could hardly be considered propitious; the next one back to India some five years later took the usual time, and its embarkation was the kind of event I can myself remember: the excitement of the ship leaving; the paper streamers tossed across the water breaking as the vessel edged out; the crowds on the dock waving to friends and relatives leaning against the ship's railings; the stacks blowing smoke and blasting out long, painful goodbyes; the massive numbers of steamer trunks, wooden crates, black hatboxes, green canvas suitcases crossed over with curved wooden struts; the flowers and fruit and chocolates and no doubt bottles of whisky and champagne. Travelling was not to be taken lightly.

Before that voyage, Enid had had two years in her English boarding school. Unlike any other India people I know, she looked back on those years as a time of marvellous joy and never quite escaped them. The friendships, the "crushes," the small intrigues, the nicknames, delighted her. The educational aspects were entirely secondary. Long afterwards, she claimed she'd wanted to be a doctor and had told her father she studied Latin under the bedclothes at night so she could qualify. He said that was ridiculous and since she looked like a waif on boarding school food, she was to return with him to Mussoorie, a hill station outside Dehra Dun. Charles Gregory was a kindly man, and I'm sure he would have taken her seriously had she been serious, but in reality to her as to almost everyone else, academic achievement was looked down upon: a girl was a "blue stocking" and a boy a "sweat"—both derogatory terms—if they studied, even though boys were expected to do well and were rigorously disciplined if they didn't. After what must have been a truly sadistic training in their public schools, the young men were to rule the Empire. For their part, the girls were to marry them. Enid's father stated: "No daughter of mine will work," and he would have considered her doing so, as she did after his death, a personal failure.

When Robin met Enid, she was seventeen, no doubt missing her friends, and he was thirty-three. She had honey-coloured hair and blue eyes and recited a poem about a dog that had to have its ears and tail cropped. She'd had elocution lessons and been taught to place heavy emotional emphasis on every word. I never heard her recite that poem, but I did hear her recite another about fairies having never a penny to spend, so know what it must have been like—excruciating to a modern listener, but in 1922 that was the style. In any case, it went down well and my father, when he told the story, said he thought she was "perfectly sweet." He was now at the right age and rank to marry (this was not permitted until an officer had reached the rank of captain, which occurred at a specific age, no matter what qualifications and aptitudes were present), so he did.

There's little doubt she was attracted to him because he was a romantic figure. One of the first pilots to be granted a civil licence (#320), he'd been known as "Mad Murray" by brother officers in the RFC, to which he'd been seconded for part of the war, had been highly recommended for the VC and had been awarded the DFC and MC. Good at athletics, he was a champion shot, amateur boxing champion of India in his category, and a renowned polo player. He never spoke of these accomplishments and the only reference I heard my mother make to them, after conditions were less romantic, was that he gave up boxing "after he killed all the people he boxed with." Apparently one of them did die.

On the night before her wedding, Enid was being bathed by her ayah, Jamuni. Sitting in the tub filled by the *bhisti* she asked Jamuni where babies came from. One can only suppose she'd been puzzling about this for some time, although she claims now that neither she nor anyone she knew ever thought about sex at all. In any case, she knew by osmosis that this was a topic to be avoided under almost all circumstances.

Jamuni, squatting by the tub, asked her where she thought they came from.

"Out of my tummy-button."

Jumuni rocked back and forth, gasping with laughter and covering her face with her hands at the deliciousness of it. Finally she said, "Missi-sahib, Missi-sahib, if the memsahib hasn't told you, I won't."

Enid insists she could never have asked her mother, so she went to her marriage as ignorant as she'd been before the bath. Robin had chosen Manasbal Lake, a remote and private area in Kashmir, as the place for their honeymoon. He loved natural beauty and gardens and she loved shopping, particularly finding bargains, but men made the decisions and she wasn't consulted. They went there by train, and during the journey hints of her vast ignorance emerged (for example, she'd come to the conclusion that God would let her know she was to have a baby by writing a message on her tummy). From that point on, Robin jumped out of the carriage at every station, and she wondered why. He must have been thoroughly disturbed, because he was trying frantically to find the only book available at the time on sexual matters: a publication by Margaret Sanger. That he should expect to find it among whatever journals were sold in Indian railway stations is beyond belief. He didn't.

To my knowledge, his and my mother's conversation never moved beyond the day's trivialities, so it must have been impossible at that point for him to discuss sex with her. They had to wait for the wedding night, which was obviously far from successful. Robin's father, Robert Murray, a Colonel in the Indian Medical Service (IMS) stationed in Calcutta, was in charge of hundreds of lives, but knew no more about the female psychological aspects of sex than Enid did. He'd told his sons women were incapable of sexual pleasure and could not experience orgasm, although some might pretend to do so. It was a general view that women co-operated as their marital duty and men had conjugal rights. Robert Murray had, however, recognized the need for male sexual relief and the problems late marriages caused: he'd given Robin a list of Indian prostitutes who were free from venereal disease.

Much later in her life, Enid, in some respects an emancipated woman, still could not say the word "sex" without lowering her voice an octave and speaking in a whisper while looking around to check who was in the room. She looked on the sexual act as "a part of married life, which doesn't take long, you know," and remembered Robin's anger on the boat going to India after I was born, when she'd told him it was too much trouble to take off her clothes so they could make love. Her mother, Louise Gregory, had a favourite saying: "The back is made to fit the burden." She had aborted without knowing she was pregnant while travelling by bullock cart from Bombay to Poona and was told she would never bear more children. She did after several years: five of them, with one dying in infancy. Mary McInnis Mackay, Robert Murray's wife and my other grandmother, whose father was also a medical man, a Surgeon-General in the IMS, must have conceived her six children without pleasure — or at least without admitting to any; she never bonded with them in any real sense, leaving them for years in England in boarding schools during the term and with tutors and governesses in the holidays, apparently without regret.

With this background, it's hardly surprising that few marriages of the time were emotionally satisfying. They were not expected to be fulfilling in the contemporary sense, but to be held together through surface detail, endless small duties, entertainments, physical activities. Maintaining them, however, was not as difficult as it might today appear to have been because education and expectations were so different. My aunt, Gwen Fraser, Enid's younger sister, pointed out recently that at the time people didn't question who they were or whether or not they were living fruitful lives. Freud's work had been published but had not reached the general public, and certainly had not reached India. Havelock Ellis would have been considered obscene and irrelevant had anyone come across him: irrelevant because, according to Gwen, "Everybody held the same opinion. One didn't run into ideas or concepts. We didn't read, and we didn't think in a way that might be different from the way other people thought. There were some individuals who did read, like my father, but he was a man and he wasn't in the army. For us, thinking and reading were not encouraged so there was no bursting out to have careers or leaving husbands to discover oneself. I don't think there was any — or at least very little — sex before marriage, if only because pregnancy was such a disgrace. Divorce was a disgrace, too, especially for the woman, even if she hadn't done anything wrong.

Women had some power if they were cunning and could please, but they were always taught to put their husbands first, to 'consider' them. That was the important thing."

Enid and Robin never, until I questioned them, talked about their honeymoon—not, as far as I know, because they wanted to avoid the topic, although this is possible, but because my mother seldom spoke about the past and when my father did, it was in anecdotal terms, not about what shaped him as a person. I once tried to open him up, to ask if he had had any sexual instruction, apart from the questionable information his father gave him, at school or elsewhere. His face closed up instantly, and he said only: "No, never." It was a taboo subject. Extremely loyal to his family, he never criticised them for his ignorance on personal matters—to do so would not have occurred to him—or for an upbringing that lacked affection, but felt, rather, that he'd been caught in a ridiculous system, which years later he tended to laugh at although he was still haunted by small social gaucheries: attempting as a very young man to tip in a club, being trapped on public transport by a deaf aunt who wanted to know how much money he was making when to talk about money at all was considered indecent. It was the small embarrassments, failures, and successes that surfaced, never the vast depths beneath them.

I was born in London ten months after their vigil by the lake. They went because I would have been the first child of the third generation on both sides to have been born in India, and this was considered, especially by Charles Gregory, my grandfather, to be unlucky. He insisted the risk should not be taken. His insistence grew out of a superstitious belief, but that belief is hardly surprising when one considers the numbers of white babies and young children whose graves are scattered across the subcontinent: going through old graveyards, one may discover three, four, five headstones placed for infants and children, and then another commemorating their still young mother. On the other hand, it's perhaps more surprising how many survived, considering dysentery, diphtheria, smallpox, typhoid, cholera, malaria, and other discomforts such as hookworm, to which 45,000,000 Indians were host in the 1920s.

Chapter Three

*T*WO INTENSE IMAGES OF my earliest years have been retrieved for me through hypnotism. They vividly contrast the ways in which the Indians and the British nurtured children.

The first is of a very small child—myself—standing in front of her ayah who is seated in a rattan armchair. They are outside in a garden with rather long grass and shrubby trees. The ayah puts her arms around the child who lays her head in a large, comfortable lap. The woman's breasts seem very big above the child's head and her face below its sari seems enormous: a round, dark face with gold earrings in the ears and a gold ring through the nose. It's a warm, not hot day, with insects making buzzing noises. No one else is close by. The child's sense is one of being content and secure in a love which demands nothing. It doesn't matter what she does: she can't do anything that is either "good" or "bad," right or wrong. The ayah, who must have been Gangadi, sent to meet my parents at Bombay, sings to her as she half sleeps in this protective cocoon.

As an adult under hypnotism, I was astonished by my hunger to find the forgotten language Gangadi used. The craving for the words, my first, was so intense that I wanted to cry out, to burst into tears, aware that they were locked, apparently irretrievably, at the brink of my mind. Very slowly, in bits and pieces, the lullaby returned: *Acha baba, acha baba, / bene baba, bene baba / nalli-nalla / nalli-nalla-nalla.* I could hear her voice singing it. Then a few spoken phrases emerged, very few.

That language was the language of the first sights, sounds, and smells; it was the language of the feel of a white sari, of the uncluttered taste of sweetness. The lost child words of a lost paradise. My ears were sharper than they are today, and my eyes could see every bright detail of daisies in grass and leaves on shrubs a few feet away.

I don't doubt the image, partly because other, related images emerged. A child sitting on a sisal mat, following a pink pattern on it with her index finger while an ayah stands beside her, holding something in a bowl for her to eat. The hem of a sari hangs just above dark ankles, the feet are broad, almost black, and the skin is cracked and dry, particularly near the soles. They appear very large. The scene shifts to a child in an ayah's arms. She's aware of the breasts above her and of the big, tender face looking down at her. She's entirely comfortable.

The next image is based on an incident I remember consciously, but I had forgotten the actual feel of the paralysing fear that went with it. When I was three years old, my parents returned to England on leave and engaged a nanny, always called Nana.

The image is not set in Dehra Dun, but in what I remember as a room in a strange house or hotel in Gulmarg, a mountain resort in Kashmir, or in Peshawar on the North-West Frontier. The child is in a small bed beside her sister's bed and is under mosquito netting. She's uncomfortably conscious of how she lies down, trying to do it correctly so she won't get into trouble. She's not allowed to sleep on her left side because her heart is on that side; she's not allowed a pillow because if she has one she will get round-shouldered; she's not permitted to sleep with her arm beneath her body because she will get pins and needles in it. Most of all, she must not suck her thumb because if she does the Scissor Man will come in and cut it off. The Scissor Man has scissors the size of garden shears. He's tall with hair that flies back from his head, and he's dressed in a blue jacket and red breeches. He runs extremely fast and comes at any moment. There are pictures of him in a book called *Struwwelpeter*. When he cuts your thumbs off, they drop on the ground and great gobs of blood fall on the ground too. After he's cut the thumbs off the little boy who is also in the picture, Mama comes home and looks at him from the doorway and says, "Ah! I knew he'd come to naughty little Suck-a-Thumb."

The child is sucking her thumb, and somebody (no doubt Nana) who cannot be seen comes into the dark room very quietly. The child whips the thumb out of her mouth and clutches it with her fingers, hiding both her fists under the bedclothes, terrified. The enormous scissors are under the netting. They seem to be disembodied as they hunt in the darkness over her head, looking for what they want.

"Scissor Man," "scissors," "hair," "thumbs," and so on, are English words. If my sister, Dawn, and I spoke our first language, Hindustani—and at eighteen months, she was barely speaking—or if I spoke it to the servants, Nana would mock, screwing up her face, gabbling, and poking her hands at me like a monkey. With unremitting visual and aural censorship, she attempted to take the language away from me, substituting her own. She needed to know everything I did and said. Dawn was less vulnerable, because she was the adored baby, still almost speechless, who had been faithfully nursed through a nearly fatal bout of dysentery by Nana and thus had established close bonds with her. But for me, the connotation of English words must be associated with this new regime during which I was being whipped into shape after being "spoiled by ayahs."

Curiously, Nana was a Cockney with a Cockney accent. This did not appear to worry my parents so much as our picking up a "chee-chee" accent, for fear of which they'd preferred, when we were with our ayahs and other servants, our speaking Hindustani to English. Even so, Robin said later that he'd been disturbed by her senseless gabbling as I, at least, was speaking a perfectly good language. However, he did nothing about it. It was understood that parents abdicated control if they wished to keep an English nurse who was there not only to give them freedom, but also because she knew so much more about children than they did.

They hired Nana while in England, despite her Cockney accent, for a curious reason. First they interviewed a Norland nanny. Norland nannies went through a rigorous training for two years and also came from a class which spoke acceptable English. Enid said, much later, "Robin would have paid—that wasn't the trouble. But she came to tea for the interview—if you had one of them, they were supposed to be part of the family, to eat with you and so forth and so on. But that girl was so nervous she had a terrible accident. She made a mess—you know—all over the chair. A bowel mess. We really couldn't have her living with us if she did things like that, especially when we had to pay her so much."

Enid was twenty-two at the time and not autocratic. She was probably almost as nervous as the nanny, who must have been eighteen or nineteen. It's extraordinary to think she could have had such a terrifying effect on anyone and causes one to wonder what kind of pulverizing background that girl must have had.

We all tend to live by tradition, and if tradition is followed blindly we continue in established patterns, learning little or nothing from experience. So it was with the tradition of keeping nannies. Enid had had her own, Carry Sharp, who'd made much of her childhood a hellish experience. Robin, in England away from his parents as a very small child—eighteen months—had a nursery governess who took down his trousers and beat him constantly; surprisingly, he told my mother he thought this woman received sexual pleasure from doing so. The Brandons had their governess who was spiteful and unsympathetic. My father's cousin, Jessie Murray, also an India child but one who spent some time in Scotland, remembered being yanked by her arm along a street in Inverness and being told by her nanny that if she didn't behave she would be stripped of her skin and hung up on a hook like the carcasses of beef in a butcher's shop they were passing. She was dragged into the shop with its sawdust-covered floor and bloody aprons. She claimed she screamed with such terror the muscles of her eyes were damaged, and she was cross-eyed from then on. When I knew her as a middle-aged woman, she was not cross-eyed, but did have weak eyes with a cast in one of them. I've no idea if terror could actually have sustained such damage, but she certainly believed it had.

There were undoubtedly lovely Mary Poppins nannies, and perhaps for Dawn, Nana was one of them since the pattern was also established that there was the favourite child. In any case, my aunt, Gwen, who is astonishingly direct, says I was a brat and something had to be done about it, and my other aunt, Irene, said, shocked when I questioned them about the need for English nannies: "But you couldn't have been left alone with ayahs." Of course, we were left alone with ayahs, and other children—Gillian, Pamela—never had nannies, so it may have been a question of prestige or expectation. Fortunately for me, two years after joining us, Nana died, and we were left once more to comfortable ayahs and, briefly, to a gentle and ineffective governess, Beatrice, a member of the "fishing fleet," who found herself a handsome officer whom I, with a child's intuition, secretly and thoroughly distrusted.

Even my mother had forgotten Nana's name until I found a signed letter from her recently. She was always "Nana." She was very small and was over seventy when she came to us. This was in 1927, which means she was born in about 1857 and trained in 1877. The dates suggest that I am one of the few people who knows today what a Victorian childhood was all about. The impression on me has been indelible. For example, her entry into the family was possibly one of the reasons Dawn and I fought continuously throughout our childhood and later. I was no doubt jealous when she was born—apparently my reaction to the happy event was "Take that horrid baby back where it came from"—but what followed could have done little to change my attitude.

If in the two years she was with us, Nana tamed me on the surface to the point where I was disciplined enough to react to life with some grace, she also, I think, left me with feelings of unlocalized guilt, a sense of the unpredictable, a discomfort in expressing emotions, and an occasional deep-seated loneliness. I also grew up with the conviction that adults did not like children and was honestly astonished more than once when later told some "grown-up" or other actually enjoyed being with us.

Nana had an infallible knowledge of how things should be done. If they were not done according to her rules, she left her employers, justified in her own stubborn certainty. She had at one time been nanny to the two illegitimate children of Ellen Terry, the famous actress, and the architect with whom she lived. One of those children was Edward Craig, the romantic dreamer who designed theatre sets on such a grandiose scale that they were much admired but seldom used. It would be interesting to know if she had any effect on him. In any case, this was obviously a very different world from ours, where illegitimacy would never have been countenanced, but her attitude was the same, and she didn't stay long. She left when Ellen Terry insisted on bringing the children down to show them off to her guests at parties after the evening performance.

It's romantic to envision the scene: children wrapped in soft blankets brought downstairs into a Victorian drawing room, lighted by gas lamps, to join a party consisting of the elaborately dressed women and famous artists and writers of the time. Possibly Oscar Wilde was there. Bernard Shaw probably wasn't: despite their long and passionate correspondence, Ellen Terry put off meeting him, saying that she was afraid he would be disappointed in her.

But Nana would have been left in the nursery, fuming at such frivolity and angry that her children had been disturbed.

Living at a time when there was no welfare system for the unemployed and, in fact, really too old to be employed at all, Nana told Enid much later that when she came for her interview, she had not eaten for three days. At the time, she said nothing of this but instead, out of pride, stated she would not be free for two days and then she'd take over. So she starved for two more days. At least, that's the family story and quite likely to be true.

Take over she did. From then on, our parents were to see us for ten minutes a day only, for a visit before dinner, with our nanny present. Enid and her sisters, Gwen and Irene, all agree that one reason these English nurses wielded such power over children — and they did — was that the child never saw its parents alone so could not complain. Nannies never had a day off or any time to themselves. Enid says the only indication she ever had from me that I was not entirely happy was when I asked her in Hindustani why she had bought a white nanny for me when I liked my black one. She also said that my speaking Hindustani may have been part of the problem: I could tell her things and Nana could not understand what I was saying. She also pointed out, keeping her own experience in mind, that "these women" were very clever and never attacked a child in front of its parents.

At that time, in the professional classes, attitudes towards children were quite different from those of today. Today conscientious parents tend to put children first, to worry abnormally about their diets, their psyches, their education, their clothes, their toys. They are taken to doctors at the first sign of a cold and are X-rayed if they stub their toes. As infants, they are shut inside warm rooms and as they grow older they are fenced in, in case they have an accident or run into strangers. Their parents may, because of so much information on the subject, suffocate them with attention when they are small and with their own expectations or fears as they grow older. In the 1920s, there were no books on parenting so mothers and fathers could remain relatively guiltless on how they fulfilled their obligations. Children were not an integral part of their lives. They were sheltered and watched, of course, but not with the kind of fear, guilt, and anticipation of failure that are prevalent today.

In fact, children were regarded as a kind of sub-species. Soon after hiring Nana, my family, including Grandmother Mary Murray of the six babies, went to Majorca. One day, Mary Murray remarked that the grapes were going mouldy. As a good Scot, and therefore unwilling to waste anything, she said without a second thought: "You'd better give them to the children." Enid, in recounting this episode, obviously felt virtuous because she didn't give them to the children. However, she'd been brought up under the same system and had not escaped her own childhood. With the extraordinary mixture of thrift and spendthrift which is the nature of the family, she insists still that she prefers rotten bananas to fresh ones, but she takes pride in never having made us eat them.

However, in general, unless there was something edible to be disposed of, children, like Samuel Johnson's hypothetical ones, who he said should be put into barrels and fed through the bunghole until they are twenty-one, were out of sight, out of mind. The parents' responsibility was to have them well looked after by someone else. However questionable the system was, it was perceived as being at least partly to the child's advantage. Gillian Hodge said she had a Norland nanny "aunt" who insisted parents were bad for children — that they "spoiled" them — and that she, before she was forced to, could not imagine raising her own children. Enid said with remarkable candour, "I suppose we were not prepared to bring up our children. We didn't know how to."

Each system has its weak and strong points. The British system of the time was hierarchical, anti-intellectual, snobbish, and often unimaginative, but it did raise adults who were largely fearless and had few neuroses, people who could handle most situations. Even so, on the obverse side of the coin, I've talked to few people who would choose to live through this upbringing a second time.

Nana's objective, gleaned from a letter she wrote nearly sixty years ago and which I found recently, was to train her children so they would grow into women whose parents would be proud of them and whose husbands would consider them "prizes." She was ferociously loyal in her attempts to turn out these prizes, and she was a devoted nurse to the baby of the family, but she was also ferocious in undoing the "damage" caused by the ayahs.

Once again, isolated images are all that are left to me of such early experiences.

The first must have taken place in England, soon after Nana's arrival, but not so soon that I wasn't already bowing to her will.

I was running in a private garden or a park — if a park it was Kensington Gardens where we were taken with other nannies and children in the afternoons — when I fell down and scraped my knees. I ran back to Nana, crying and expecting sympathy; she told me I was being a baby and that as punishment I was to run and fall on them again. I did, making sure the small wound was intensified. I even seem to remember satisfaction in doing so. Oddly contradictory, the next image occurs in Majorca. I was left for a few minutes with the gardener and while with him fell down and hurt myself. Afraid that he had failed in his duty, he rushed and picked bunches of flowers and offered them to me as a distraction. But Nana arrived and gave him a furious tongue lashing, which to my astonishment cowed him as much as a similar attack would have cowed me.

There was no question of being consistent, but there was the question of power, and in that hierarchical system, Nana had the power. While she was with us, I remember very little of Indian servants—we returned to India after my father's leave—although Gangadi must have been somewhere because she surfaced again as Dawn's ayah after Nana died. In any case, they were not there to go to for complaint or consolation.

Power, isolation, and unremitting pressure are the requisites for brain-washing. The curious result is that it appears as if the recipient of this treatment may become enamoured of his or her tormentor. I wanted to please Nana quite apart from any punishment I might receive if I didn't. Occasionally on Sunday mornings, Dawn and I were allowed to get into bed with her to be told stories. I remember only one of these, my favourite. It concerned a very spoilt little girl—spoilt by ayahs—whom she'd made into a reasonable human being within a week. I'm sure she did.

Not long ago, I read *Victorian Murderesses*, a factual account by Mary S. Hartman. In it, a governess with complete control of four young girls abuses them, but when neighbours report this to their father, who lives apart from them, and he comes to investigate, his daughters stand, literally as well as figuratively, behind their tormentor, and he goes away satisfied that his children are having the best care available. It's impossible to disentangle the interplay of various emotions in these circumstances.

In order to gratify, I would do anything. Eating outside while staying at a hotel in Gulmarg, the children were placed at a table with their nannies while their parents ate elsewhere. There is little doubt that children are far more fastidious than most adults realize, because I remember being forced to sit in a place where some child had spilt milk and where the wet, wrinkled, white cloth wrapped itself about my bare legs, filling me with disgust. We were given spinach and most of the children were fussing over it. Nana said with pride that her child loved spinach and to prove her point gave me an enormous plateful, which I ate with equal pride, delighted to back her up to the admiration of her peers while revolted by every mouthful.

Mortification of the senses was part of the process. When we travelled, if there was only one bed, Dawn was given the top with its pillow, because she was frail, while I was packed into the bottom. This was particularly unpleasant since she was not yet toilet-trained, and I would wake up to find my feet damp and occasionally stuck, giving me a thrill of horror, with faeces. When Nana curled my hair, she did so with strips of rags, pulling hard on each strand as she wound it up. The rag strips became a form of torture and years later if someone played affectionately with my hair an involuntary shudder would pass down my back. Similarly, buttonhooks were used to button up boots: thrust through the hole, searching for the buttons, they dug into the tender bones of the foot before being triumphantly withdrawn.

An isolated memory has to do with a children's party. Our outer clothes—again, this must have taken place in Peshawar—were left on a bed in a bedroom. I had just been given a new blue outfit of trousers and jacket; it was made of a furry wool material, and I was proud of it. Dawn had my outgrown pink outfit, well washed with much of the furry texture worn off. After the party—one of those occasions when children sat around a large, white-clothed table and ate appropriate food—we were taken into the bedroom to be put into our heavier garments. Dawn vomited over hers, which was stripped off her and rammed, evil smelling and damp, onto me, after which she was put into mine. I appear to remember a somewhat disconcerted mother watching this exchange but not interfering.

This disparity in the way children were treated, although curious, was not in any way exceptional. My mother had been the "terrible" child and her younger sister, Gwen, the adored baby. In both our cases, the elder was considered responsible for what the younger did. A hard, white hairbrush sat on Nana's dresser, and if either Dawn or I misbehaved, I was spanked with it (another was used for the same purpose in my mother's family), presumably to teach me to look after children smaller than myself. At the same time, I had no control, of course, over what my sister did; I in no way was taught to look after her or, I think, encouraged to love her. Similarly, my mother and her sister, Gwen, have never been truly comfortable with each other.

Finishing one's food was also always stressed, both by nannies and later in boarding schools, as part of the English fixation on eating and defecating. As a child, eating became a painful ritual for me, and I was very slow in attempting to force food down my throat. To cure this tendency, on at least one occasion Nana picked up my spoon impatiently and pushed it into my mouth. When I vomited into the bowl she was holding, she spooned the vomit back into me. I've never forgotten the slimy, sickly taste, the undigested lumps, the white bowl held close to my face, the metal spoon forced between my teeth.

Mocking was another tool: mocking the child's language, appearance, abilities. Given what was then called a fairy cycle (a small bike), I was passionately attached to it but slow to learn to balance; because of this inability, I was made to feel like a fool and it was taken away from me.

Extraordinary as it seems, prudishness was so extreme that some nannies did not bath their children naked. I recall Dawn and myself being bathed while a younger nanny was there watching and talking. The conversation had to do with how she washed her children. She said she put them in the bath with their vests on so they wouldn't be exposed, and then she'd wash them up under their vests. She was sure this was how it should be done (perhaps she was a Norland nanny) and was subtly critical of Nana who, to my surprise, took it with reasonably good humour, not objecting but obviously feeling that it wasn't necessary to keep children clothed while she bathed them. Even so, it goes without saying that we were taught to regard our bodies with extreme modesty and never to touch our private parts except by necessity with paper or a cloth after going to the toilet or washing ourselves. This training was so stringent, I had no idea I had a vagina until I was married. Although I'd taken courses in biology, the inference must have been blocked out.

Possibly the euphemisms we were taught to use in our family for bodily parts and functions also came from Nana, although they may have been of long standing and perhaps were used by other families. They certainly appear to be idiosyncratic since I've never heard them from anyone else: we did "big tronie" and "little tronie" and referred to the unmentionable part of the body as "my Sunday face." However, in all fairness, there was no shame attached to these words. They could be used with impunity, whereas "toilet" was considered to be in very bad taste.

Nana did introduce a curiously unhygienic custom into the household. We didn't have flush toilets in India; the pots, held in wooden structures, were emptied and cleaned out by the sweeper, an untouchable. Possibly due to frugality or to save them from being stuffed up with paper, Nana suggested — and the suggestion was accepted — that Dawn and I should have small cloths, to be hung up under the washbasin stand, of different colours so we should know which was to be used by whom, to wipe ourselves with after we had done "little tronie." They hung there getting stiffer and no doubt smellier with each application. My parents were fastidious and I'm surprised they agreed to this. I also wonder what the servants thought, knowing now that Hindus regard whites as revolting for using the right hand both for cleaning with paper, in itself regarded as a "dirty" way to do it, and for eating. Even the use of a handkerchief for holding mucous is considered filthy.

But then there was that other generous side of Nana. One Christmas she gave me a life-size baby doll with a German bisque head which no doubt cost her a month's wages. It was wrapped in a delicate blue shawl and placed in a crib. I was told it was a real baby and can remember the magic of that moment, the mystery of looking but not daring to touch it. It was a long time before I played with "Bobby"—in any case, I never really knew what to do with dolls—and he still seems half alive to me, a member of the family. Judgements are never simple and no doubt should not be made at all. After all, that dragon of my childhood who inspired nightmares and inhibitions, who to me exemplifies the questionable way in which many British children were raised, was also an old woman stringently and even heroically doing her duty as she saw it, one who should, in fact, have reached the age where she was being looked after herself.

She had a weak heart, a fact she'd never divulged to my parents. It was first recognized after an earthquake when everyone in the house rushed outside. Dawn and myself, wrapped in blankets, were carried in our parents' arms. We were again not in Dehra Dun, but in a house with a tin roof which made a deafening clatter when it was attacked during hail storms dumping enormous ice stones on it. The night of the earthquake was calm and warm and when I asked why we were outside in the dark, my mother told me we'd gone out to watch the birds which were reacting to the quake with far more frenzy than we were. To me, it seemed like a special and wonderful occasion, perhaps because Nana was not with us. She'd been forgotten, and was later discovered in the house suffering intense pain. She died not long afterwards and became another of those countless foreigners buried in a British graveyard in India.

Memorable events appear to have taken place while we were in the bath. Again we were being bathed, but by an ayah, or perhaps by two, since we each had our own once Nana was in the hospital, when my mother came in and told us she was dead. Dawn, catching my mother's sorrowful mood, started to cry. Filled with overwhelming relief but showing, I thought and still think, no emotion, I sat in the tub, staring down at the water. Years later, my mother said, still shocked, I had smiled. I don't think so. I was five years old, already old enough to be perfectly aware of what was expected, aware that I should look sad, but stubbornly refusing to do so. The only way I could respond was to give no response at all.

Going through old photographs recently, I came across Nana's letter (normally my family kept no letters, so this was a bonus) written in a cramped, careful script from an address in Peshawar in 1929. It is charming, misspelled, ungrammatical: written by an old woman in love with the family for which she is working. It's discovery was distressingly ironic after what I'd been recalling and writing:

My dear Mrs. Robin:

Just a line to wish you the same old wish that everyone else can wish you, very many happy returns of your 24 Birthday, and may God give you health and strength to live to see Jean [myself] and Dawn grow up to be lively Women and do you credit for your training and cair, and that you may see them settle down in life. If they turn out like their Mother. They will be a very great prize to the men that is lucky enough to get them. That is my great wish for you, and I am sure I cannot wish you or the Mager a better one, for I know that is what you both wish best of all. Nor however can I thank you enough for all your kindness to me in every way, even if you were my own daughter you could not have been kinder. have you ever had a feeling when someone is very kind to you and always showing their Hearts kindness to you it pains you and you want to cry and you would like to put your Harms round their neck and tell them how you love them and not to do any more for them for they never can repay it, that's the way I always feel towards you. and I cannot do all these things for I would look such an old fool. So this is the only chance I have had of telling you how I feel towards you and hope I always shall. For the Mager and yourself have been nothing but kindness since I came to you. but if ever I can do anything in my power to show gratitude to you please let me do it for if it is in my power I will do it. and that's for Mrs. Chone [Irene], and Miss Gregory [Gwen] they have always been very kind to me in helping me in every way they could although I tease Mrs. Chone I am very fond of her, I like to see her ruffled and to see her proud little flush and Miss Gregory is my Bar black sheep with a little black divel sometimes, playing ring-a roses in her inside until I get a thisel and prick him of the playground. Well I hope there will be a dance tonight so as you may finish up the day happy once more wishing you many happy returns of the day with every good wish for your happiness. I am yours respectfully,

M. E. Merton

or to make it not stiff love from Nana.

So that's what her name was.

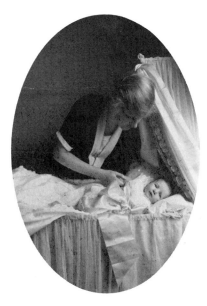

Enid Gregory (Murray) with
baby Rona, c. 1924.

Robin Murray, Rona's father, as a
young officer in the Ninth Gurkhas.

Warm-hearted Ayah,
Pranciena Hami and Rona,
London, 1924.

Rona, Nana—looking typically
severe—and Dawn, in
Scotland, c. 1927.

Eric Gregory in his Gilgit boots, North-West Frontier.

The old Maxwell car, Dehra Dun.

Bide-a-Wee, the Murray house in Dehra Dun, *c.* 1930.

Ninth Gurkha Mess Hall, Dehra Dun, Birpur.

Major Robert (Robin) Murray, fourth from the left, front row. Ninth Gurkhas, Dehra Dun, Birpur.

Robin Murray leading battalion on parade, North-West Frontier.

Rona on Lucky, Dawn in background, Gulmarg, *c.* 1930.

Rona and Dawn at a fancy dress party, 1929.

A tiger hunt. Note the rather large tiger in foreground.
Dawn and Rona in front. Michael is the tall man in the centre.

Enid Murray checking stores at last camp, Erin Nullah,
Zanskar area, *c.* 1928.

The wedding of Gwen Gregory, *c.* 1929.

Houseboat *Lotus Eater*, Dal Lake in Kashmir.
From left: Irene, Enid and Sam, Irene's second husband.

Chapter Four

*A*LWAYS, DURING HOT summers, the acrid smell of a tall, multifoliate, white weed (tansy? cow parsley?) evokes an instantaneous sense in me of somewhere else, of heat and insects and drowsy timelessness. I stop walking or pull up the horse if riding and pause, trying to remember details, to remember any small thing I can. And there's another plant, a shrub, also multifoliate, with tiny dark blue, purple, and reddish petals that I know has a strong scent. To reach it, I walk unashamed through park flower beds, packing down earth and bending back branches. But it has no smell in this North American country. Cheated, I try to recreate the heavy, distinctive fragrance. Bees toil through the florets. Concentrating, I rediscover a cloud of perfume and am lost in a garden planted around a long white bungalow.

Its cement floor powdered with dust and a few dried leaves, a verandah runs across the house front. Large circular wire baskets lined with moss and holding maidenhair ferns and bright flowers hang from its roof. One of the *malis* waters them with a heavy-snouted watering can. He wears a *dhoti* and long shirt. He talks to me while he stands on a ladder, carefully pouring a stream of water into the baskets. I am six or seven years old and sit on the step. Up above me, men crawl over the roof, replacing thatch. They call to each other and laugh while they work.

Our beds have been brought out onto the verandah because it's hot, even though it can't be the really hot weather yet, or we would be in Kashmir, not Dehra Dun. We sleep under mosquito netting which is now tied back. Being outside at night and having our parents sleep where we do, is like being released on a holiday, a difference, because the room I share with my sister, Dawn, is at the back of the house, and is small, and because we don't often see our parents in an intimate way. Off our room, a dank cement bathroom has a hole in the floor through which water is emptied out by the *bhisthi* who fills the tub when we bath. To keep down the dust and cool the house off, he also sprinkles the verandah and the drive with water out of an enormous goatskin bag. He wears a turban and dresses in white; all the men wear white, and while the bearer and *syces* have jackets, the sweeper wears only a loincloth. The sweeper is an untouchable. While he sweeps he squats down, using a brush made of long, pliable strands of thin wood tied together with dried rush into a short handle. He sidles along on brown, skin-cracked feet, making a swoosh, swoosh sound. While he sweeps, we talk to each other, his small, dark face smiling. He's never in a hurry; he often sits back on his heels, his hands hanging limply with the brush in them, while he gives me all his attention. I cannot recall what we talk about. He swooshes most of the day, or he seems to. When he doesn't, he's emptying the bathroom pots after they've been used. Nobody else would do that, but he doesn't seem to mind. He doesn't seem to mind being untouchable; that doesn't come into the conversation. I can touch him, but I don't remember if I ever do.

The *malis* and the *bhisthi* and the sweeper live with the other servants in their own village at the foot of a hill which drops down behind the house. There are banana trees on the slope, and quite often my father goes to them to see if the bananas are ripe. They never seem to be, or if they are, they're eaten by somebody or something else before he gets to them. On the top of the slope there's a row of eucalyptus trees which drop their thousands of small, clean-scented knobs and thin leaves onto the earth. My father likes to have a branch from one of these trees put into his hot bath to soften and scent the water.

Also at the back of the house, yellow roses grow on a long trellis, and to the left stables stand above the servants' quarters. We have four horses: Fairy, my father's chief polo pony, as well as two others and Bunty, who's mine. We also have a donkey belonging to Dawn. Once, when she was giving it a lump of sugar, it bit her finger and she made a terrible fuss. I thought she was too old to scream and cry like that, which she also did when she ate a red pepper she found in a field. I didn't feel the least bit sorry for her. In any case, she should have held her hand flat.

Sometimes Dawn and I eat outside, under a peepul tree. My father told me the tree has that name because it talks continuously, whispering secrets, like people. It's the kind of tree the Buddha sat under. While he was sitting there, snails crawled up him and made him a hat like a *topi*, but without a brim, to protect him from the sun in the summer and from the rain which battered down on him in the monsoon season.

When we eat outside with our ayahs looking after us, Bunty sometimes comes up from the back and eats off my plate. She's a bay pony and was given to me by Paul, a boy I didn't like very much, who has now gone to school in England. Paul also gave me his bicycle and his *syce*, but my father got angry when I insisted he had been given to me; he told me I was being ridiculous and the *syce* belonged to him. I don't know why he was angry, because he has his own *syce*. There's one for each horse and, as well, a man who cuts their hay. All these people live in the village with their own families. I'm not allowed there alone, but once my mother took me down. The houses are small and are made of mud, painted white, with thick walls attached to each other. The low stoves are on the outside and are also made of mud; they have two round holes on top where pans are set to be heated by the fire inside them. It was the first time I ever saw lovely, neat stoves and somebody cooking. I can't go into the kitchen up here and neither can my mother, because the cook would be offended and might leave. He's a brahman and the most important of all the servants.

Down in the village, the children were shy and stood back in doorways or against the walls and stared at us. Some of the little boys wore only shirts. I asked my mother why they didn't wear trousers and she said, "Perhaps they're too poor." It seems to me that if they are too poor, they should have trousers and not a shirt, because then they would cover that part of their bodies. I would never let anybody see that part of me although I had to once.

My ayah, Asha, lives in that village. She has a beautiful sari for special occasions. It's white with a heavy blue and gold border and tiny gold flowers painted all over it. She taught me plain knitting—not purl—the German way and told me about being shut up in a cage when she lived with Christian missionaries. I have a vision of her like a child bird in a cage hung on a tree. She didn't like the missionaries who wouldn't give her enough to eat, but they did teach her English and she's proud of that. Even so, we speak Hindustani. I had another ayah I liked better; she was tall and beautiful and laughed and spoke loudly. My mother said she stole something—my father's handkerchiefs, I think—so she had to go away. I like Asha, but she doesn't laugh often.

Gangadi is Dawn's ayah. She's big and dark and wears plain white saris. She used to be mine, but now she doesn't pay me any attention. Some of the time, she has a little girl with her, just walking, who used to call my mother "Mummy" (I don't think she liked that) and thought she belonged to us, but she was given to Gangadi. She was found thrown away in a small white house across the riverbed down below one side of our garden. She'd been born two or three days before and left on the earth floor with lime in it, which made holes in her body. My mother told the servants to bring her here and then they fed her milk through a fountain pen. My father said she would never live and to let her die, but she did live. My mother says she's very high caste but I don't know how she knows that. Gangadi has no babies of her own.

I can count up to twenty in Hindustani so I know there are usually sixteen servants. I also know they have to have very clean hands because my father looks at their nails when he takes them on. I watch while he pays them. He has a table set up on the verandah and takes money out of a small metal box while he writes down the name of everyone who goes by in the line. As well as the cook, the ayahs, the bearer, the *khidmatgar* who waits at the grownup table, the *syces* and *malis*, the *bhisthi* and sweeper and *chaukidar* who walks around at night with his *lathi* guarding the house, there is the *dhobi* who beats the washing against stones on the riverbank and does the ironing, and is the driver for the car. Sometimes there is a *darzi* who makes our clothes on the verandah. When he twists long cords, he stretches out one leg and holds the end of the strip with his big toe and the one beside it. He squats in front of his sewing machine, whirring the handle, or sews without it. His son sits beside him, making dresses and pyjamas and dressing gowns for our dolls out of bright, silky material with small, perfect stitches. He's about my age, but he never plays with us. He doesn't even look at us. He doesn't seem to play at all, but sits there all day beside his father.

❧ ❧

None of the children played with us. I doubt if they even thought about it, and neither did we. I knew I was not supposed to touch them, although physical contact with adults was not outlawed, but have no idea when I was told not to, or why. What I do remember is going to a children's birthday party where we rode elephants. I was put on a young one without a *machan* and was alone with the son of the *mahout* who was some years older than I. We all went off along the road while our mothers sat on a verandah having tea or drinks and talking in a wildly enthusiastic way to each other. The young *mahout* must have been in training as well as the baby elephant, because the boy lost control and the elephant turned around and raced back to the house. I threw my arms around the *mahout's* waist, clinging like a burr, and when the mothers saw this they burst out laughing. I felt abashed, knowing I was doing something shameful, but also indignant because I would have fallen off if I hadn't. He was probably as embarrassed as I was and avoided looking at me or admitting anything had occurred. The only other real memory I have of Indian children is of being in the car going through a village with my mother when she drove into a pram loaded with babies. It was being pushed by a girl of nine or ten dressed in a ragged cotton dress, her long, black hair in a pigtail. The car tipped the pram over with three or four startled faces looking up from it. No one was hurt, but my mother, quick-tempered and upset, was enraged with the girl who simply stared at her without comprehension.

❧

The *mali* squats on the ground under the jacaranda tree at the side of the house. He has a penknife with him and he cuts a lizard into two pieces with it. The two parts wriggle off in opposite directions. The head with its tiny eyes and front feet crawls under some bushes and the tail with its little feet goes off across the grass. The *mali* is saying, "Look at it, Missi-Baba, it isn't dead. You can cut it up and it still doesn't die." I like squatting there in the shade with him watching the two live pieces crawl away. There was a little white stuff where it had been cut.

It's difficult to know when something is dead and when it isn't. Like the snake. The snake happened when I was riding up to Gulmarg with my father. I sat on Lucky, the piebald horse—all piebalds are lucky—I always have when we go up to Kashmir, and I watched while Dawn and my mother got into the *dandy*, one at each end. They looked very comfortable; my mother was laughing. They were to be carried up by the men, and I was proud to be riding with my father because it meant I was a good rider and was growing up. Then we started up a steep, stony road with Luke, my sausage dog, running with us (my mother doesn't like Luke; she says he smells). After we'd gone quite far, Luke started barking and wagging his tail at something hidden in grass and bushes by the side of the road. It was a long snake which wriggled out across the gravel. My father got off his horse and beat it with his riding crop while I sat there and watched him. While he was doing this, a caravan of men and donkeys came down the hill and stopped. The men talked with my father about whether the snake was dead or not, and decided it was. I didn't know how it could have been, because it went on wriggling while we rode away.

One day we found a heap of rabbit fur and the long, sharp porcupine quills that can be used for making pens. There must have been a fight. I don't know if the porcupine and rabbit were dead, but the jackal must have died the day Bunty ran away with me. I like it when she gets away, because every afternoon when Dawn and I ride, Asha and Gangadi and a *syce* walk with us along the road. It's hot, and they go slowly, so we plod along with dust coming up all around us. The day I raced with my father along the side of the polo field, I knew how different that kind of riding was. Then it was easy to forget the heat and the itchiness because it was like flying on a bird with everything flashing past so quickly all you could think about was staying on without holding the pommel—which is shameful—and rushing so that you could hardly breathe.

They were throwing stones at a jackal in a place cleared out of the trees by the side of the road. I heard a yelping noise that I'll always remember because it was so full of pain. Bunty stopped and we watched. Men and women were throwing the stones and shouting at the jackal which was struggling in a cloud of dust. It was on its back with its feet waving in the air and blood coming out of it. The people were furious, their faces screwed up and their hands filled with rocks. When I told the *syce*, he said it must have been killing chickens. He didn't think anything about it.

The other *syce* was here this morning but he's gone now. He's always called the "three-fingered man" because he was born with only three fingers on one of his hands. He doesn't work here any more, but goes from one place to another begging for food. The reason he doesn't work and has no money is because he's mad. Some people say he's only mad when there's a full moon. He galloped into a bridge when he was on Fairy and crashed his head which made him the way he is. I heard my mother and father asking each other if I should be allowed to talk to him—he's another person who has conversations with me—and they decided it was all right. To me, he's not at all different from other people except for the three fingers. One day I was in the car with my mother, and we were going along the same hot road when we came to two policemen marching with the three-fingered man chained to them with handcuffs. My mother stopped the car and asked what they were doing.

They said they were taking him to prison because he'd been found burning papers in the Mess. My mother was furious and said they couldn't put him in prison because he was mad so he didn't know what he was doing. She made them take the handcuffs off, and she put him in the car and drove him to our house. But he knows what he's doing. I'm glad she didn't let them take him away.

I was also in the old Maxwell, as they call it, with my father and mother when the locusts came. They were so thick against the wind-screen that my mother had to take out the cellophane window on her side and lean out and try to brush them off while my father drove. I was sitting in the back and one got inside. It stuck against the back window and then flopped around on the top of the back seat. It was quite big and was gold, looking like the amber beads with little shell things in them my mother sometimes wears. You could hear the locusts crunching under the hard wheels of the car as it crushed over them and left a trail of dead, gold bodies on the road. The *malis* were lighting smoky fires all over the garden to try to keep them away from the flowers, particularly away from the sweetpeas—two long rows of them which are so high that when my father sits on Fairy and holds up his riding crop, he still doesn't reach the top of them. He's proud of the sweetpeas and certainly doesn't want the locusts to eat them.

When I go down to the little black box on a post by the gate to fetch the calling cards—some have corners turned down and some don't; they mean different things—I put my hand in carefully, because it's filled with geckoes that run away making cheeping noises exactly like birds. High up on the electric wire, there's a small owl which sits there night and day, never moving. It seems to be perfectly alive, but it isn't. It's been electrocuted on the wire.

Sometimes the garden is filled with monkeys. They don't stay long, they just pass through, but when they're here there are hundreds of them, swinging through the trees and screaming at each other. After they've gone, the green parrots come. The sun flashes on their wings and they fill the trees with screeching and rustling noises. Then they go, and it's quiet again until the monsoon time when hailstones batter down and rain rushes onto the garden and down the windows. Then the worms come out of their holes so they won't be drowned and you can hardly step between them, particularly on the driveway. They are all sizes and some seem to be knotted together in clumps as they poke up in the squishy mud. Then all the Indians run up and down between their village and the house in their soaking-wet clothes. When the monsoon first comes, some of them just stand in the rain, looking up at the sky, smiling.

One night we were at the Club at a party when it must have been monsoon time, because my father came and took my hand and led me out onto the verandah. First we went down to one end of it where it was black and clear and there were huge, bright stars in the sky. But at the other end, rain was pouring down. It was quiet and mysterious being out there with him while everybody else was inside talking and laughing in the rooms with lights.

It was like being on the boat coming back to India after a leave when we passed another one, going the other way. It was a black night and that boat was filled with lights and people leaning against the railings going one way, and we were filled with lights and people going the other way. We waved to each other across the sea.

And once, my father took me into the garden and led me to the flower bed along the drive and showed me a certain tiny, whitish flower. I was surprised he'd even noticed it; it wasn't at all like the trees of scarlet poinsettias with their milky stems that have to be put in boiling water when they are cut, or like the great trailing vines of purple flowers. When he told me to smell it, I knew why he'd shown it to me: it had a warm, lazy, delicious perfume that made you dizzy.

Sometimes he lets me have a sip of his beer when they are sitting outside in fold-up chairs on the lawn under the banyan tree and they have visitors. The *malis* put the chairs and tables out and the *khidmatgar* brings out the glasses on a silver tray. He carries a white napkin over his shoulder and with it he flicks the table and wipes anything that's going to be used even if it's already clean. Dawn and I don't sit with them, but we stay around and listen to them talking, leaning back in their chairs with the tall, cool glasses in front of them. The beer has foam on it that sticks to your lips after you drink it and has a bitter taste. Beatrice, who is our governess now, sits with them.

She gives us lessons under that tree, which has a circle of flat stones around it to keep away cobras. She teaches us the alphabet. I make the letters in a special printing book and write down stories. I can't spell anything or read. She tells me which letter to use. The stories are almost all about a small, crooked man who lives in a tree in the garden. He has a hump on his back and wears a green jacket and a tall hat.

I don't tell Beatrice or anyone that I dream about him almost every night. Sometimes he takes the long chain snake somebody gave me and beats me with it. Sometimes he pushes me off a cliff and when I reach the bottom, he's already there, smiling with his crooked face, waiting to kill me because I should have been killed already, falling over the cliff. When he isn't doing those things, he's waiting in the tree to do them.

Beatrice also helps me to catch butterflies. We trap them in a net with a handle and then put them into a bottle with chloroform in it until they are dead, and then we stick pins through them and pin them onto boards. She's told me not to stroke their wings because then the lovely colours will come off, and they do. They come off on my finger: a tiny dust which is red or yellow or purple. Once, when it was almost dark, we caught a moth that was as big as a bird. It was furry and soft and fluttering and very dark, not the colour of a butterfly. At night, there are bats as well. They hang upsidedown when they aren't flying.

It was dark when the Indians skinned the tiger on the tiger hunt. There were rushlights set up on posts so they could see what they were doing. They slit the skin down its tummy and then peeled it back so you could see its insides. The colours were almost like the colours of the butterflies: orange, and red, and blue red, like flowers, not at all like the meat you eat. The Indian mothers took out lumps of fat and rubbed them all over the naked little boys until they were shining. My mother said they did it to make them strong, and she also said you had to watch closely or they would take the whiskers because they thought if they wore them they would have lots more boy babies. The man who shot the tiger, whose name was Michael, wanted to keep the whiskers on the tiger. I watched carefully because I like Michael.

On the hunt, we slept in green tents—a long row of them—which were comfortable and cosy. Dawn and I shared one, with beds made of straw along each side and blankets and sheets and pillows. Everything was carried into the jungle by the beaters and we had our ayahs and the *khidmatgar* and other servants and people with us. The grownups had their table with a white cloth and folding chairs and plates and glasses and the *khidmatgars* looked after them. They had green canvas baths slung on poles.

The camp was set up in a clear space, and at one end three elephants munched on huge banana leaves and grasses all day long except when they were being ridden. It you gave them something to eat, they would curl the soft nose ends of their trunks around it to hold it and then loop up into the air and put whatever it was in their mouths. But one of them would hold his trunk up high and open his mouth between the long, sharp ivory tusks and expect you to put a banana right into his mouth, which I could only do if I was held up. It made me a little afraid. Their legs were like huge columns with toes on them, and I was told not to go right up to them in case I was stepped on and squashed flat. I was careful not to, but I could stand back and stroke the rough, bumpy, grey skin with the ends of my fingers. So you could get on them, they crooked a front leg up into a knee for you to climb on. Then you could get onto the ladder down their sides. But the *mahout* would let an elephant take him in its trunk and swing him up onto its head. Once one of them did that to me. I was astonished at how quick it was. It grabbed me around the waist and swung me upside-down and then up again so I could sit down. It made me dizzy.

We would ride in a *machan* on top of an elephant with our ayahs when the people were hunting the tiger. The *machan* was flat and had a rail around it. The *mahout* sat in front of us, on the neck, and he told the elephant what to do with a heavy, pointed metal rod. I thought it must have hurt, but was told it didn't. We would go off through the jungle where it was dark and cool with the sun coming down through leaves and thick trees all around us. When we came to a heavy branch that the elephant could go under but we couldn't, it stopped and twisted its trunk around it and broke it off.

It was safe sitting up there. The only thing that wasn't safe, we were told, was that if we were playing outside and heard a high whistle it meant a tiger had been wounded and would be dangerous, so we were to run into the camp and into our tents. Once the whistle did go off and we ran, but it was a mistake.

One day we were taken to see the goat. It was small and white and was tied up on a short rope to a fallen tree. It had a pile of hay and was eating it. We were told this goat was the bait for the tiger, that it would come and kill it. When it was found dead, the shooters would know the tiger would be back to finish eating it, so they would get up on their *machan* in the tree with their guns and then kill the tiger. The beaters were there to make a circle around it on the ground and drive it towards the guns by shouting and hitting on pans. It seemed unfair for the goat because it was small and tied up and didn't know what was going to happen to it. But it was lucky in a way, because the tiger didn't kill it for a long time and the hunters thought they wouldn't get a chance to shoot. They were particularly upset, because if Michael didn't get a tiger this time he never would since he had to go away afterwards.

My mother told me I should find him a four-leaf clover for luck. Everybody knew I was good at finding them. So I went off by myself and looked until I found three, which I gave him. The next day, the goat was dead and he shot the tiger. She still says it was because of the clovers, and she told everybody that, but I don't think he thought so. I didn't either.

◆◇◆

Tiger hunting was supposed to have ended for all but VIPs by the beginning of the thirties—and this must have taken place in about 1930, when I was six years old—so I don't know why we were there at all. Possibly Michael—I don't know his last name—was a VIP since he was a godson of George V and had been sent to India because he was in some kind of trouble at home; I was told later that he'd fallen in love with the "wrong" kind of girl and needed to be separated from her, but I don't know if this was true. He was a young, tall, good-looking man and must have been friendly since I fell childishly in love with him. He was killed in the Second World War.

My father, Robin, discussed tiger shooting at some length, saying that there were four methods, varying in price. The first and most expensive shoot was generally financed by a rajah. In this case, there would be several *machans* built into trees spaced about fifty yards apart in a locality where there was not too much underbrush. The beaters—and there could be a couple of hundred of them—armed with trays, rattles, and tins advanced slowly in two converging lines, beating gently so the tiger would slink, thus offering a target, rather than race through the jungle. A refinement on this method was to place the marksman in a cage, through which he would shoot, on the ground. The second method was somewhat more sporting: the guns were placed on elephants which moved slightly ahead of the beaters. The third method was much like the one I've described, but it did have its hazards. Robin knew a forestry officer who put his wife in a separate *machan*, some thirty yards away from his own, where she could watch what was going on. The tiger noticed her in the tree and—unheard-of behaviour—sprang at her, getting its forepaws onto the nearest side of the *machan*, where it hung momentarily. The terrified woman drew away from it and fell to the ground. In his panic, her husband moved suddenly and upset his carefully piled-up cartridges, leaving him with only one shot in his single-load elephant rifle. When he pulled the trigger, the tiger dropped, but he didn't know whether or not he'd hit it. Both it and his wife had been hidden by the long grass. When he went to the foot of the tree, he found a dead tiger but no sign of his wife who'd run a remarkable distance by the time she was discovered.

There was a final method, which Robin claimed only the very young, very broke, and very foolish attempted. When he was in that situation, he went off with a bearer and two Gurkha orderlies, Ran Bahadur and Shamsher, to shoot in the Terai, on the Nepal border, an area noted for tigers and malaria.

Originally intending to be judicious, he tethered a goat and in the afternoon climbed into a *machan*, supplying himself with food, drink, and a book to read. There he stayed all night, with the goat bleating sadly and the mosquitoes attacking him unmercifully. In the morning, too uncomfortable to have slept at all, he was rewarded by the sight, through the early mist, of a tiger frolicking in a stream some yards away. He'd believed that tigers, like other cats, abhorred water and was so astonished at its splashing in and out of the wadi that he forgot to shoot at all. In any case, it completely ignored the sleeping goat and disappeared into the jungle.

He repeated this manoeuvre the second night, during which he decided the mosquitoes were having more fun than he was. At this point, Ran Bahadur came along and suggested there really wasn't much point in sitting in a tree when he could take him to exactly where the tigers were. Robin was shamed into doing what he'd been warned never to do—go after the tiger on foot. He ended up crawling with the two orderlies in single file through a tunnel of grass with no field of fire, and with Ran Bahadur, who was in front, turning round with a grin while he pointed out tiger-pugs in the moist earth and indicated, by touching his nose, that he could smell the animal. Soon afterwards, the Gurkha touched his ear and made lapping indications with his tongue, and sure enough, listening closely, they could all hear it drinking.

Robin, with his gun, took the lead and they went on, he claimed to his abject terror, until they finally discovered they were stalking a rivulet in the jungle. The orderlies were dejected and wanted to find the real thing, but by that time he pointed out it was too late and went home to nurse a bad case of malaria.

My mother calls us "pig-dogs" when she loves us, and she calls other people "chaps." When she's at home, she seems to spend most of her time at her desk, writing letters. Her desk is in a corner of the drawing room. The room she and my father sleep in goes off that room. It's large and airy with a big bed and we are allowed to go in there. My father and mother have different smells. I can smell them, even though they both bath every day and sometimes more than that. My mother's smell is warm and suffocating; my father's is more like one of those white, tall weeds, but fainter. I don't suppose grownup people notice it, but I don't like either smell very much. We aren't allowed to go into the bedroom my grandmother stays in when she visits us. She wears long dresses and jet black beads and diamond rings. Her white hair is always piled up on top of her head. To me, she's a distant person. I never remember sitting on her lap or kissing her and I never remember my mother kissing her, but my father does sometimes politely. Of course, he's her son. She laughs when she tells stories or remembers something funny and she knits my father hundreds of pairs of socks. She has teeth that click.

I've had malaria and dysentery and measles and tonsillitis and they think I've had smallpox, but nobody seems to be certain about that. It may have been chicken pox. My hair was cut short so I looked like a boy because hair takes the strength out of you. I wanted to be a boy anyway, so it was all right looking like one. (My father's moustache prickles when he kisses me. I don't want a moustache when I grow up so perhaps it's better to be a girl.) But even though I've had all these things, Dawn is much frailer than I am, so they get angry if I fight with her. One day my father and his friends played a game throwing her to each other like a ball in the drawing room. I asked them to throw me, but they wouldn't. I think they like her better.

Perhaps that's because I'm not frail, even though one day I was on my mother's bed and a doctor came and tried to stick a tube into me.

My mother held me down on my back by my shoulders. There were all kinds of people there, standing behind and in front of me, where they could see what was going on. The doctor had a black bag and he took out a tube made of rubber and tried to stick it into my Sunday Face. One person held one leg down and another person the other leg, open wide. I was so ashamed everybody could see that part of me I always keep hidden, I tried to kick and stop them and I screamed, not because it hurt although it did, but because those people were watching and talking and didn't seem to know at all how I felt. At last I heard the doctor say, "I can't get it in. She's too small," and my mother and the others let me go. They left me alone and I turned over and wouldn't look at anybody. I don't know why they did that to me.

That may be why I didn't like Paul but I don't think so. I think I didn't like him because he kept telling me he was bigger and stronger and better than I was because he was born when the war was on and I wasn't. He was better at climbing trees, even though I'm better than anyone else I know. He said if I didn't do what he wanted, he would kill Dawn. I don't like her much, but killing her was going too far. I told Asha who didn't pay any attention. Also, Paul got under a blanket with me and felt that part. I didn't feel him. We were in a hotel somewhere. There was a couch in the hallway with a cover over it and we got into it. A tall lady with lots of long beads round her neck came by, and I was frightened. I knew we were being so wicked I couldn't think of anything to say, but Paul knew what to say: "We're looking at something very beautiful under here."

She smiled at us and said, "Are you?" and went away.

❧

In actual fact, there was a great deal of sexual interest and gratification among children when they were, on rather rare occasions, together, and I know that Paul sneaked me into corners more than once. Probably the ayahs, if they knew, thought nothing of it. I assume now that I was far more guilty about it—probably well rebuked or spanked by my nanny before she died for touching myself in some way—than the others involved. Had I been told that adults did anything of that kind, I would have utterly refused to believe it, thinking as I did that only particularly awful children became involved in this way. There were degrees of wickedness: it was worse to experiment with a boy than with a girl, for instance. One little girl stated casually that she'd drunk a boy's urine, and I was aghast, wondering why she hadn't died on the spot.

When Paul went to England at seven or eight, he was in the same public school, Wellington College, to which Lionel Brandon was later sent. Lionel was about three years younger, and he told me he and Paul never spoke to or acknowledged each other, although they'd played together in India, where Lionel had also been somewhat afraid of, and impressed by, him. It was simply "not done" for an older boy to have anything to do with one who was younger. Lionel also said that later Paul played rugby for the school, and his parents—who must have been on leave—came and watched the matches with pride. This, he says, must have been all they saw of their son, who was killed in the Second World War. Paul was not, of course, born during the first war but a few years after the armistice.

•⊰ၓ⊱•

Our garden has two large lawns, one in front of the house and one beside it. Sometimes my father brings his Gurkhas and they drill on the side lawn. There are about four hundred of them. I've seen some of them without their hats on when they play soccer so I know they have all their hair shaved off except for a topknot. My father says they leave that much on so they can be pulled up to heaven by angels when they die.

He usually wears khaki shorts and puttees or a khaki coat and trousers and boots and sometimes a thick brown belt around his waist and over his shoulder. This is his uniform. His friends are dressed the same way and one of them, Brandy, plays with us. He gives me Chinese tortures and the game is to see how long I can stand it before telling him it hurts too much. One of these friends actually likes children and took Dawn and me to a toy shop and told us we could choose anything we wanted. He bought us suitcases and dolls and gave us so much it made me feel funny because I didn't know how much money he had.

When the knife sharpeners and magicians come, they go on the other lawn. The knife sharpeners have a large wheel and a strap for sharpening. All the servants come up to see the magicians and they stand behind us while we sit on carpets that have been brought out and put on the grass. The magicians tear their *pagris* into strips and then pull them out from their chests or pockets whole again. They have a mongoose and a snake in different baskets and they let them out to fight with each other. Their best trick is to grow a small tree with mangoes on it. They plant the seed in a pot and cover it with a cloth. Then they do some other tricks, and after a while one of them takes the cloth off and there is a thin little plant with two or three leaves growing on it. Next time they take it off, there's a small bush. And the last time, there are mangoes growing on the bush.

71

I know the servants are worried. In the village I galloped into once by myself when Bunty got away with me, there's a man who is young and who is more than asleep. He doesn't seem to breathe, but he isn't dead because he doesn't rot away. He's lying on a mat in a house. A travelling holy man came by and put him into this other world that he's in. The holy man said he was to stay like that for quite a long time, and then he would come back and wake him up. Now the time has gone, and he's not come back. Asha says this person will die soon if he isn't woken up.

❦

There are some family stories, but not many, concerning Indian "magic." My mother's brother, Eric, told us about having seen a holy man treat an Indian who'd been bitten by a venomous snake. He said the healer stroked the man's leg away from the wound, as if he were drawing the poison out. He then shook his hand as one would shake off drops of water. Miraculously, the patient lived. Eric and his second wife also said they watched a woman being levitated off a bed. They were close and could sweep their hands under and over the body, testing to find out if this were a trick and the woman was being raised by invisible cords. Their hands were unobstructed. Neither of them approved; they obviously felt uncomfortable over what had occurred.

Years after Asha's story about the young man who was not "woken up," I heard more about the incident. Apparently, it was not unusual for a guru to train a disciple by putting him into a state of suspended animation during which his soul could wander at will outside his body. Only the guru could call the soul back. In this case, the guru had not returned and couldn't be found, even with the help of the police. In the meantime, the disciple had become an object of concern and curiosity, and many people were travelling to see him. There was no sign of life about him, but neither was there any sign of death. He remained in that hot climate looking like a frozen corpse.

My father spoke of being nearby when one of the great Indian festivals took place and of seeing an image that affected him. A young woman without a hair on her body stood perfectly possessed and stark naked in the middle of the crowd. No one paid her any attention. Indian women are extremely modest, and I can only think she may have been a nun in the tantra tradition.

《》

We go to Kashmir in the hot weather. Then Dawn and I are more with other people, particularly with my mother and our aunts, Irene and Gwen, in a houseboat called "The Lotus Eater" on the Dal Lake. This isn't really a boat, because it doesn't move around much, although once I remember it being pushed to another part of the lake by men with long poles. It's very rich inside, with carpets on the floors and red seats and cushions with embroidery all over them. Outside, on the deck, there's a diving board and a water shoot. When we swim, we wear water wings or float in round tubes. The lake is warm, and the lily leaves are so large with such strong stalks that if we sit on them they hold us up and there are bubbles in the water. If we aren't swimming, we sit on the deck and fish with hooks. The fishes are small and are put into a tub of water and then dumped back in the lake. Sometimes blue kingfishers fly around us and dive into the water, and dragonflies swoop onto the boat, and sometimes my mother swims with us.

Once I went into the living room part of the boat and found her there and she was crying. I started to cry too, to be with her, and she stopped, saying, "Don't do that or the others will hear us." She laughed and wiped my face.

Every day men come by in boats called *shikaras*, selling vegetables and fruit and mushrooms and silk and things made of brass and small boxes with round edges which have animals and fruit on them. They are lovely to feel because they're so smooth. And they sell little brass cages with beads that you can twist and make into different shapes. If anyone wants to go to another houseboat, they go in these *shikaras*, which are very comfortable, with red seats and cushions.

Most of all, I love walking in the fields which are full of irises. They have pointed leaves and purple flowers—thousands of them. And once when we went up there, there was snow. We rode in a toboggan. There's a golf course where my father plays when he's with us, but usually he's in Dehra Dun. I saw men laying down new grass in squares up there and my mother gave them some money. I asked her why she had done that and she said the money wasn't worth anything anyway because it was English, but they took it. Once she gave money to a blind man with a big white beard. He was being led around by a little boy. But usually she and my father don't give money to people.

When we aren't on the houseboat, we go up to Gulmarg and live in a hotel or a cottage. We ride up or go in *dandies* and the Indians—even

73

the women — carry everything up. They carry crates on their backs with straps around their foreheads. My father thinks the Kashmiri women are beautiful because they run so straight with great bundles of wood or pots on their heads.

◆§ ੩◆

Another woman belonging to the Anglo-Indian brigade later talked about these coolies. She said they carried immense weights balanced on their backs with the help of a single strap around their foreheads and that in time this strap made a deep dent across their frontal bones. She swore she once saw a woman carrying a grand piano up the steep incline into the mountains. This appears to be quite impossible, even if it were a baby grand. I do not remember any resentment on the part of the Indians at this back-breaking labour or any other kind of work.

Much of the time it was very cold in Kashmir, Himalayan country, and the people carried little containers of hot coals under their clothes to keep themselves warm. When my parents were on their honeymoon, in April, a girl child, badly burned, was brought to my mother who tried to doctor her with a Girl Guide kit, all she had. They never knew if the child survived. My father was particularly upset by and often talked about the danger of these small stoves.

The golf course at Gulmarg, outside Srinagar in Kashmir, set in the mountains and running up peaks and through valleys, was famous for its beauty. My parents apparently went to Kashmir rather than the exquisite hill station outside Dehra Dun, Mussoorie, where my mother was born, because of my father's desire to play golf on his short leaves. The Brandons went to Mussoorie and said they thought Kashmir was more expensive and more "upper." In any case, it was an idyllic place, filled with flowers and water and gentle people.

The only other town I remember at all as a child was Peshawar, on the North-West Frontier, where my father served at the Khyber Pass during my "nanny" years. My family must have driven from Srinagar in their Maxwell because they had a car while they were there. My mother told me that since none of the other wives could drive, she was permitted to go up with the officers, including of course my father, to the Pass when they went on duty and then drive herself back. Generally, entry into the tribal areas was by permit only. It was problematical territory and women were normally restricted.

74

In *Plain Tales from the Raj*, compiled by Charles Allen, Irene Edwards describes nursing on the Frontier in 1929, when my parents were there and anti-British feeling was growing. Peshawar was known as "the city of a thousand and one sins." She says, "I had heard of family feuds [among the tribesmen], now I was to see the results. You would get a case coming in with all the intestines sticking out. They used to get the skin of a chicken and wrap the intestines in this skin to keep them fresh. We used to have to cut out part of the intestine, pick out shrapnel and pellets from gunshot wounds and sew them up. We used to have jealous husbands cutting off their wives' noses, breasts amputated, even pregnant women with their abdomens ripped open. . . . Our gardeners were prisoners. These men had heavy chains around their waists, down each leg and around each ankle. The clanking of these chains used to be our waking bell as they came into our verandah watering the pots in gangs, always with an armed guard."

My father must have been involved when the Peshawar Riots erupted in 1930, since I have a photograph he took of the gruesome results. However, as children we were never aware of any violence. I do remember being in a crowd of people with another white child who became agitated and pointed out to me a man without a nose, saying he must have leprosy. This was before it was known leprosy is only contagious if one is in contact with it over a long period, and we both wondered why he was allowed to go free, shuddering to think we might get it.

Peshawar was also the location of the famous Vale Hunt Club, in which my father took part. Years after we had left India, at the approach of Partition in 1947, an official of the Club went around the stables and kennels putting down all the horses and hounds, afraid of what might become of them when the British left. And it must also have been the area in which my uncle, Eric Gregory, worked when he was in the Intelligence Service, because he wore tribesmen's clothes, still in the family, on his forays into the marketplaces to gather information: baggy trousers, a long striped shirt worn outside them, a short embroidered jacket, turned-up shoes, and a *pagri*. A fair man, he darkened his face with walnut juice. He had blue, Nordic eyes, but apparently there are blue-eyed people in that region, perhaps stemming from the Aryan invasions.

Although we generally travelled by car, horse, or *dandy*, I can remember an intriguing incident which took place on a train. We were travelling in a small compartment of the British type in which seats faced each other. Our family was settling down when two Indian women, exquisitely dressed in saris and jewellery, got on; they wore make-up and nail polish, which I'd never before seen. They were extremely shy, gentle, and apologetic in asking permission to sit with us because the train was full. My parents must have granted this but I felt they were uncomfortable. It was legal, but probably not the custom for Indians to travel with Europeans. In any case, these women sat close together on one side of the compartment and we on the other side. I found them incredibly beautiful and couldn't help staring at them. Possibly they were prostitutes.

I know it was legal for the two races to travel together because my father wrote an amusing story about a newly arrived and arrogant young officer who threatened to have a polite Indian thrown out of what turned out to be their joint compartment. The Indian left quietly, but the upshot was that a sergeant-major was waiting for the officer at Quetta station: "'Sir, the Colonel sends his compliments and has ordered me to take delivery of your sword.'

"The new officer, who had gone to Oxford, not Sandhurst, was mystified by this request. The sergeant told him in non-military terms that he was under arrest. He, completely confused, explained that his sword was packed in his luggage and offered his pistol instead. Of course, all this was regarded as a huge joke. The fledgling officer had chosen the wrong man, a knighted politician on the Viceroy's Council, on whom to impose a legally non-existent segregation."

⋠§⋟

It was Beatrice, our governess, who, in 1932, told Dawn and me we were to leave India. She opened an atlas and pointed out the six weeks' journey in front of us: from Bombay around the Malay Peninsula and through the China Sea to Japan, where we would stop for a few days, and then across the Pacific to Canada.

When we were preparing to leave, the servants packed everything up. Asha was told to clean my doll's pram, to be sold, and my mother was critical, saying she'd done a rotten job. Asha's feelings were hurt, and I was definitely on her side. We had to leave our horses and dogs and most of our toys. Huge wooden trunks sat in the rooms and on the verandah. My father had taken early retirement—he was forty-two—and he and my mother were engrossed in selling the house and starting a new life.

I remember looking into the drawing room from behind a curtain and seeing them sitting down and talking to an Indian, and I remember being surprised. Social intercourse of this kind was outside my experience. My mother said much later that he was ruler of one of the princely states, enormously wealthy and of far higher caste than they were, who was interested in buying the house. However, I don't remember saying in Hindustani, as they claimed, "Bring me my gun so I can shoot that big black man." This rather surprises me as I never remember thinking of Indians as black.

He didn't buy the house but must have been amused at this rudeness because he gave me a splendid life-size doll, which I had to leave behind. I don't think I cared. In fact, I don't remember having any regrets about leaving the animals or the toys or the servants who were my friends. All the service British in India were travelling people. They moved from one part of the country to another on a regular basis as well as going away on six-month leave every three years. I'm sure I didn't realize that we should not be back and I was, of course, completely unaware that the garden with its perfumes and birds and insect noises would haunt me all my life and would eventually draw me back as India has drawn so many others in our attempts to discover who we are.

Even so, to put the balance right, I also recall being hot and intolerably bored, dressed in a red striped sweater and pleated flannel skirt, no doubt sent from Daniel Neal's in London, in that garden. Life in India appears romantic and varied in retrospect, and no doubt was, but there were also endless hours of having nothing to do. Dawn and I seldom had other children to play with, and I think we were not imaginative in any games we may have played with each other. We must have been more entertained when Beatrice arrived and we hunted butterflies and learned the alphabet, but what I chiefly remember are the plodding rides, always down the same road, escorted by ayahs and *syces*, my mother at her desk writing letters, my father occasionally sitting on the lawn with friends having a drink, the interruption and excitement of Christmas when we would find a pile of presents on the chairs by our beds. Everything was done for us. We had no small jobs, little to learn.

I don't ever remember being deliberately entertained by ayahs, apart from being taught how to knit, or by other servants. I do remember that when I was with the three-fingered man or the sweeper or the *mali*, they gave me all their attention, listened to what I had to say, and talked to me as if I were indeed a person with things to tell them. This attitude may constitute one of the differences between Indians and most Westerners, who generally make only half contact with children while involved in their own affairs. The Indians I knew lived in the moment, and the moment always gave them time to be wholly where they were, even if that was merely sitting on a verandah, brush in hand, listening to a small child, or showing a little girl how a lizard was still "alive" when its amputated sections moved off in different directions.

Chapter
Five

OVER HALF A CENTURY
stretched between the period of my childhood in India and that of my
return. As far as I have understood, in a country which is considered to
be basically changeless, many changes have occurred and many which
one would have expected, have not. Despite Mahatma Gandhi's passionate work, and even though it's now illegal, the Hindu caste system
has been based on tradition for so long that it's not been possible to
eradicate it, and the position of women, despite many political gains,
and of female children does not appear to have improved greatly. On the
other hand, the division between British and Indian has, of course,
disappeared so returning travellers, and there are many, have far more
freedom than they had before Partition when sticky protocol and
accepted racism divided people.

To help come full circle in this search for roots, I went through my
father's papers, read accounts, and interviewed friends and relatives.

❧

In the 1920s, the Indian population was 319,000,000. At the same time
the total British population in India numbered only 200,000. This
modest figure included an administration of army and police number-
ing 67,000 as well as the Indian Civil Service—highly regarded by
historians as being incorruptible—consisting of under a thousand men.
Those I've talked to agree that with such a wide discrepancy in numbers,
the British couldn't have ruled India if the majority of Indians hadn't
wanted them there. The two peoples to a great extent understood each
other. For one thing, the Hindus—comprising about eighty per cent of
the native population—and the British both formed caste societies,
with the following rough equivalents: the brahmans corresponded to the
civil servants; the *kshatriyas* (warriors) to the army; the *vaisyas* (merchants) to the English businessmen, most of whom were looked down
upon by the two upper castes of both races since they handled money:

the derogatory term *box-wallah*, referring to a European businessman, was derived from the Indian door-to-door salesman. This British group divided into two, those in commerce and those in trade, with the latter working in shops, an occupation which was considered "beyond the pale." The Eurasians were at the bottom of the heap and could be considered more or less analogous to the *sudras*, the lowest caste, or even to the untouchables, since they were without caste, being referred to as "out-casts." This hierarchy of castes in India had developed through the ages. Originally, the term simply denoted the occupation a man followed, and one was not considered to be above or below another.

The term "untouchable" had originally been applied to an indigenous people, the Dravidians, the splendid temple builders of the South, who did not know, or naturally abide by, the strict taboos regarding cleanliness of the Aryans who conquered India, and were therefore considered unclean. By the 1920s, Gandhi had given these people the gentle name *harijans*,[2] meaning Children of God, in his attempt to combat the non-physical violence the caste system generated. The British, I think, didn't recognize this type of violence. In 1988, one of my aunts still referred contemptuously to a woman who had become a member of the family through marriage as "that little half-caste." Missionaries were looked down upon by the higher British castes and no doubt by the Hindus as well.

In 1930 India, tabulated with Burma, consisted of two hundred and twenty-two distinct peoples, each with its own vernacular and no common language but with English probably having the widest currency.[3] In addition, there were eight principal and several minor religions. Within the Hindu religion, the major castes were subdivided into 2,300 minor ones with little opportunity for a person to move from one to another: boys followed their father's profession or trade, and that was set by their caste: for example, the potters' sons became potters and therefore belonged to a lowly sub-division of the *sudras*. My father claimed, incorrectly (for us, an enlightening comment on how separated the two peoples were), that there was no possibility whatsoever of mobility in the Indian caste system: in actual fact, a *vaisya*, for instance,

---

[2] Known today as the Unscheduled castes. The government is running into great difficulties in attempting reforms in their conditions, which have remained largely unchanged.

[3] Indian Statutory Commission.

who had a wealthy father and a splendid education, could rise in the hierarchy, just as a British child could.

The rich men of the country, apart from the rajahs, were generally the *banyas* who were merchants (*vaisyas*) but were also moneylenders to whom most of the poor paid huge interest rates. Robin Murray claimed one could recognize these *banyas* by their enormous paunches. He spoke of driving frequently through a bazaar and noticing one who squatted in his corn shop but was known to own a fleet of cars running between Rawalpindi and Srinagar. Robin employed a young brahman to clean and drive his own ancient vehicle, and he claimed that whenever this driver was sent to fetch something from the bazaar, the *banya* was forced to heave himself up and *salaam* by bending low and placing the palm of his hand on his forehead in obeisance. Had he offended the brahman, who could equally well have been a beggar, by breaching the caste code, he could have been brought before a *durbar* (court) and tried for the offence.

However, this may have been how Robin, who lived in the country as an adult for over twenty years, saw India, rather than its reality, although certainly the *banya* may not have been "twice born," in which case he could not have been distinguished by the sacred thread[4] and would have been inferior to the brahman. If so, an amusing aside comes to my mind. Since most Indians were miserably poor, they were also very thin. As a result, a man of great girth was looked upon with envy and presumably with concupiscent affection since he had, and could provide, plenty to eat. I met an extraordinary Sanskrit scholar, Agehanandi Bharati, when he left India to go to the States in the 1950s. A German, he'd been accepted as a brahman monk because his exceptional knowledge of Sanskrit and Indian tradition persuaded certain Hindus that he'd been one of them in his last incarnation. A very tall man, he was also heavy, weighing about three hundred pounds. After some experience in his new country, he said ruefully, "These stupid American women do not like obese men." With great self-discipline, he cut his weight down by a third. The *banya* who amused Robin by his girth, no doubt had his compensations.

In any case, the caste system, combined with other factors, kept the Indians themselves apart, as well as separating the two races, and the

---

[4] "Twice born" refers to a ceremony in which a boy takes on the privileges and responsibilities of the brahman caste, during which he is invested with the sacred thread.

demarcation demanded by the Indians was in some respects at least as powerful as that assumed by the whites, although high-caste Indians, some of them educated in British public schools, were beginning to gain a foothold in the Civil Service, the army, and the clubs. The men of both cultures occasionally mingled in business and in some regiments (not the Gurkhas). The women, except the few who met through church or charity groups, barely communicated with each other.

The Hindu religious system was inextricably bound up with caste and was at least partly responsible for the gulf between the two peoples. The British were eaters of the cow, and therefore contact with them for high caste Hindus was defiling. There is the story of an Indian prince who wore white gloves as protection while in England but removed them to eat. When sitting beside an English lady at a dinner party who admired his ring and asked to see it, he took it off his finger and gave it to her. After she'd examined it, he asked her to place it on the table and then indicated to his servant that he should remove and wash it so no pollution would take place when he replaced it on his hand. A Maharajah in Rajasthan took with him large silver vessels filled with water when he visited England so that he would not be forced to drink what was "defiled." This had nothing to do with physically polluted water.

Beef-eating was only a small part of the taboo system. Bipinchandra Pal, in the *Soul of India*, written in the early part of this century, discusses the spiritual life as being absolutely conditional upon the purity of the physical life. He says the Hindus had long known the organic interdependence between the body, particularly of the nerves, and the mind. For spiritual growth, therefore, it was necessary to follow a strict course of discipline (*deha-shuddhi*) which consisted of a complex set of religious sanctions and taboos. The British, of course, were not subject to these taboos so that close contact with them could endanger the spiritual life. These included eating only certain types of foods — those "likely to be conducive . . . to the higher life" and cooked by high-caste individuals — and avoiding other kinds. Even when family members did the cooking, they tied clean cloths over their lips after bathing and changing their clothes, and when a man returned from the street to his house (his temple), he left his shoes at the door and changed his clothes. Daily ritual bathing was essential for spiritual as well as physical cleanliness. Liquid was drunk out of *chatties* which were then thrown away. Hands, used for eating off banana leaves since utensils were contaminated, were washed and the mouth rinsed after eating. Furthermore, the Hindu ate only with the right hand, while the left was used for washing the genitals and rectum and other such tasks.

Gillian Hodge spoke of her shadow defiling the *mali's* food if it fell over it. Robin Murray talked about untouchables having to keep a literal distance—200 yards—between themselves and caste Hindus, or the "twice born" would be polluted and their spiritual life endangered.

The British honoured the caste system imposed by their servants. They had, of course, no choice if they were to conform to the usage of the country. My father pointed out the Indians' inherent wisdom and how effective a union their system created:

> It must be remembered that Britain never conquered India. Englishmen merely injected themselves, through trade, into the Indian pattern of life, which, in the interests of the people, they changed as little as possible; but in the natural course of events they became the predominant influence on that sub-continent of mixed races, owing to their innate political capacity. They came into a country innocent of running water. The prevailing custom was to hire a *bhisthi*, or water-carrier, a man of lowly caste, and pay him the current wage, a custom to which they conformed. Similarly, there were no drains, so a sweeper [an untouchable] was hired at a recognized wage to carry away every form of waste. Again the white man fell into line. So, if it were a servant for this abhorrent task that the sahib required, he would glance through a pile of chits, and perhaps read that Ram 'took great interest in his work' or some such other acrid irony before hiring him. But do not think these people were downtrodden. They earned more income than they could obtain in any other way, even if it were miserable by western standards. What is more, they knew how to look after themselves. I remember reading of the loyalty and self-sacrifice of such Indians as remained true to the British during the Siege of Lucknow, 1858, when, although the garrison was on the verge of starvation, they begged the British to keep all the available rice for themselves, saying they would make do on just the water the rice had been boiled in. Their heroic self-denial was extolled for generations. It is only recently that our brilliant food analysts have discovered that when rice is boiled all the nutriment goes into the water. The faithful humble native got away with both the substance and the kudos; the grateful white over-lord dined off the shadow.

> Similarly, the self-created servant class in India developed the most complete trade union that ever existed, without any fuss, or talk, or union bosses. They gradually brought it into existence by their inherent talent for self-preservation. It worked in two ways. On the one hand wages, which in the beginning were merely their accustomed pittance, gradually crept upwards. They were never allowed to go down again.

The second method was more crafty and relied on caste. The Englishman did not know much about caste; it was a mystery to him; so he accepted it as inevitable when his *syce*, or groom, informed him that he would exercise and groom his horse, and feed it grain, but that it was against his caste to feed it grass. That was the task of the "grass-cut." Again it was against the caste of either of these servants to water the horse. That was the task of a *bhisthi*. So each horse was waited upon by three servants. The grass-cut and *bhisthi* might also work for other horses, but it never occurred to anyone that a *syce* could look after more than one.

The same system applied right through the servant world. A man's bearer would look after his clothes and even wait at table, but never dust his room. That was the work of a sweeper. A *khansaman* would cook, but not wash the dishes, that was the work of the *masalchee*. A *khidmatgar* would wait at table, but never, say, lay the fire, that was the task of the *mali's* coolie, the *mali* being the gardener, who pointed with his finger but was above doing any rough work himself. An ayah would care for a baby in the house, but would never push a pram, which was a boy's task. Furthermore, an ayah would specialize for an infant-in-arms, but would not work for a baby that could toddle. That required a different class of ayah. In addition, if a memsahib wished to conform, and in effect she had no choice, she could not look after her own babies or dare to work in her own kitchen, generally called a "cook-house," which was always a separate building joined to the bungalow by a covered passage. Had she done so, she would have been outcast, and unable to procure any servants.

Naturally, at some stage her husband discovered that he had the choice of having his house pillaged periodically, or of hiring a thief to keep his friends away. The salaried thief then called himself a *chaukidar* (watchman) and collected chits saying how honest and reliable he was. One could multiply these cases until they become tedious. Back of it all was the idea of reducing work to the bare minimum while drawing enough pay to subsist. The Indian servant was supplied with quarters, enough to shelter him. His clothes were a strip of cotton fabric which he washed himself and made last for years. His bed he made for himself with bamboos and rope and called a *charpoi*, meaning literally "four legs." He walked bare-foot. His wife waited on him hand and foot, and occupied his every thought apart from his food, and so long as he could exist he was not interested in exhausting himself. So the upshot was that a married sahib had to live in a hive of servants who choked him economically with a surfeit of honey.

My wife one day found one of her ayahs of whom she was very fond, playing a strange-looking game with pebbles on our verandah. She enquired what she was doing. The ayah replied quite candidly that she was calculating how much money the sahib had left when he had finished paying the servants, which, believe me, was not very much! The pay rolls were drawn up by a *babu*, or Indian clerk, and everybody knew what everybody else drew.

On returning from parade one morning I was greeted by a very agitated bearer, who rushed out to meet me, fell on his knees, clasped me around the ankles, thus halting my progress, laid his head on my feet and sobbed as though his heart would break. He seemed demented. When I could at last prevail on him to speak he sobbed that he had done me a most terrible injury. He had. My servants' quarters were behind my bungalow, which was built on a ridge, and were about thirty feet below, down a short but very steep hill. Our stables also were there, and at that time I was using a loose-box as a garage for my new car, a Chevrolet which I could ill-afford, but which was very necessary because our bungalow was the most outlying in the cantonments. Between his sobs, the bearer explained that the weather looked threatening and he was afraid my new car might get wet, so he summoned all the servants and together they proceeded to push it down to the cover of the stables. At this stage I knew what to expect and hurried round the house to see what I had expected, my new car standing on its head against a mud wall, having somersaulted over the first obstacle.

This was the kind of thing the so-called nabobs of the east had often to put up with, in addition to malaria, enlarged livers, sun-stroke and what-not; so don't be ready to judge them harshly. There were, however, compensations for this kind of life. With his fifteen or so servants the sahib was kept perfectly *khush* (happy). If his shoelace unfastened, there was a plunge of someone to tie it up. Very likely, his stable produced three or more polo ponies whose satin coats and resplendent accoutrements would not disgrace a horse guardsman, and would also be a joy to ride.

The indigenous English caste society mirrored that of the Indian, and was no doubt exaggerated on the sub-continent. Protocol in mess, club, and at government functions was followed heroically: everyone knew his place and what was expected of him. Gillian Hodge says that at formal dinner parties in Calcutta members of a family were ranked according to the occupation of the head of the household. People in commerce were placed at the bottom of the table. Her father, a jute dealer, and his family had only one caste below them: that of the coal dealer. She remembers flirting with a delightful young man below her at the table and joking over their status. Those in trade were not included at all.

She claims that it was impossible to walk into a brahman household; to do so would have caused a riot. The system also led to problems in policing. Only a high-caste police officer could arrest a brahman, so there had to be at least some high-caste police. Similarly, only Moslems could arrest Moslems, so there had to be Moslem officers who would, of course, live apart from the Hindus.

She says her father met business-caste Indians but never over lunch and her mother met, through the Anglican church, certain women, such as Lady Bannerjee, who had forfeited their caste by becoming Christians. Together they attended the superb cathedral in Calcutta and belonged to a group involved in good works. Apparently their major charity lay in raising money for "old cow farms." It's doubtful if they ever actually visited these *gaushalas*.

Since the cow is regarded as sacred (in the *Rig Veda*, Aditi, the mother of all the gods, is portrayed as a cow), to kill her is, of course, a particularly sinful act, deicide, which engenders many penances and much bad karma. In actual fact, she was probably in past ages given her high status by wise brahman priests because her secretions and excretions were, and are, of immense value to the well-being of humans. In India, her milk is drunk as well as being made into curds and *ghee*; her dung is used for heating, cooking, firing pots, cleansing wounds, and insulating walls; her urine is believed by some to be the most intense of all purifiers, both internally and externally. In addition, Nandin, the bull, is the special mount and companion of Shiva.

However, by the early part of this century, much pasture had been ruined and there was little forage for cattle. In *Mother India* Catherine Mayo[5] describes in gruesome detail the fate of many of these animals, which, while they could not be killed, could be left to starve and could also be abused in unspeakable ways. She quotes an acquaintance: "The suffering in these places is terrible. In one of them I recently saw an old cow lying helpless, being consumed by maggots which had begun at her hind quarters. It would take ten days for them to eat up to her heart and kill her. Till then she must lie as she lay."

These "old cow farms" could hardly be looked upon as alleviating suffering. Possibly there were charities shared by women of both cultures which had more successful results. For the most part, however, the women lived separate lives and knew little of what went on beyond their own coteries. My mother, after seeing a spate of films on India which

[5] Mayo, an American, wrote her exposé in 1927, angering the British as much as she did the Indians. Even so, she cannot be discounted since her research is largely based on official documents and many of her conclusions regarding the treatment of women have resurfaced today.

came out in the 1970s and '80s portraying the poverty of the country, said, "Well, of course, we didn't know anything about that because we lived in the cantonments," and my Aunt Irene, who all her life was fascinated by metaphysical questions, said she would have loved to know more about Indian religious beliefs, but that as a British police officer's wife it was impossible for her to make the necessary contacts. The prevailing attitude, in my mother's words, appears to have been, "Because, I mean, you just didn't."

Gillian Hodge, born a generation later, also spoke about being quite unaware of how other people lived while she enjoyed her own luxurious cocoon. Even so, she was more aware than most because her family was independent of the administrative system and freer to do as it liked. Also, unlike me—I left India when I was eight years old—and most British children, she was in India during her teens. She had been sent to boarding school in England at six and during the next seven years saw her parents, like so many other British children, at only brief intervals on their leaves. However, in 1940, because of the war, she was shipped back home. She said that on her arrival she didn't recognize her mother and remembers thinking: "I don't know what this lady looks like."

At thirteen, she settled down to life in Ballygunge, a "second stage" suburb of Calcutta which was still the business centre of India with fine old buildings on the one hand and appalling poverty on the other. Calcutta, called by Kipling the city of dreadful night, was known as a metropolis of divisions where no one had anything to do with anyone outside his own particular social (caste) or racial sector. To quote from Charles Allen's *Plain Tales from the Raj*: "The civil servant didn't hob-nob with the businessman. The Indian businessman didn't hob-nob with the British businessman. The Bengali businessman didn't mix in with the Marwari businessman."

Above all else, high-caste Hindu women kept to themselves; nevertheless, some women did find ways of overcoming these restrictions. Gillian's parents had rented a large house attached by a common wall to another which belonged to a brahman family. Her mother and her female neighbour, who was in purdah, talked to each other every day on the phone and became fast friends without ever seeing each other. When Gillian asked if they couldn't actually meet, her mother said that was not necessary. The brahman was well educated, active in her own community, and could observe their house through her lattice. Gifts of flowers and fruits were exchanged, and when Gillian was about to be married some years later, her wedding gifts were arranged so that they could be scrutinized and commented upon by their neighbour, who ran constant interference. She insisted, generously, that she should be responsible for the *shamiana* to be raised by her servants, under which the marriage was to take place. This structure, built of poles twined with leaves of the neem tree, symbolic of male and female genitalia, was reputed to enhance fertility. Gillian later claimed she knew exactly why she had four children in rapid succession.

When cholera broke out in the village after the British had left, or were in the process of leaving India, the government did little about it, so the two women took it upon themselves to institute measures which should contain the epidemic. Gillian's mother was able to get hold of serum and needles and her neighbour to enforce their use although injections were contrary to much "stuff." She hired two sikhs with *lathis* who forced immunization upon those villagers unwilling to be treated. The epidemic was successfully alleviated. Neither woman could have acted on her own, but together, although physically apart, they made a formidable pair.

Gillian went to The New School which operated in Calcutta during the winter and to Darjeeling in the summer. It had been hastily put together by the British so their children would be segregated from Indian and (worse still) Eurasian children; this enforced separation, so important to the British, was based less on educational standards than on the usual terror that their children might pick up the "wrong" (chee-chee) accent.[6]

Finally, after graduation, Gillian was able to mingle socially with Indians to a degree. She went to an art school where she was the only European. Male and female students were segregated. She never ate with her fellow female students, but they did share classrooms and instructors as well as an ancient Sikh, armed with a stick, who was there to protect them from harassment: he was so old that after sitting for hours outside their instruction room, he couldn't get to his feet and had to be helped to stand up by those he was "guarding." And later still, she acquired a studio in a jail where she said a fairly open system prevailed and the prisoners moved around with comparative freedom.

[6] My parents fought the same kind of rearguard action when they went to Canada, where my sister and I were instantly deposited in a boarding school of the heroically Spartan British type, partly at least so we would avoid contamination with the Canadian accent.

Despite there being this almost impenetrable gulf between the two races, occasional social contact occurred. A few years before I was born, my father's cousin, Jessie de Goutiere, produced her first son in Nainital, a hill station in northeast India, and had some interchange in the nursing home with Indian women who were also confined there. What remained in her memory above all was the plight of a young bride, not yet in her teens. This child delivered her baby, recovered, and had to leave. She never stopped weeping at the prospect of returning home. The nuns were equally unwilling to give her up to her large, ageing, and unpleasant husband, but could do nothing about it. The problems were sexual; he was insatiable, and she found his demands terrifying and painful. However, she had no choice but to satisfy him, and would no doubt be pregnant again almost instantly and dead before many years were over. Jessie was powerless to help her.

Had she known more herself, she would have realized this girl was better off than most in that she delivered her baby where she did; most births, even among the wealthiest, took place in the worst room in the house—a dank hole with old rags used during delivery. In this instance, it was not a case of women being devalued, as Mayo suggests, but because it was better not to attract the attention of the gods, who might react negatively to the propitious event. Jessie talked about another encounter which supported the same superstitious fear, as well as a very real devaluation. She watched a little girl being treated with harsh disdain by her mother—an unusual circumstance—and managed to ask why she was being so unkind. It transpired the unhappy woman had lost several sons and was terrified of losing this child, who was in fact a boy. In order to deflect the bad luck or the gods' anger which had followed her, she dressed her son as a girl and treated him as worthless.

Since the British and Indians lived such separate lives, it must have been comparatively straightforward for the British to interfere as little as possible with the religious and cultural lives of the people they ruled. However, there were some exceptions. They had interfered with thug-gee and suttee. About a hundred years before, William Bentinck as Governor-General had outlawed both. But by the 1920s, nothing had been done about child marriage, a more amorphous ethical problem than the other two. All three customs had religious sanctions.

Thugs killed as ritual sacrifice to Kali; they strangled their unsuspecting victims with a knotted cloth containing a coin consecrated to the goddess. Untold thousands were killed in this way, one man alone admitting (or boasting) to having made 719 sacrifices.

Wives who walked, or were forced, into the flames of their husbands' funeral pyres were considered to re-enact the role of Sati, one of the incarnations of Shiva's consort (Kali is another), who immolated herself in her father's sacrificial fires when he quarrelled with and humiliated her Lord. She is the prototype of the perfect wife, and those who committed suttee were considered equally perfect: their act would, in addition, save their husbands countless incarnations. Some of these wives were still small children—and may have been yoked to ageing men—whose marriages had not been consummated.

Long outlawed, suttee—restricted to the highest castes and particularly prevalent among the Rajput *kshatriyas*—takes place even today, and in my parents' time there was the odd personal encounter with the remnants of the custom. One of these came through the fair-haired tennis player, Cuckoo Wall, mentioned earlier, and her lovely dark sister, Pat, whom I remember well. It's a remarkably romantic story. Twenty or thirty years after suttee had been legally outlawed in 1830, a young soldier whose name was Angelo was out with his platoon when they heard terrified screams in the distance. They galloped towards the disturbance and found a woman being burned alive on her husband's pyre. Angelo and his men rescued the widow, who was about fifteen, and he married her, making her in time the grandmother of Cuckoo and Pat. The mixed marriage in no way interfered with his career—he finally became a brigadier general—or denigrated his descendants: in the earlier years of British rule, when there were few white women in the country, mixed unions were fairly common and were not regarded with the snobbish disdain they incurred later when the fishing fleet moved into high gear.

The marriage bond, sacred as it was in conservative Western society, was sanctified to its limit in Hindu culture. Whereas the Englishwoman was supposed to look up to her husband, to "consider" him, to follow his decisions, and to be sexually available, the Hindu wife was expected to regard her husband literally as her god. Her duty was to please him utterly, responding with love and admiration to his needs and talents, doubtful though the latter might be. She was expected to be cheerful and meek under all circumstances, and to rely on him totally:

She should do nothing independently
even in her own house.
In childhood subject to her father,
in youth to her husband,
and when her husband is dead to her sons,
she should never enjoy independence. . . .

Though [her husband] be uncouth and prone to pleasure,
though he have no good points at all,
the virtuous wife should ever
worship her lord as a god. (*Ramayana*, ii, 57)

If a man died, his widow, often still a child, was considered responsible and her life became even more difficult than it had been previously
in her mother-in-law's domain. She become more of a slave to the
household than she'd been as a wife, and she cast a pall over all who came
in contact with her since she was considered to bring them bad luck. As a
result, she was not allowed to take any part in social or ritual life. If she
broke her vows, it was believed she imperilled her dead husband's
spiritual welfare and was thus constantly watched by her lord's relatives.
All through her life she was to remain humble, chaste, discreet, isolated,
and hard-working. People speak of seeing these widows, with shaved
heads and clothed in mandatary white saris, flitting like little ghosts
as they ran their errands and then disappeared. In 1925, there were
26,834,838 of them; recent statistics place them at 23,000,000. One can
only assume that most girls and women tried and still try desperately to
keep their husbands alive, no matter how unspeakably awful they might
be.

I recently asked my mother about child marriages and she said that,
yes, of course they knew about them and she'd heard some of the little
girls did suffer. She said they could be married before menses and would
move into their husbands' family homes, but the marriage was not
supposed to be consummated until puberty. However, Katherine Mayo,
again in *Mother India*, unearthed a petition regarding child brides
presented by Western women doctors to the Viceroy in 1891 and
brought forward as applicable in 1922 when some members of the
Legislative Assembly were attempting, against strong opposition, to
raise the marriageable age of girls to thirteen. The bill was thrown out as
impinging upon the sacred vows of matrimony. The petition listed the
following cases (extracted):

A. Aged 9. Day after marriage. Left femur dislocated, pelvis crushed out of shape, flesh hanging in shreds.

B. Aged 10. Unable to stand, bleeding profusely, flesh much lacerated.

C. Aged 9. So completely ravished as to be almost beyond surgical repair. Her husband had two other living wives and spoke very fine English.

D. Aged 10. A very small child, and entirely undeveloped physically. This child was bleeding to death from the rectum.

   Her husband was a man of about forty years of age, weighing not less than eleven stone [154 pounds]. He had accomplished his desire in an unnatural way.

E. Aged about 9. Lower limbs completely paralysed.

I. Aged about 7. Living with husband. Died in great agony after three days.

M. Aged about 10. Crawled to hospital on her hands and knees. Has never been able to stand erect since her marriage.

A bill was finally passed in 1925 fixing a girl's age of consent at thirteen. Later the age was raised to sixteen but official regulations mean little in India, particularly in rural areas. Recently (1989), a news photograph showed a two-year-old girl suckling at her mother's breast after her marriage to a six-year-old boy had been celebrated.

Arranged marriages were general. Love, not unwisely perhaps, was considered to grow after, not before marriage. Rabindranath Tagore explains the premise in *The Book of Marriage*:

> For the purpose of marriage, spontaneous love is unreliable; its proper cultivation should yield the best results . . . and the cultivation should begin before marriage. Therefore from their earliest years, the husband as an idea is held up before our girls, in verse and story, through ceremonial and worship. When at length they get the husband, he is to them not a person but a principle, like loyalty, patriotism or such other abstractions. . . .

Virtually all girls were to be married. The few who were not were those given as offerings to, or were chosen by, the temples to become *devadasis*—prostitutes of the gods.[7] Their function was to attend the god's person—for example, to wash and clothe him—to sing, dance, and help the devotee achieve union with the god.

---

[7] Recent literature claims they are not and never were prostitutes. However, the word is translated as given.

The *devadasis* formed a tiny exception. In general, a father had to find his daughter a husband. If he failed, he was socially stigmatized and was believed to incur frightful karmic penalties. Added to his problems was that of raising a dowry as well as an often vast amount of money to pay for the nuptial festivities. This was the case in all classes: in *India As I Knew It* (1925), Michael O'Dwyer speaks of the marriage of a Maharajah's sister which was to cost thirty to forty thousand pounds. He objected to the expense and asked for precedents, but there were none. For over two hundred years the daughters born into the family had not survived.

Poor fathers were naturally in greater difficulties than rich ones so infanticide of girl babies was inevitable. Enid found her "thrown away" baby and was told by Robin when she was in some way involved with the Gurkha hospital in Dehra Dun that she should not be surprised at the numbers of stillborn little girls. They were far from stillborn: at birth the custom was to lay them on a nearby table with their heads hanging off its edge until they died. They were too great a liability. The British obviously ignored this custom: Enid must have been warned so she wouldn't ask embarrassing questions. She didn't appear to be shocked by it.

To bear a son who would carry on the family name, support his parents in their old age, and perform the last rites at the funeral pyre, was considered of even more importance for a woman than that she, as the perfect wife, remain chaste. Without a son, she was nothing. Sometimes, through no fault of her own body, it was impossible for her to conceive. Agehananda Bharati told me that when he served in the temples, men whose wives had not become pregnant would bring them to stay overnight. The wife was then visited by the god, who hopefully impregnated her, chancing that the offspring would be a son. The child would, of course, be taken as that of the husband, who was probably infertile due to venereal disease.

Babies were delivered by midwives, castigated by Mayo as filthy and of low caste as befitted their defiling occupation. But Pamela Clay was successfully birthed by competent Indian women in Darjeeling despite a difficult delivery which produced twins, and Enid says nothing of filthy conditions when she once went to help with the labour of a young Gurkha woman whom she'd heard screaming with pain. She said the custom was for the mother, lying on the floor, to place her feet against a wall while bearing down for the birth. At midnight, she was told by the two midwives that she should leave as the baby was about to be born. Apparently they didn't want her there for the actual birth—perhaps because she knew little about it or perhaps because at one time the Gurkhas believed if a white woman lived among them some vital essence would vanish into the air. By morning, the baby had still not appeared and the girl was still in agony. Enid contacted the regimental doctor who had the young mother taken to the hospital and successfully delivered. The doctor was not enthusiastic: "Please don't send any more of your women to me, Mrs. Robin, because they might die and then I would be blamed."

No one of my acquaintance or in the accounts I've read of the period mentions dowry deaths, although Mayo noted that many young women died under questionable circumstances. Since recognition of such deaths has been so recent, it's impossible to know if they have always taken place.

Of course, this brief examination of the life of Indian women earlier in this century is totally one-sided, relying as it does on observations by Westerners. An account, including details of her mother's traditional views, by Shudha Mazundor, in *A Pattern of Life in India* (1977), covers the same period and gives a charming picture of childhood and marriage from a Hindu viewpoint. Shudha Mazundor's story is of a woman who was born into a wealthy brahman family and who married a liberated and sympathetic man, so naturally it's also limited, but it does illustrate the success which could attend upon Tagore's belief that spontaneous love is unreliable and that girls should be trained from their earliest years to cultivate love "through ceremonial and worship."

Shudha's childhood appears to have consisted of a gentle, constant training to mould her into a perfect wife who would fit cheerfully into her in-laws' home, no matter how irksome that might be. Her mother stressed that a man may do as he chooses but a house is doomed where a woman follows her own desires: it is her duty to be entirely true to her husband's family traditions, so she will never disgrace herself or her own family when she moves to her new home. The vocation, Shudha was taught, of every girl is to be a wife and mother and to be of service to others. Her training hinged on religious thoughts and practices, embedded in *bratas* (vows). As a tiny girl, she was educated in simple duties through, for example, the *tulsi brata* which taught her how to care for the household bush of sweet basil, or the cow *brata* which made her familiar with the friend who nourished her. Her prayers were naïve and practical: "Cows in the cow shed / Corn in the store house / Vermilion between the parting in my hair / Every year a son and may not a single one die / And may not a teardrop fall from my eye."

Shudha was allowed into her mother's *puja* room with its pictures of gods and goddesses only after she'd washed and changed her clothes. Lakshmi, goddess of plenty and wife of Vishnu, was kept in the sacred room along with her toilet articles and gay ribbons in a basket emblematic of a happy marriage. This basket, also containing a mirror, cowrie shells (symbolic of wealth), collyrium for the eyes, and precious vermilion for the married woman's hair parting, was carried by the bride when she left her father's house. Soft Ganges mud, out of which the child was to mould each day her Shiva in *lingam* form, was also in the room. The phallus (lingam) would have become an expected and intimate male property. After it was sculpted, it was worshipped with flowers, holy water, lamplight, and *pujas* for it was believed Shiva's benediction would bring his devotee a husband as great-hearted as himself. These attributes were stressed in the legends and stories told to young girls in order to prepare them for the excitement of meeting their own "god." All was carried out with tender ritual that sometimes included Shudha's small friends, although she was not encouraged to associate with certain girls (were some of them white or Eurasian?) at school because they didn't have the standards of cleanliness that her mother insisted on.

She says girls were married between nine and twelve after lengthy consultations on breeding, health, education, and horoscope readings. The event was crowned with an enormous feast, and for some time after her marriage the bride was dressed in gold ornaments, fine saris, and a veil that was to be held at a certain height over her face, depending on her intimacy with her visitors. Above all, she was to be bashful before her husband. In fact, every time he passed by, she was supposed to run away. On the auspicious night, she was to wait for him to speak—and she was told he would probably ask her her name although he of course knew it, simply because he had to say something—and then they were to whisper: many people in the extended family would be straining to hear what was said and would desire to be the first to announce all was going as it should.

In all this time, the bride and groom did not see each other except by dim lamplight, and the bride was never to be found with her husband in daylight: she would leave the bed at dawn each day and sleep next to her mother-in-law in another room.

Shudha's training in the mystery and devotion of marriage was justified, or her parents chose the groom wisely, or she was simply lucky. In any case, according to her account her marriage was happy, quite possibly far happier than those of British couples who'd joined together without any preparation whatsoever.

Of course, that's pure conjecture. It's impossible even to consider the possibility that Indian and British women ever discussed their intimate lives: they simply lived side by side with minimal communication. It's revealing that *Mother India* was written by an American woman who went to India for purposes of investigation. Unlike the outsider, the thousands of British women who lived in India for most of their lives appear to have taken little interest in these domestic affairs. The memsahibs, it seems, stood behind the system and "considered" their husbands, submerging their own views, if they had them, as their Indian counterparts did. And no more than they, fewer than two per cent of whom were literate in the simplest sense, had they been encouraged to think by an education which stressed character-building for future wives of the Empire rather than intellectual or imaginative faculties.

Sexual taboos possibly also stood in the way of Englishwomen finding out more about the country in which they lived. The Hindu religion is firmly based on sex, which is celebrated as a creative act: in the process of creating life, the entire universe is recreated. My mother once wrinkled up her nose in disgust when she mentioned *Holi*, the Indian spring festival, saying that the red powder thrown over people and animals was "supposed to be menstrual blood." She was so offended she didn't want to know anything more about it.

◈

My father, Robin, didn't mention the divisions caused by caste when he spoke admiringly of visiting an ashram in Rishikesh,[8] not far from Dehra Dun, where he found an excellent library. He said that anyone could go there and would be given a chair, a table, and a rope bed. All one had to do was to spend four hours a day in meditation—he

---

[8] In the sixties, the Beatles made Rishikesh famous when they studied transcendental meditation there with Maharishi Mahesh.

appeared to think this might be quite a simple undertaking! To his surprise, when he spoke to a man covered in ashes, with filthy, matted hair, he discovered that he spoke excellent English. Another, lying naked with his face in the grass, turned out to have been a Calcutta High Court judge who had "got religion."

My parents had been invited to this ashram by an Englishman who'd been studying for the church at Cambridge when he was caught up in the First World War and served in India. After his unit was disbanded, he wanted to find out more about Indian philosophy and was told by a Hindu family to buy a robe, a bowl, and a rosary, and then to go out, otherwise empty-handed, into the streets and beg. He claimed that he walked out of one world into another—a world of love. When he was hungry, people fed him, and when he was tired, he was given a bed. When the time was ripe for him to go somewhere, means were found, as my parents later discovered for themselves when he in turn visited them. All he had done, he said, was to walk to the railway station where a Hindu asked him where he was going, bought his ticket, and sent a telegram to the Dehra Dun *mahant* (the wealthy Hindu office holder in each district) who in turn sent his own car to drive him to his host's bungalow. After his stay, having presented my father with his begging bowl and rosary, and my mother with a small rare dog (I have no idea why he had a dog attached to him; it certainly wasn't a pi dog), he left in the same way.

Robin and Enid were excited by their visit to the ashram. This was, for them, an unusual opportunity, proving that had they not had a specific invitation, they wouldn't have considered themselves free to enter such a place. Once there, however, they discussed yogi practice with their host, who obviously made a profound impression on my father. In his account, he says this man told them the practice consists primarily in recognizing, as other religions do, the divine spark in all men and in developing that spark in order to foster union with God. He stressed that success depends entirely on the self: no one may do it for anyone else.

First one must discipline the body and purify the soul by abstaining from those things—strong drink, drugs, tobacco—which pollute the material part of the mind. Next one must rigidly control one's thoughts by, for instance, never thinking evil of anyone:

If one cannot think any good of a certain individual, then one must cast that person out of one's thoughts. How often does one hear one person rail against another? And to what purpose? The person railed against does not hear, but the person who rails works himself into a passion and loses his own tranquillity. The person who abuses another in his absence only advertises to the world his own state of mind.

The yogi also talked about what he considered the more difficult practises intended to widen the gap between the body and the soul. By dint of willpower—helped by bodily positions and breathing exercises—and constant practice, the devotee learns to focus all on God, moving in the process through three stages. The first is "I am His"; the second "I am Thine"; the third "I am Thou." In the second stage of realization, the devotee is already holy. In the third he is sacred, but few reach such elevation.

The Englishman claimed, as others have done, that the great masters could leave their bodies in a state of suspended animation while they travelled in the soul region, and that he himself was able to rise out of his body and look down upon himself, adding that the first time this happens it is a never-to-be-forgotten experience.

Robin wrote about another visitor to the ashram, Lieutenant Lal Bahadur Thapa, a Gurkha of the Chettri caste, who told him there was a large yogic ashram near his home. The Gurkha said that in it there were people who could perform miraculous healing, which he himself couldn't understand, but which certainly occurred. This man was drawn to the practice, but felt he was too materially minded at the time to become a wholehearted devotee.

Lieutenant Thapa had been one of those selected to represent India at the coronation of George V and talked enthusiastically about what an experience it had been to be shown the greatness of the Raj: battleships being constructed on the Clyde, secret defences of Gibraltar, and aeroplanes, which he'd never before seen. "It was all *bahut achcha bundobust* [very good organization]."

Robin asked him how long he had been in England:

He replied that he'd been there only three weeks. I asked him what had been his predominant impression, what stood out above everything else in his memory? He pondered for a moment and then replied that he thought he could never forget the little urchins running about Glasgow with bare legs and feet, and streaming noses, selling newspapers.

I had already heard the story of the answer to the same question put to one of his companions of that expedition. This was a grizzled old Subahdar who replied, "There were no flies in the bazaar [London], and the women spoke with soft voices."[9]

Robin considered his Gurkhas to be wise and humorous people, although he was amused over their inflated reputation as soldiers who "stormed walls in the face of gunfire and cut off the heads of the enemy with their kukris"—a report in the papers during the first war when, in fact, no Gurkhas had been present. He said they were just as frightened as anybody else during action and would have been fools not to have been. He added, however, that they were well disciplined and excellent to work with.

The Gurkhas—the word originally designated "defenders of cows" —are a tough mountainous people with an indomitable will to survive, no doubt due to their poverty and hardship as children. In a pamphlet, *My Life Story*, Rambahadur Limbu, the first Gurkha to win a VC,[10] writes: "My childhood was sad and unhappy. It was not that there was no love for me in the family, but it was evident that Death was determined to wipe out my whole family in no time. A large family of ten members died one by one . . . leaving only three young brothers. . . . We were not sure whether we were going to live either . . . but Death had indeed decided to spare [us]. This I was to know after many years while I was under a shower of bullets, but not a single bullet had my name written on it."

As young boys growing up in Nepalese villages or across the border in India, always hungry and cold, they subsisted by grazing cattle 8000 feet above sea level in areas infested with leopards and other predators and by trekking great distances for fuel and water. This experience combined with their religion—most are Hindus, some are Buddhists—made them possibly the most fatalistic people in the world. Their great hope was to be picked, at fourteen or a little older, for the army by a *galla walla*, a British recruiter, and they would go to any lengths to be chosen, having been brought up on tales of far-away places, plenty to eat, and heroism. If they failed to be taken, or if they failed in their training, they felt intolerably disgraced. Even so, fatalism prevailed. As one of them

[9] With reference to the first remark, historians suggest that those Indians who served in the two world wars and actually saw England realized Raj power and wealth were not as great as they had thought and their knowledge subsequently helped fuel Independence.

[10] Over 70 per cent of all VCs conferred in both world wars went to Gurkhas and Sikhs.

wrote: "How he picked me I can only attribute to what is written on my forehead—that which the gods write at birth and the skin hides all our lives—but he did pick me."

Fatalism in the Gurkha culture is backed by religious belief in a God who decides it all: Lalhabadur Limbu, another highly decorated soldier who looked on his being promoted and demoted with indifference, as nothing he'd asked for, wrote: "I thought to myself what we say up in the hills: 'In matters of God, Government and Games, there is neither victory or defeat, but that the Referee wills it'" (Sandro Tucci, *Gurkhas*).

Like others, Robin Murray found his young soldiers to be optimistic, open, resourceful, and cheerful. He told a story of climbing in the Himalayas when he took two Gurkhas with him. This was a long, fast trek during which they walked away from their supplies. He offered one of them some chocolate, which he carried with him for just such a contingency, but it was refused. The Gurkha said, "I'd probably like it very much and would want some in the future when I couldn't have it, so it's better not to know what it tastes like."

On the same trek, he heard the two men joking and laughing and asked them why they were amused. They were embarrassed, didn't want to tell him, and went on laughing. Finally, they admitted they'd been discussing the reason for such late marriages among Englishmen and had decided it was because Englishwomen were so ugly. They found it entertaining that the powerful British had to put up with such women while they had their own beautiful wives. As well as respect, some at least, of the British, had an amused and tolerant attitude towards the Gurkhas. Outside the Mess there hung what appeared to be an ordinary bell. One day an officer was informed that the bell had been scratched, and on examination found it was made of gold. Someone had been carefully shaving the bell during the night. My father said, "They're very clever people, you know. And they're very poor."

My father's anecdotes to do with his regiment are few: the Gurkhas, with their regulated caste system and military hierarchy, fell into the same category of general separation between Indians and British. On the other hand, the yogi (who was, of course, British but had become Indian in his outlook) had a profound influence on him. In his obituary, his former commanding officer wrote: "He was never known to say a nasty word about anyone." Being human, he certainly did not admire everyone, but he managed to keep quiet about how he felt.

Gandhi, who succeeded in so much, who fought against caste[11] and for women as fiercely as he fought for Independence, had not succeeded, by the time of his death, in wiping out hierarchical and sexual attitudes which had existed for centuries. In the twenties and thirties, undoubtedly admired by some of the British, he appears to have been known to those in the army as a nuisance and something of a joke. I doubt if military families were interested in the social issues he raised, not because they were indifferent to human welfare, but because they were unknowing. One of my aunts said, "We thought he was a funny little man. But now we are forgotten, and look at him!" In a letter written to my father in 1931, the English yogi says: "Compared to Gandhi, Vaswani [an Indian spiritual leader] is a garden of flowers whereas Gandhi is a bundle of commercialized humility."

Robin wrote about an incident which occurred in the same year. He and Enid were riding along a narrow bazaar road when they became aware of a rumpus on ahead: men shouting in unison, a swirl of people even thicker than usual. They were confronted by a procession with men marching four or five abreast carrying tattered cloth scrolls. He said there had been some talk of hostile political demonstrations against the British by followers of Gandhi, but that those in the cantonments had only read about them in the papers. In this confrontation, he and Enid, white and obviously of the ruling caste, were defenceless. There was no room to pass and their horses, unnerved by the mob, started to act up, endangering the merchants' stalls. At this juncture, their *syce*, who had been following them with the mid-day feed for all three horses, caught up to them and abused the crowd, shouting *chhup raho* (shut-up), and so on. The crowd silenced and parted instantly:

> Subsequently, I sent my servant back to the village to ascertain discreetly what that business had been about. I received the report that some *bad-mashas* (troublemakers) had come into the village and paid the inhabitants four annas (eight cents) an hour to walk around the streets shouting, "Gandhi! We want Gandhi!" and other similar remarks.

> "What did the people think of it?" I enquired.

[11] He was assassinated by a fanatical brahman because of his attitude towards caste.

So far as he could find out, nobody seemed to think anything at all, but it was grand fun; many of the men had no jobs, and as for the others, they were being paid the same wages as they would have got for toiling in the fields.

Divorced as they were from the Indians and experiencing this kind of incident, it's hardly surprising that many of the military British did not take Gandhi and Independence very seriously or that they had little intimate knowledge of the lives of those with whom they shared a continent. The two peoples lived their separate lives, staring at each other for a moment, as my childhood friend Lionel Brandon and the little Indian boy did, one in the train about to go on his way, and the other in the station, remaining where he was.

PART II

India Now

Chapter
Six

*E*ARLY IN 1987, FIFTY-FIVE years after leaving India, I finally returned. Jenny Colbourne, born in Calcutta and taken to England as a child in 1945, and I had often talked about going back, and now we felt time was running out. Neither of us knew exactly what we were looking for, but we did know we had to explore submerged memories—perfumes, landscapes, people—and examine the roots out of which our lives had grown. For us, India had become a mythic country, set in the past. We wanted to discover its reality and the changes, based on our fugitive memories and those of others, that had taken place. Jenny went ahead, and later my husband, Walter, and I followed her.

We travelled, sometimes together and sometimes separately, for three months. Even so, it was impossible to uncover all the territory that had been with me since childhood. Spring came late that year, and Kashmir was still under snow; we didn't have the time or money to reach Peshawar, now in Pakistan. I returned with Walter and another friend, Dale, eighteen months later.

My personal quest ended unexpectedly in a graveyard in Peshawar, but even then I had no idea how profound an emotional turmoil remained until I returned to my second country, now experienced differently because I had changed.

Shortly after our return, a man selling frozen food—steaks, salmon and sole, prawns and stuffed chicken to be put into a microwave oven—drove his van up to the door. I picked up a container and asked him what it weighed. He said he didn't know. I estimated four pounds. He agreed. All those neatly wrapped packages weighed about the same amount and each sold for between $50.00 and $100.00. In India, the price of one package would keep a large family in food and accommodation for more than a month. And few families are so favoured.

Unbidden, images sprang to life: a small boy giving his baby brother a bottle on a dingy Calcutta street at night, a monk met by chance on a road in Mussoorie, dying puppies with their dying mother in Varanasi, lepers holding out filthy rag-wrapped stubs of fingers, a man with elephantiasis, brilliantly alive children, a corpse sitting in flames, a tiny craft of flowers sailing down the Ganges, a young girl with her first bar of soap, a fire ceremony, a woman with one eye in Madurai.

Opposed to these images was that of a man at the door, rude and bad tempered because he hadn't sold outrageously priced dead fish and pieces of animals to be put with minimal effort into a microwave oven. A few months earlier he would have been taken for granted. But now we stood outside a house altogether too rich, in a street too quiet, in a country where children are not permitted to speak to strangers, where animals are either pampered or silently destroyed, where many adults live behind double-locked doors, where unsightly individuals are cloistered away, where no sacrificial flower boats sail waters, no monks pause on a hillside transmitting their joy to others, and where, certainly, if a woman has no natural eye she will wear one made of glass.

This North American country, where we are so fortunate, seemed, at that deadweight moment, to be so packaged, wasteful, orderly, concerned with the easy at any cost, so neurotically insured against possible disaster, and so unknowing, that its people have forgotten how to taste life before they die.

My voice was ugly with emotion—"We've just come back from India"—and I had to rush back into the house to hide my face.

Chapter Seven

*W*E WERE TO ARRIVE IN Calcutta. Before we left, we had read *Days and Nights in Calcutta* by Clark Blaise and Bharati Mukherjee and as a result Walter told me in all seriousness that he couldn't let me get into a taxi first because the door would be banged shut and I'd be whisked away to some terrifying destination. I pointed out I was too old for that kind of adventure. Who would want me? He dwelled on the authors' descriptions of murderers who haunted the road between the Ramakrishna Mission, where we intended to stay, and Calcutta itself. We'd also read Dominique Lapierre's *City of Joy*, a sympathetic and appalling account of slum life in the most poverty stricken city in the world. We'd seen articles in newspapers and journals depicting starvation, riots, diseases, lepers, and beggars. An Indian student studying in Canada had demonstrated how we were to place a foot through the straps on our luggage when we lined up for tickets: we'd certainly have our cases stolen if we didn't. Nightmares woke Walter up night after night. Why, he asked, if we had to go to India did we choose to land in Calcutta, the most deprived and terrifying city in the world? We were landing there because that's where we'd arranged to meet Jenny Colbourne. It was too late to change our minds. In any case, I wanted to go to Calcutta.

The flight on Aeroflot from London — the cheapest way — didn't bode well. Large, aggressive, white-uniformed stewardesses, reminiscent of Big Nurse in Kesey's *One Flew over the Cuckoo's Nest* pushed wagons down the aisles over sleeping feet and into jutting elbows. At five o'clock in the morning, they woke us up, if we'd managed to sleep at all, insisting we eat greasy lumps of stew, accompanied by red caviar, in heavy bowls. At Moscow airport, we moved in a line to have documents examined by a grim man who appeared to be a member of the police. When my turn came, he held up the procession a good fifteen minutes, scrutinizing passport, visas, inoculation forms. It was the first delay. Everyone else had passed through rapidly. Ridiculously unnerved, I began to wonder if by some Kafkaesque circumstance I was to be summoned before a tribunal which would inform me I was guilty without telling me what crime I'd committed. He finally asked if I knew I could stay in Pakistan only three months and upon my confirmation, let me through. This question made some sense after we'd travelled for a time, discovering Pakistan was in the U.S. sphere of influence and therefore suspect to the Russians.

Locked into the monolithic steel and glass airport for eight hours, we were served inedible food by sullen waitresses who pushed dishes back and forth desultorily. The lights were turned out and we tried to sleep on linked, tubular chairs while loud voices and clicking heels echoed off cement walls. I remembered the ship leaving England for India when I was a child: the streamers, the flowers, the porters, the immaculate stewards jumping to attention, the crane swinging enormous loads of luggage on board (here, we had a small suitcase each), the festivities.

Even so, hardly recognizing them at the moment, gestures were made which should have indicated something of what was to come. An Indian restaurateur, returning to his birthplace for an arranged marriage, insisted on buying us glasses of wine. The price boggled us. We wanted to return the gesture, but the wine was undrinkable. Separated on the final leg of the flight, Walter and I sat next to Indians. He is so large—six foot four, weighing over two hundred pounds—that an aisle location was essential then and even more essential later. Our seatmates individually offered us rides into Calcutta from Dum Dum, where we were dreading difficulties since we didn't know if letters sent to India had arrived. We were also convinced a taxi driver would cheat us unmercifully. We had to make our money last three months.

The offers were comforting but unnecessary. When we emerged from the airport, we picked out three faces at the front of a vast crowd; they belonged to Jenny Colbourne, Kalyan Pal, whom we'd once met briefly in Canada, and his friend Mr. Chatterjee. The three of them were ecstatic: they hadn't really expected to see us, or at least not both of us. On their first enquiry, neither Walter nor I was listed as on the flight; on the second one of us was, but they didn't know which one.

They had booked a taxi. They'd taken care of everything. Human nature being what it is, we felt ridiculously superior to a distraught traveller who came up and asked us if there was a hotel of some kind in Dum Dum. He was there only briefly and had obviously read the same kinds of accounts about Calcutta that we had. When Kalyan directed him to nearby accommodation, his relief was so apparent we wanted to laugh. We shouldn't have. After all, we'd been told by a world traveller that when she had to be in Calcutta for a couple of days, she'd locked herself in her hotel room and hadn't come out until her taxi took her to the airport.

❧

We drove through the dusk of Bengal's winter (January) with Mr. Chatterjee, overcome by excitement, reciting Gray's "Elegy," the poem, oddly enough, General Wolfe was reading, a few years after it had been written, in the small boat which took him to the cliffs fronting the Plains of Abraham where he was shortly to die. Mr. Chatterjee had, of course, no knowledge of Wolfe or of Canada as his voice intoned the opening verse: "The curfew tolls the knell of parting day. . . ." The day was parting, and as he recalled the poem we saw people apparently already asleep, sharing their space with ghostly white bullocks and cows on the median of the highway. For the first time we saw these figures, later to become familiar, wrapped in greyed-over white shrouds which covered their entire bodies, lying down or sitting stiffly as if they were corpses. Images stand out in retrospect. Mine that evening is of a figure sitting immobile on a section of ground between two crowded highways with his knees raised to form a triangle, looking like a dusty phantom. Accompanying the image, is Mr. Chatterjee's voice breaking into fragments from Keats and what he believed to be Tennyson's "Charge of the Light Brigade"; it wasn't, but I didn't have the heart to correct him.

Jenny had told her acquaintances that I was a well-known Canadian poet. I do write poetry but am far from well known. However, no matter how much I demurred I was not believed; my protestations were put down to modesty, and soon I was not merely well known but famous. To the Bengalis, to be a poet is the ultimate pinnacle to which one can aspire. Soon people were asking me where they could buy my books — I had brought none with me. I'd seen no point in doing so. In Canada people sometimes buy poetry books, but they seldom read them. Often bookstores refuse to stock them. The change in attitude not only astonished, but also made me wretchedly embarrassed. Had I not been put out by Penguin? Penguins are almost the only English books available in India. An additional embarrassment occurred when Mr. Chatterjee asked Walter, politely, what he did.

Walter is a potter, and better known than I am as a poet. However, a potter belongs close to the lowest subdivision of the lowest caste in

India. When he told Mr. Chatterjee what he did, there was an embarrassed silence: how could a potter be connected to a poet? Should he even be riding in the same car as a potter? We later discovered the response was always the same. Talking to a fellow guest at the YMCA, into which Jenny had booked us rather than into the Ramakrishna Mission, she again dropped the "well-known" poet when we introduced ourselves. She seemed, quite rightly, to think it gave us some kudos. The man, who had insisted he was a radical and didn't believe in any deity or tradition, clasped his hands exultantly, saying, "You don't understand. I have met God." Then he asked what Walter did and on receiving the answer shrank back and was silent. From then on, Walter said he was an artist.

Kalyan Pal, our mail-drop and later our mentor and friend, lived near Dum Dum and had to return many miles that night, but he insisted on making sure we reached the Y before he went home. On the way, stunned with lack of sleep, we passed a slum in the growing darkness where individual dwellings had tiny roofs of thatch and tin. Each appeared to be little more than a yard square. We discovered later this was a not far from accurate estimate. Mr. Chatterjee told us they were the homes of refugees from Bihar. We came upon a wedding. January-February is an auspicious time for weddings, and later we came across many more. The splendid groom, followed by his male friends, was mounted on a wretchedly thin white horse. He wore richly coloured clothes, an elaborately carved white head-dress, a garland of marigolds. He sat on a gaily coloured saddle and held decorated reins. Behind him, a lighted house front was also decorated with marigolds. Lakshmi, the goddess of plenty, requires many lights for a propitious union so that it may be materially prosperous. No matter how poor an Indian family, electricity, often run off a generator, is essential. Mr. Chatterjee said the groom was not from their parts, where a white horse was not mandatory, but that in some areas the groom's family had to obtain one at any cost or it was considered mean-hearted and was shamed.

When we reached the Y, we parted company from Kalyan and Mr. Chatterjee. A beggar followed us to the steps. He was a young man immersed in a dark shawl. One hand held the material about his face, the other was slightly outstretched. He later became familiar, we were on his beat, with his whining voice, his crooked arm. He called me "Mother," and the skin crept across my back.

◆◈◆

In historic terms not long ago, Calcutta had been the City of Palaces, the British centre of government until 1912, and after that still the business centre of the country: enormously wealthy, with wide streets, emporiums, parks, gardens, magnificent temples and an Anglican cathedral. It had also been, and still is, the cultural Mecca of India. An old Englishman who was returning for a visit told us that when he'd lived in Calcutta as a young man it had been the cleanest and most beautiful city in the world.

Jenny had been born in Calcutta. Her mother, when she was over forty had insisted on riding in the Ladies' Plate until, to her daughter's relief, she broke her leg thus putting an end to her wild ambitions. Here, Gillian's mother had helped raise money for "old cow farms," Pamela Clay's father had run an educational system, and my grandfather, Robert Murray, a Colonel in the Indian Medical Service, had conducted a lucrative private practice in which he was particularly successful at removing cataracts, at that time a difficult and problematical undertaking. He needed a lucrative practice; he was supporting his six children and two nephews, none of whom saw him in their formative years, in England.

This city had been the home of my grandmother who had a rhyme attached to her which made it easy to remember her maiden name: Mary MacInnis MacKay, Queen of the Island of Skye. She was probably reasonably typical of many Anglo-Indian women at the turn of the century and looking at her briefly should give some indication of what life used to be like, and the kinds of people who lived it, then. She was pretty with brilliant blue eyes, spoiled, unmaternal, sociable, conventional, humorous, and without self-doubt. She loved to dance, particularly the Highland Fling, and to laugh. She appears to have lived on a Tolstoyan stage without the self-questioning and growth into maturity of Tolstoy's characters. Lucky enough to have been dealt a hand that suited her admirably, she made the most of it, throwing herself into the social life in India, into bearing six children, all of whom survived, and into travelling back and forth across the world when visiting her offspring who were brought up — my father from the age of eighteen months — by nursery governesses and English public schools.

Being separated from her children didn't appear to upset her — it was an accepted fact of life — although she must have been aware of an often lack of sympathy among governesses and of the harsh discipline of public schools. Apart from her own experiences and those of her siblings, she recounted meeting Rudyard Kipling, a renegade regarded with scorn by most of the caste British, who had been sent from India when he was five and did not see his parents again until he was seventeen. He told her that he still couldn't stop himself from ducking automatically if anyone passed behind his chair, he was so used to having his ears cuffed for no discernible reason when he was studying or reading.

She was a conventional woman—in her old age, convinced the world was about to end, she hedged her bets by reading the bible every night— but open to surprises. When she met D. H. Lawrence in Majorca, where she was having a holiday with my family, she came back to the house one day in a state of high excitement, saying she'd met that "frightfully wicked man." She was charmed by him, and for him to have charmed a woman who regarded Kipling with reservations, he must indeed have had a quite wonderful way with him.

Mary Murray had been born in Madras, where her father, Surgeon-General George MacKay, as astute Scot, was secretary to various medical and military institutions. It was he who instituted the Widows' and Orphans' Fund after the Indian Mutiny in 1857 (a pension my mother still receives), but he must have been well settled there by 1850, when he was presented with a gold clock by "grateful patients." A community-minded man, he helped establish the Medical College of Madras for training Indians and also the first libraries. His children were destined for the life of the ruling class and the code which governed it.

That code included a gallant attitude towards women, who were considered to have been entrusted to their husbands by their fathers. Much freedom appears to have prevailed, partly at least because of this trust. Other men's wives were free to be admired, flattered, flirted with, but after that were out of bounds; women were expected to be charming and even flirtatious but scandal was to be heroically avoided, so if an infringement occurred it would no doubt have remained unacknowledged by all concerned. It's possible an infringement occurred in my grandmother's case, according to family gossip; if so, it was ignored.

In any case, a woman's charm lay in her frivolity, a gender rather than a sexual attitude, and she was treated with what today would be regarded as affectation: a kind of jolly patronizing. She was not to be taken seriously as a person, but as a member of the weaker sex was to be provided for, guarded, and treated with good manners and solicitude. Mary Murray loved to point out that in the Black Hole of Calcutta the one or two women involved were placed close to a single tiny air vent and survived, whereas most of the men died. History does not bear this out (in actual fact, the "hole" was a room opening onto a verandah, and no women are mentioned as being present), but the tale was typical, and this kind of story was capped with the sentiment that Englishwomen were looked after by Englishmen, whereas those of other nations were not so fortunate.

It would never have occurred to anyone that these women were second-class citizens without voting rights, and that their power lay in charm and cunning, or that their own sexual, and perhaps maternal, needs were not admitted to exist by their husbands or by themselves. Their education consisted in learning a kind of solid endurance, in knowing how to behave "correctly," and in imbibing attitudes which, for the most part, were never lost: one of these was certainly a sense of British, and even family, superiority. Another was contempt for unmarried women and particularly for "blue-stockings," who were regarded as opinionated, plain, and unable to get a man, or at least the "right" kind of man. The traces of this attitude still exist.

They spent their time in social activities: in leaving cards, returning calls, attending the Viceroy's balls in gorgeous gowns and jewels, going to dinners and dances, driving carriages, riding horses, painting water colours, playing the piano and singing—but never professionally. They were expected to be thrifty in small things and to live harmoniously with their husbands. For the right woman it was the ideal life—great fun with little responsibility, and sometimes had extraordinary rewards.

One day Mary Murray was driving her carriage through Calcutta, presumably with her *syce* in attendance, when she was "abducted" by an enthusiastic throng of men. They gesticulated and called out with excitement, the sun brilliant on their arms and faces, on their white cotton garments. They took her from her carriage, led her into a temple, covered her with ornaments and jewels, and paid her homage as if she were a goddess. The story gives no indication that she knew ahead of time what was going to happen, but she must have been warned and her husband must have known. If not, she would at the very least have been astonished if not frightened, even though Calcutta, the city of palaces, was considered absolutely safe despite its appalling poverty: poverty was not noticed by people like Mary Murray, who had grown up with it.

These men were thanking her and indirectly Robert Murray for his work in removing cataracts and thus giving sight to the blind, indicating he must have treated the poor for nothing because English doctors' private fees were considerable. I thought the story apocryphal until I went to India and learned that anything can happen there. Mary was presented with a turquoise ring by the Dalai Lama for the same reason.

That was my grandmother's Calcutta.

Today it is at least in part a city of refugees fleeing abject poverty in Bihar or persecution in Bangladesh. No one knows how many people live there. In 1985, statistics estimated over ten and a half million, with well over 200,000 people per square mile; according to Lapierre, in the slum areas each person has a margin of three square feet. This margin may now be smaller. When we walked through the streets, we found shops of perhaps six feet cubed divided horizontally: two men squatted crouched over at street level, and another sat cross-legged in the upper half selling his wares.

We made our way among crowds of walking people, buses, cars, three-wheelers, handcarts, motorbikes, bicycles, rickshaws, cows, bullocks, goats, and dogs, along streets rampant with potholes—one so large a car had fallen into it—partly caused by leisurely men meddling with drains or putting through underground transportation: a project which had so far taken eighteen years and would doubtless never be completed. Once Walter looked up, pointing to something he wanted us to see, and fell into a gaping cavity. We couldn't take our eyes off the two feet in front of us, particularly since we hadn't acquired the sixth sense of the Bengalis who manage to avoid each other, whether walking or as part of the insane traffic. To go a couple of blocks was exhausting—and this in the cool winter. Certainly in the summer, when rats may be broiled alive, or during the monsoons when a man could fall into a rushing manhole because its cover had been stolen for iron content, it would be inconceivable.

Apart from government buildings, which are kept in reasonable repair, we found brick, stone, and iron crumbling to the ground. Early in the day, water from pumps where people wash forms puddles and rivulets in broken asphalt. Trees grow through buildings. Beggars inhabit every conceivable spot. Telephones almost never work, so if you want to see somebody you send a messenger. Constant power cuts plunge everything into darkness. The homeless live anywhere and everywhere. Without public lavatories, men urinate against walls and into open drains. Most debris is disposed of by dogs and cows—I watched a sleek white cow steadily eating a long, filthy rag—and the rest (scraps of paper, old nails, bits of glass, nuggets of coal, cow dung) is carefully gathered to be sold or used.

But also, children laughed and collected around us; people we met on the street asked us to their homes; flowers and shrines glowed from nooks and crannies. Above all, it seemed to us a city where people operated from the heart, where the Bengalis look on their teeming "guests"—most of whom are Moslems—with a kindly resignation. And where, when we talked to a stranger, he didn't open the conversation with a remark about the weather and then turn away, but with something on the order of "Do you believe in the Almighty?" and that question naturally led into fascinating ramifications. Finally, when we left India, but particularly Calcutta, we felt deprived on returning to a sanitary, ordered existence in our own cities with their often isolated and lonely inhabitants.

❧

Surprisingly, since there is no space anywhere, the Y is built around a tennis court complete with players in their mandatory white sports' clothes. An upper balcony where guests sit in the evening and talk to each other, surrounds it. We found its rooms clean and adequate, with a lighted coil to deter mosquitos. However, its breakfast was quite horrible, its water supposedly filtered and purified, but when Walter went to the kitchen to refill a jug he found it came straight out of the tap. He was dismayed—above all else we'd been warned to avoid untreated water. From that moment, we doctored it with disinfectant and were wise. We discovered later that most educated people carried their own water with them when travelling. Indians, too, are subject to delhi-belly.

Outside the Y, a woman sat on the sidewalk with two boy babies and an exquisite little girl. All day they were there and late into the night. The babies, lying naked on bits of white cloth spread on the sidewalk, were pale brown, immaculately clean and chubby: they were little chips off the sun, perfectly formed. We never heard them crying. The girl in her ragged green dress did most of the begging: she would run after us, cupped hand out, smiling. In the evening, the babies were shrouded in their cotton cloths, asleep. Three feet away endless traffic shot its exhaust into their bodies. The family had a tin cup and a tin plate. We had the feeling, after a few days, that at some time late at night they disappeared and returned early in the morning, and we wondered if they actually lived somewhere else.

Danny, an Indian film-maker staying at the Y, was documenting poverty in Calcutta. He told us there was a syndicate that looked after beggars. In return for being given the take, this Mafia minimally housed, fed, and clothed them. During good times the Mafia flourished; during lean times the beggars didn't starve. He said he had offered this woman a small job, accommodation and food, but she'd refused. To our concern as we thought of the traffic, noise, dirt, he saw this as laziness—it was easier to sit on a street corner. Others pointed out that beggar women always had small babies and suggested they were not necessarily their own—they were possibly lent to them by the syndicate which was accused of stealing children. Dr. Manna, whom we met soon after arrival through a contact with his son in Canada, told us the same thing. He and Danny both asked us not to give these beggars anything: doing so encouraged the system. We were to give only to the very old and to lepers. I asked Dr. Manna if it were true that children were sometimes crippled at birth to make them more pathetic and he said, yes, that was the case. Lapierre writes of this organization in *The City of Joy* and claims it runs every aspect of the lives of the poor.

But when we returned to Canada, I asked Agehananda Bharati about this syndicate.

He exploded with impatience: "I suppose you were told some kind of Mafia organizes beggars, cripples children, and all that nonsense. It's quite untrue. There may be a small syndicate that looks after perhaps one tenth. Possibly. But these people are professional beggars. They always have been. They provide the givers with merit. That's the way it is."

Whether a syndicate exists or not, at the time we became aware of feet twisted sideways or backwards, of broken fingers, and preferred not even to consider far worse distortions which indeed were probably birth defects. From then on, we felt guilty if we gave alms and guilty if we didn't. In the country of the blind the one-eyed man is king, and in India, we, with our little bundle of travellers' cheques, were wealthy beyond imagining. We were told if we offered food instead of money, it would be turned down. This was not true.

Tara and her friends found us almost instantly. Intelligent, lovely, perhaps about ten, she apparently lived on the street. Wrapped in an ancient muslin shawl and skirt, her black hair drawn off her face, her feet without shoes, she was an actress, a spark of joy, a survivor. She went everywhere with us except into the Lal Market where an attempt is made to keep beggars out. There the licensed guides are the beggars—it's their territory. She waited outside, and then, skipping along, held one of my hands, her friend the other, talking in Bengali the entire time. Since we were not supposed to give them money we bought them bananas and *samosas*. They were delighted. When a wretched little boy wanted to join our entourage, Tara screwed up her face and shook her head—no, he's not worth it; you belong to us.

"Mama? Papa?" we asked.

She burst out laughing: "No Mama, no Papa."

That could have been true.

ـﻬﺟﻬـ

Jenny had already been in India for two months and had seen the south, where we were to go, so when we went on she stayed behind and rejoined us later. Having travelled alone, she was unravelled by the time she met us, her straight fair hair flattened to her head, her long, attractive face without colour. She'd slept in cheap hotels and eaten all the things we were warned against without experiencing delhi-belly but had contracted a low-grade pneumonia.

She told us she was sometimes amazed at the way she behaved: she was much nicer than she was elsewhere, but also she did and said things she would never dream of in other places—she could be impatient, unkind, rude. We saw this for ourselves one day when we were going to the market, followed by a hoard of children. She turned around and hissed at them in a fury: "I'll get the police. Go away." They scattered instantly.

But later, after we'd left, Tara pestered her and explained through gestures that she had only one dress so she could never wash it: "So on the last day, off we went to the market and I picked out a frightfully practical dress with a zip to the waist. It was expandable, and long. I suggested she put it on. She shook her hands and head, indicating she needed to have a bath and wash her hair, so that meant we had to look for soap—you know, they usually use a lump of clay and ashes. Might as well go the whole hog, I thought, so I bought her a bar of Lux. Then we had to find a pump. By this time there was a procession. After some shyness, she lifted her dress and scrubbed herself, and then a girl carrying a baby wanted the baby washed, and her clothes, and so on. By this time, we were surrounded by children and when I left they were all bathing, blowing bubbles, jumping up and down, and pumping water like crazy. Tara got more fun out of the soap than out of the dress."

In England some months later, Jenny watched a documentary on an Englishman, Dr. Prager, whom we'd met working on a street close to the Y. Early in the morning, people lined up for treatment and medication. One of his patients in the film was Tara, a subdued shadow of herself, listless and quiet, and he said, "This child is suffering from tuberculosis." We wondered if she was still alive.

We also wondered what had become of Dr. Prager, who had far outstayed his visa and was threatened with extradition. He wasn't overly concerned when we met him, saying, "Well, you know India. I hope to be here for years before they finally, if they do, turn me out."

While he talked, he looked at the long line of people in front of him, one with his foot in a basin of water, others women carrying children. Renting a room from an English lady of eighty-seven left over from the Raj, he'd adopted the Indian attitude: let the day look after itself. His only regret appeared to be that he didn't have a "surgery" and some necessary instruments.

Chowringhee, now officially changed to Jawaharlal Nehru Road but unrecognized as such, is one of the chief roads in Calcutta, wide and once handsome with grand hotels and shops. As night came on, we passed sleepers under its Esplanade: each about eighteen inches from the other, shrouded in ageing cloths, faces covered to discourage insects and rats, they lay in a row. Similar to those on the road from Dum Dum, they were like corpses in a slightly foetal position, without movement or sound. Against a wall, we noticed an odd pile of what appeared to be refuse—old cloth, a newspaper—but the pile was a child, or more than one, asleep for the night.

We asked about taking photographs and were told, gently, that people didn't like their poverty exposed. Even so, one evening I found it impossible to resist. A boy of four or five was sitting alone on the pavement with a baby in his arms. Beside him was a bucket of what appeared to be filthy water or paint, a pile of rags, an old cooking pot, and a baby's bottle. I gestured with my camera—I had to use a flash and was nervous. The street was crowded, men were pushing past us, the traffic was nerve-wracking. We'd been told small things could lead to sudden tensions.

The child was very sleepy. He smiled and uncovered his brother's face, showing him off proudly. Almost asleep, he held up an arm for *baksheesh*. I gave him a rupee, adjusted the camera, and took a couple of shots. Men approached me, watching. But they only wanted to know how the camera worked, and one of them, a well-dressed man, said sadly, "They are so good."

And that is one's primary impression of the Indian poor despite strikes and occasional riots. In 1918, a British Under-Secretary of State, Edwin Montagu, made it his business to attempt to stir "the masses of India out of their state of pathetic contentment." The subsequent bill based on his report doesn't appear to have succeeded. We also took photographs of a couple who lived in a back alley. They were delighted to pose, pulling out the crosses about their necks to indicate they were Christians. This appeared to be important to them—as if we were fortunate indeed to have chosen people of our own religion. Often it's the very poor, the Untouchables, who are Christians: they have nothing to lose. Later we returned with prints. No gift could have been greater. They called to their neighbours—everybody must see this miracle— and begged us to come again when their son would be with them. This was impossible and we made them understand that a boy was with them in one of the prints, but they shook their heads contemptuously—he was not their son. Boys, we found, loved to jump in front of the camera just as the shutter clicked.

We breakfasted in a tiny restaurant used by foreigners travelling on a limited budget and discovered "lassis," a delicious concoction like a milkshake. Later, travelling south, we watched out for them on street stands. It took us weeks to realize they were made with untreated ice and the glasses were washed in old buckets. Sugarcane juice sold everywhere bred the same problems. But tea was safe. Boiled with milk and insuffer- able heapings of sugar, it was sold in *chattis*—cups turned out in the millions by potters and thrown away ("It's only earth") after use.

Sometimes we treated ourselves to lunch at one of the grander hotels, The Park or The Great Eastern, or we had a Raj tea at Flury's. Jenny remembered going to Flury's as a child—the silver service, the cakes, the "separate, separate" tea: meaning we could administer our own milk and sugar without reverting to boiled tannic acid. These "great" hotels were clean and comfortable in their front areas but were fraught with the contradictions we were to find everywhere: to get to the cloakrooms, we had to pass into malodorous, water-spilled passageways, and sometimes through kitchens where rows of men were working. The cloakrooms themselves were tiny, swimming in water and refuse, without paper, towels, or soap.

To reach these hotels, we passed major hangouts for the dispossessed and became familiar with some of them.

Walking down the Esplanade, we heard a rapid patter of small feet behind us. We didn't want to turn around. We knew it would be somebody wanting something. When the sound was right behind us, we felt forced to turn and were confronted by Socrates, or so it seemed: a man with a large, intelligent face, handsome eyes, thick white hair brushed back from his forehead, a full white beard. His torso was well formed; his legs, no longer than six inches, terminated in the feet of a small child. When we gave him money, he took it proudly, as his due.

We passed lepers, some on their feet holding out stumps of hands swathed in bandages covered with blood and suppuration; others, their legs gone, travelling on boards with small wheels, pushing themselves along with their stumps. They congregated together, cheerful friends.

A young man with an exquisite face lay on a shred of cloth in the hot sun. He had no arms and his small legs were joined together into a kind of fish's tail. He didn't move or speak. He simply lay there all day, his tin cup for alms beside him, earning his family their bowl of rice.

A man with elephantiasis sat all day, too, but he had a chair. The exposed leg stretched in front of him was as large as an elephant's, its crinkled grey skin in folds, like an elephant's. Later we saw a young boy with the same hideous disease, contracted from mosquitos, with his useless arm a yard in circumference.

Sometimes in the evenings, we sat with Jenny in our bedroom at the Y, drinking gin and smoking cigarettes. "It is impossible for a woman to smoke in India," we'd been told. Few people drink: both indulgences are outlawed by Hinduism. Wherever we went, our bedroom was to become a refuge.

We found it oddly difficult to talk about what was happening to us. Perhaps we were too bombarded by chaos or too tired; perhaps living it was enough. I wanted to keep a record on tape and could occasionally persuade the others to join me on it.

"Is it what you expected?" Jenny asked one evening soon after we arrived.

120

"I don't know. Of course, I never lived in Calcutta—just heard those stories. It all seems vaguely familiar—perhaps the kind of constant music and the noise—but at the same time unknown. What really upsets me is I don't even recognize the language. I hoped it would come back."

"But they speak Bengali, not Hindustani."

"Oh, of course. I do remember blind beggars so perhaps the impact isn't as much as it would be if I'd never lived in India. And that strong marigold smell floats me back. But I don't know where. I don't know what I'm looking for."

"It's exactly what I expected," Walter said. "Wall to wall people. But they're not starving, thank God."

Jenny said, "No. And they're not diminished by their poverty because they don't expect anything else. They just keep on, endlessly trying to keep clean, washing themselves and their clothes on the street, and being so—cheerful. It's astonishing, really."

"No wonder the Indians are surprised at leftover hippies—that people actually choose dirty hair and ripped clothes," Walter said. "Fuck, why shouldn't they be?"

The clink of a bottle filled with duty-free gin is recorded on the tape. Then Jenny's voice goes on, telling us that one day when she was in the south in a temple filled with people, she suddenly felt terrified at being out of control. "I thought I was going to make a scene, throw myself on the ground in tears and submit. Submit unconditionally to a God I didn't think I believed in any longer. I don't know why—I'm not a great submitter. Just the reverse. And it was so unexpected. Whatever is happening to me, it's turning me inside out. It's not the poverty or the beggars—I expected all that. It's something quite different: a return to some kind of faith that was lost. It's very painful. I think it has to do with the way the poverty and pain is accepted. The cheerfulness."

"It all becomes blurred—I suppose it has to, or one couldn't bear it."

Danny, the film-maker, had told Jenny he concentrated on one family: the husband picked up scraps of waste paper that were made into containers for fruit and *muri*. His wife searched for used nails and then hammered them out and sold them, and early in the morning the children went through the piles of ashes and used coals that are raked to the side of the road at night. Their job was to sort and wash any unburned bits. The family makes about 600 rupees ($60.00) a month.

Jenny said, "I suppose it's enough to keep them somewhere and buy their rice."

"I saw some tiny girls looking for drinking straws in those heaps of refuse." I said.

Jenny laughed with an edge of hysteria: "Don't tell me they're the ones we use. Nothing's wasted. When I was in Goa, I stayed at a cheap place with an outdoor biffy where you crouched down. When I used it, the pigs came, squealing with delight, their snouts about six inches from my bottom. It was unnerving the first time but I got used to it."

"The *bhangis* are supposed to take them out, or used to, in the mornings to scour the ditches, but that was in the villages. I don't think I'll eat pork."

"Shit, no," Walter said. "I've never seen such hideous bristly black pigs." In his agitation he was finding four-letter words comforting.

Jenny had talked to the film-maker more than we had: "Danny said giving alms is very important to both Moslems and Hindus. It's a kind of philosophy. You can do terrible things with the left hand and make up by doing good things with the right. Beggars are at other people's disposal so they can gain merit—good karma. Perhaps that's why they don't usually thank you."

Walter said, "Remember Kalyan said some beggar was found after his death to have a lakh of rupees stowed away. Kalyan said, 'Why shouldn't he have? Why shouldn't he be able to save everything when he has no overhead?'"

Jenny started to laugh again: "Literally no overhead."

And I said, "I bet that's just another story. Where would he keep them? I've been wondering where the beggar women keep the babies' diapers. I've never seen any."

"They don't use them," Jenny said firmly. "Even the middle class."

While we talked we were thrust into darkness. Another power failure. The little snakewick lighted against mosquitos had burned itself out.

I said, "In the Lal Market today, Walter and I left a parcel behind after drinking some coffee. We thought it was useless to go back for it after all the stories we'd been told, but in the end we did, and there it was, waiting for us."

"I haven't lost anything," Jenny said. "And after travelling for months I feel safer here than anywhere else in the world. Just the same, it was nice to see you at the airport and it's incredibly nice to drink gin."

She felt her way to the door in the dark, still talking: "My mother said the Indians are happy people. I told the drugstore man I was taking lots of photographs to show my parents when I go home. This was really their city. He begged me not to. He said, 'Oh, don't. It will break their hearts.'"

I turned off the tape. The interminable noise—traffic, ghetto-blasters, loud voices—reverberated off the walls. We were already so used to it, we hadn't noticed it while we were talking.

Chapter Eight

*T*HE DRUGSTORE MAN helped us out in many ways. He sold us the disinfectant drops for our water, toilet paper—a luxury hard to find—and aspirin. It was he who first explained one of the problems to us. West Bengal has a communist government which, in its attempt to alleviate the conditions of the poor, had fixed the rents after taking office. As a result, it's not worthwhile for landlords to put money into buildings. At the same time, exorbitant prices are asked for accommodation that's for sale. He said a small, two-bedroom flat on Park Street sells for 90,000 pounds, so nobody can afford it. And then there appear to be no building regulations, or if there are no one pays them any attention: "My landlady, she was selling the roof of my building. These new people were deciding to put another storey on top above me. This new floor was so heavy it was causing all my walls to crack."

"But don't you worry about it?"

"Living in Calcutta is too much to worry just getting through a day. Who has the time to worry about cracking in the walls?"

It's the middle class—constituting now close to fifteen per cent of the population—which is aware of the problems and despairs. We talked to a bank clerk, an educated man with a passion for William Faulkner. He was on strike, and we asked him why: "God only knows," he answered gloomily.

Extraordinarily, Jenny found a particular connection with the drug-store owner. She had an image in the recesses of memory of an old-fashioned chemist's shop at a juncture where two roads split off into a Y. The shop had a rounded front window and contained big bottles of coloured water. She finally remembered it was called Bathgate and asked about it: "Out of business. It's gone. My mother, she bought or maybe was given those bottles. They were worth nothing then. I do not have them. Today, they would be buying my shop. Collectors, you understand."

Jenny had lived in India, chiefly in Calcutta, where her father was a tea dealer, until she was ten. She has that sense, which I also have, of not knowing where she belongs: "I've always had a problem when people have said, 'Where do you come from?' I go into a long spiel about how I was born in India, schooled in England, went to Germany, and now live in Canada. I always feel impelled to explain. It's the India part that's important—I suppose because of all those first impressions that are with you for life."

"Yes. And in any case, whether we were in India or Canada or somewhere else, our parents and other people always talked of England as 'home,' even if they'd never lived there."

"Exactly."

Jenny knew she had to come to terms with fugitive memories before she would know who she was. This amorphous need crystallized after her divorce in 1981 when she was in England and read in *The Daily Telegraph* column "Tall Tales from the Raj" that the Hallam School in Nainital, which she'd gone to during the war, was having a reunion in the Royal Armoury in Chelsea. She attended and suffered a shock: so many of her compatriots were so old. She was ushered into a large room filled with military portraits and balding Brits who were reminiscing about their ayahs and bearers, their lives in India. They were desperate for information and anyone who'd been back was mobbed. She said, hesitating, trying to find the right words, "There was something pathetic about it."

Later she moved house and realized how many Indian cook books she'd accumulated, how many of her clothes were in bright red and orange, and how often she'd been criticized by her parents for being inappropriately dressed. When she'd left India, before the war ended, her mother had told her, for security reasons, she was going on a picnic: the picnic had lasted forty-two years.

As a child, her idea of a railway terminal had been Howrah Station in Calcutta. She'd landed in Glasgow Central on a cold March day and was frightened because the people were so quiet and grey. In contrast, she remembered constant, brilliant sunshine (not, of course, a truthful image), the biggest butterflies in the world, the brightest flowers, the most powerful perfumes, and the most gaily dressed, talkative women. "Something is being restored to me from my childhood. I became a lapsed Catholic, but here I can believe again. I keep being struck by the devotion in people — Hindus, Catholics, it doesn't matter what. They all have a tremendous faith — God will look after you. You mustn't worry. Not just uneducated people, but everyone. And then everything is heightened — tenderness, violence, wealth, poverty, and that heightens one's emotional response. But at the same time, India's absolutely infuriating — the post office, the queues for tickets, cashing travellers' cheques. All those kinds of things."

Reliving her childhood, Jenny found her way to the Octherlony Monument, a huge column built on the Maidan — a dusty park area. As a child, she'd always wanted to climb up it and her mother had always said, "Tomorrow." Now at last, she fulfilled a life's ambition. But first she had to get police permission. It was no longer open to the public. At the station, the men were all amused — another British woman trying to recapture something that had gone forever: "I had to make an appointment — Thursday morning from eleven to eleven-thirty. It was like going to the hairdresser. But I had the whole place to myself. I could see the entire city.

"Then I wanted to find the house where I was born — it used to be #1 Clive Street, which was absolutely in the heart of Calcutta off BBD Bog, but of course all the names have been changed so it wasn't easy to locate. Anyway, Kalyan took me to the Central Post Office and we went through many rooms with people doing nothing — one light bulb and clerks with desks filled with ageing, yellow paper, and files everywhere, including the floor. I don't understand how anybody finds anything, but they know exactly where everything is. I was ushered into a room with six men also doing nothing, and Kalyan spoke to them in Bengali, but said 'sentimental reasons' in English, and they looked it up and decided it was now the Bank of Alahabad. I rushed to the window and indeed, there it was — I'd been born on the roof of that building, in a flat which my parents, as the youngest members of the staff of Findley's at the time, had lived in.

"And then we lived in a house on Store Road that was a chummerie. We lived upstairs, an Indian family downstairs. I looked for it, but it had been torn down."

"A chummerie?"

"All chums together."

"My God, it sounds like an English boarding school."

"Well, yes, it probably was like that. What happened was that many unmarried Englishmen would come out and club together and rent a house. When we were there, they were away — off to the war, I suppose. It had a grandiose staircase with hunting prints and tiger and leopard skins and boar heads. And a big, cool sitting room and then a verandah with wicker chairs and collections of blown eggs and butterflies in cases and an elephant-foot wastepaper basket. That's where the chums would have their sundowners — and my parents too, of course — while they were waited on by their turbaned bearers. They must have loved it. It was an elegant old house built in the last century."

"I don't suppose they thought twice about using an elephant's leg as a wastepaper basket."

"I don't suppose so. People didn't in those days. Anyway, it's hardly better now. I've heard exporters send Indians' skulls abroad to be used as paper weights."

"There are more Indians than elephants, I suppose."

"People will do anything for money. In any case, I managed to meet the man who lived next door — he's high up in Tata's — and he arranged for me to go around to the back where I remembered an orange tree. I wanted to take photographs. The tree was still there, big now, and there were banana trees and a tank. It was a jungle, filled with the old, wonderful smells. Once a snake charmer lost his python in that place. It was a garden then, and we'd played with a pet turkey in it that disappeared at Christmas. We were terribly upset. I'm glad the orange tree's still there — it's all that remains."

⋘⸙⋙

For Jenny the tree remained, and other, less tangible memories and emotions remained for both of us: qualities rather than objects. Passion, perhaps. A tiny girl, barely walking, clothed in a dirty dress, squatted in the dust of a back street in front of a cart selling *samosas*. Oblivious to a cow standing beside her and equally oblivious to passing traffic and people, she carefully, with her forefinger, traced the outline of a woman's face on a poster stuck to the cart. The face was that of a goddess. She moved her finger around the oval, to the eyes and mouth, and then pressing herself against the board she kissed the paper replica with the kind of passion associated with distraught lovers or with mystics burning in their devotions.

❧ ❧

We picked up the Calcutta English newspapers, wonderful for their Indian English and open criticism of government. One of them contained a brief article. It was without judgement, repeating an item picked up from an American paper which stated the U.S. authorities had broken up a ring of smugglers operating between the States and Mexico. Their booty were Mexican children whose parents had been told they would be adopted by rich Americans, and who had been paid $100.00. The children were kept in a small house inside the American border. When the Immigration authorities entered it, they found a dozen of them, ranging in age from a few months to twelve years. They were not there for adoption but to constitute a living organ bank for those more fortunate than themselves.

Possibly if we hadn't been in Calcutta, surrounded by materially poor, passionately alive children, the article might have been dismissed as improbable, or have been forgotten.

Chapter
Nine

*T*HE MASS AT THE MOTHER House was celebrated every day at five-forty-five in the morning. It was barely light, the streets were comparatively empty although people were already up, the Muezzin had called the faithful to prayer, the conch shells' long notes had woken the city, when Jenny and I went to attend. We walked as quickly as we could, trying to avoid puddles and rivulets. Young women, moving soundlessly, appeared out of the dusk. Walking singly—tall, erect, in light blue saris—they were pale and beautiful phantoms making their way to the prestigious Loretta Convent where Mother Teresa had once taught history.

We passed children going through heaps of ashes and refuse raked off the sidewalks to the edge of the roads. A tiny girl, possibly three years old, clothed in a single garment—a dress—was helping her brothers and sisters. Her face and body were coated in ashes.

The large room used as a chapel in the Mother House was already filled with silent nuns in white saris—bordered in blue for those who'd taken the final vows. They knelt on the bare floor. I wasn't permitted to take Mass—a note on the door insisted on Roman Catholics only—but Jenny joined them in receiving the wafer from the officiating priest. She was no longer lapsed. I envied her, having long left the Anglican church, appalled at what it seemed to me Christianity had become. But I wanted to believe.

After the service, Jenny edged me over to meet Mother Teresa, who took my hand in both hers and bowed over it. It was a short meeting. A young Western helper wanted a printed paper containing Mother's photograph to send to her brother for his birthday. We were instantly each given one—mine to be gone forever in a parcel posted from Calcutta and lost.

Mother Teresa was a good foot shorter than myself, and I'm a small woman. It was inconceivable that even when much younger she'd run looking for refuge through a monsoon carrying a dying woman whose feet had been eaten away by rats. But I could easily believe she'd thrown herself down in Kalighat, telling those who wanted to get rid of her to kill her; and I could believe she nursed the dying, left untended by others through fear, infected as they were by cholera and other diseases.

A practical woman, at over seventy she had little time to spare for visitors. Completely engaged in what she's doing, she brushes off lesser considerations. Whether she's esteemed as a saint or not by the rest of the world probably holds little interest for her. She's caught up in the process, not the result. She simply said, after her greeting, that we would be taken to a room where we'd help with children and would see her later. We didn't.

On our way, we passed above a courtyard where nuns were stooping over buckets of water, washing sheets, saris, children's garments. The strictest rule in the establishment is attention to cleanliness. The fairly small space we entered was filled with babies in cots. At one end an enormous hamper held well-worn clothes and diapers to be used indiscriminately. One or two children were crawling on the floor, supervised by an elderly nun. She didn't cuddle the children or make a fuss of them, and later we learned from a Canadian volunteer, disturbed in view of current findings in developmental psychology, that close contact between tenders and children is discouraged.

I was directed to a heavy, spastic girl and told to change her diaper and dress her. She struggled in my arms, frantic to get out of the crib, to attempt to walk. I had trouble dressing and holding her, but lifted her out and supported her while she tried to place one foot in front of the other. She was exhausting in her frustration: one of those intelligent beings trapped in an unresponsive body. But she was only one of many, given what scanty care was available.

The attitude in Calcutta towards Mother Teresa is ambivalent. We were told by Bengalis that by some she's loved and praised, by others resented for her high profile, which they feel gives the city a bad name. She's been accused of stealing children off the streets. Sometimes foreigners who work for her have difficulty in getting their visas extended: a young girl staying at the Y was deported while we were there. This may have been for reasons other than that she was a volunteer, but she said she had no idea why she was being sent home. The Indians do not look kindly on proselytizers and possibly this is where some of the criticism comes from: the nuns have of course accepted Catholicism.

Also, the Order cannot escape the general corruption: an item in the paper reported the arrest of two volunteers for absconding with 100,000 rupees, stolen from charitable money which is sent from all over the world. The Indians are philosophical about these kinds of events. A woman we met who'd adopted a boy from Mother Teresa said it was her karmic duty to give gifts of food and clothes to the hospice, but what happened to them—she claimed they were sold and the money secreted away—was not her concern. She was one of those wealthy middle-class women who so often appear dissatisfied and she complained bitterly it had taken much time and effort to get her little boy, whereas she could easily have obtained a girl—few people wanted them.

Agehananda Bharati regarded Mother Teresa in his idiosyncratic way: "She's the Cosmic Head Nurse. Pope Paul VI gave her a Cadillac, and what did she do? She raffled it and raised 200,000 rupees. Then she bought up all the condoms in Bengal and Bihar and had a major celebration—a cosmic bonfire."

This amusing man, a humanist, had of course his own reasons for his scorn. Brought up a Catholic, he'd adopted Hinduism and when questioned simply said Catholicism was a boring religion with its single deity. But his story does indicate the power Mother Teresa generates.

Saints are reputedly difficult people: their vision is single, their strength of will formidable. It's hardly surprising that Westerners, who need so desperately to believe in simple goodness, revere this woman, while Indians, whose country she lives in, are equivocal. The very title, "Mother," appeals to the romantic in us, but in her adopted country it's a common form of address for any ageing woman.

Kalyan took us in a rented car to one of Mother Teresa's Houses of Charity not far from his home near Dum Dum. The drive over broken roads was appalling. Cars shaved past people and traffic, swerved to avoid cows munching their cuds in the middle of the road: cows appeared to be, and probably are, treated with more respect than pedestrians, who might as well have been invisible. Our car would pull up abruptly a couple of inches from a woman carrying a child or from a man pushing a huge handcart laden with long pipes. Traffic theoretically travels on the left, but moves rapidly to the right to avoid an impasse, and after that goes in any direction at all. Our driver joked at each near miss, and Kalyan laughed at us: "You are not used to our pattern of driving—we can only go at forty-five kilometres an hour. If we hit someone it's a kiss, but if you hit someone it's a crash."

Even so, in the city that day, a bus driver had driven over two vendors pulling carts and had killed them both, driving on without comment, apparently to fulfil his obligations to his passengers.

At the House of Charity, we were shown around by a nun who had also taught in Loretto Convent and had afterwards taken up the contemplative life: to pray and meditate. In this House, one of many, the sisters look after those who are mad and children who are ill, many because of poor nourishment. Their families can visit them, and once the small patients are better they go home. Sister Ann Teresa told us, "Mother wants to keep families intact." Extensive fields are filled with vegetables, grown partly to give people work and partly to give to charity.

Jenny talked about the devotion she'd observed throughout her travelling, and the sister said, "Yes. That's what keeps it all going."

Jenny was having her private problems with the Catholic church, which was examining her relationship with her former husband. They'd gone through a civil divorce but he now wanted the marriage annulled —permitted, she believed, only for non-consummation—so he could marry another Catholic woman. She pointed out she had borne him three children. How could her marriage be annulled? The sister, undismayed by the apparent contradictions, said, "I can see how you feel, but you need to accept this as part of the suffering of life. Suffering must be accepted, because through it we grow. You will perform a kindness for this woman."

She told us she had certain landmarks by which she lived. If she found it hard to get along with somebody, she repeated constantly, "May You enter into [that person] with all Your graces." Another repetition was: "Someone is dying. May You make his death easier and allow him to repent and go to heaven." She admitted that one needs belief in Catholic dogma for this prayer, but it could be changed to: "Someone is dying. May his death be easy."

Her emphasis on the need to accept suffering reinforced a comment in a Calcutta paper by an Australian who felt the easy life lived by his compatriots was destroying the coming generation. They had not suffered, he said, and therefore had learned nothing. This points, of course, to a Western paradox: we learn and grow through suffering, but at the same time revere those who attempt to alleviate it.

A Scot who'd gone back to his original home from India, but had returned, also criticized Western society: "I asked myself what was everyone rushing around for? . . . Then I realized why I wanted to get back to India. For all its callousness, inequality and injustice, India still has time to question the meaning of existence. We may be poor, inefficient and unpunctual . . . but at least we function as humans— from our hearts. We have time for one another and for questioning why we are here."[12]

I thought of my family's servants, particularly the sweeper and the *syce* who would listen and talk to me when I was a child. The urgency we attach to time disintegrates in a country where millennia have changed life so little.

Strangers have time to go to great lengths to make you happy. Walking down a street in the heat of the day, we longed for a cold beer. Indian beer is good, and safe. We had become adept at picking out people who could speak English—generally, a man in a jacket. We asked a passing stranger where we could get a drink, and he pointed out an expensive hotel. We said we wanted a more reasonably priced place. He switched his direction, walked with us, and then joined us in a restaurant. Men sat downstairs; the occasional woman with a man upstairs. We went up, and before long were invited to this stranger's house where he said his wife would give us dinner. Still caught up in the Western world, we didn't have time. He told us his children would be terribly disappointed—he would only be able to tell them about us. Would we please let him know if we came back to Calcutta? He would meet us at the Dum Dum airport, he would show us around.

Kalyan and his friends had endless time for us. They met us on the Maidan, presided over by an enormous statue of Victoria, the Queen Empress, and took us to the Independence Day parade. The Maidan had once been a great park where our parents and grandparents drove their carriages, rode their horses, and played cricket. Now it's a barren stretch of trampled ground.

Crowds came from every direction; nervous police hovered every-where. Men were separated from women and children in case of a riot, and Jenny and I found ourselves enclosed in a crammed area where we sat on the ground and where small girls peed joyfully into the earth. Tanks, lorries, contingents of marchers passed by, and then a float commemorating Rabindranath Tagore, Bengal's beloved poet, obvi-ously considered at least as important as all this military paraphernalia.

We wanted to see the Botanical Gardens, founded by the British on 109 hectares of land. But to do so, we had to go over the Hooghly River,

[12] *Hindustan Times Sunday Magazine*, March 22, 1987.

on which my maternal great-grandfather had once been a river pilot, and on the day we chose the traffic was so heavy it had caused a jam on the Howrah bridge. Our bus had to turn back. Later Kalyan and his friends arranged for a "country boat" to take several of us over. The gardens were a disappointment, but we were learning what real wages were. Kalyan dickered for the rickshaws—three-wheelers pulled by men on bicycles—which dragged us, two in each, for miles after we left the river. Their designated fare for four or five hours of back-breaking work was 10 rupees—one dollar. Walter was so ashamed he surreptitiously slipped them more.

We also went to the Law Courts, where a High Court Judge was a woman. We later discovered more about professional women in India. At the time we merely noted and forgot the fact in our reaction to the overpowering smell of urine on the stairs, the crowds, the Dickensian feel of the place with its dusty stacks of files and documents. Self-important barristers and lawyers, all of whom wore wigs, gowns, and other regalia denoting their hierarchic positions, hurried to and fro: we'd heard that India is more what England once was, than England herself is today, and here was proof. While we were there, a siren shrilled the anniversary of Gandhi's assassination. India stood still in remembrance, and Jenny wept.

Spontaneous generosity took us by surprise. We thought we would buy some raw silk and have dresses made. Close to the Lal Market, we found a silk shop and talked to the owner, Anil Arora, who flicked his bolts of cloth open in an absent-minded manner, not overly concerned with whether we bought or not. While we were talking, Buddhism came up, and his whole attitude changed. "Are you interested?" he asked. When I said I was, he rushed to his carrying bag and brought out a pile of six or seven books.

He wanted to give me his store of constant reading. I accepted one on the life of the great Tibetan saint, Milaropa, and when we returned a few days later he asked anxiously if I'd read it. Unfortunately, I hadn't, so I could not discuss it with him. It turned out to be an extraordinary and sometimes humorous account, but to me as unbelievable as a fairy tale. Anil told us he was trying to sell his business and become an airline pilot because reading *Jonathan Livingston Seagull* had opened so great a longing in his heart that he wanted to fly physically as well as metaphorically. He later found us a *darzi*, fixed his prices, and undertook the indescribable problems connected with posting our parcels to Canada. It was "no problem," a term we were constantly to come across in India.

Dr. Manna, who'd already taken us to galleries and given us information about the "Mafia," invited us to tea in his Calcutta house. He had a family village to which he returned every other weekend to set up a table and treat patients free of charge. He said it was impossible for him to return there unless he contributed to village life, but it was also impossible for him not to return. For thirty years he'd practiced in Calcutta without remuneration. He was not a wealthy man—he drove an antique Ford—but must have had family money. During tea, he warned us about all the things we had to avoid eating. There was not much left. We asked about fried food—*samosas* and other street delicacies—but, no, the oil was often cut with kerosene and had caused many deaths. People were too poor, they couldn't afford pure oil, and corrupt sellers adulterated it.

Like others, he insisted that Hindus believe in only one God, but this God has many manifestations. Jenny had heard a homely explanation of the same thing: "To your mother you are a daughter, to your children a mother, to your husband a wife, to friends you are a friend, if you work you are an employee to the one who employs you, but just the same, you are you: Jenny Colbourne. All aspects of the same thing."

Dr. Manna has a woodblock print on his wall. It depicts three figures. On the right is Brahma, holding up his arms which are without hands. The middle figure is Kali, the goddess of the phenomenal world—of illusion—and of death and regeneration. She's often depicted as black, with enormous tusks symbolizing her terrifying aspect, and is the chief goddess of Calcutta. The figure on the left represents man. He can see Brahma only through her, so his view is distorted. Man also holds up his arms, which are without hands, and Brahma says, "You're not perfect? Well, why worry, I'm not perfect either."

Hinduism has no sense of judgement or of sin. We simply are: striving, fallible, corrupt inhabitants of an illusion. As a result, there are few of the condemnations we make in the West. If a man is cruel and dishonest, that is the stage he's reached. Hopefully, he will work his way up the karmic ladder, becoming gentle and honest. But humankind is also divine—although it doesn't recognize itself as such—because all is one: the spiritual and the phenomenal. There is no division. The *Agni Purana* states: "The wise man's God is his inner self."

135

When we discussed this later, Jenny said, "It's all very well, but when you think about the loathsome things humanity has done throughout history it's not easy to accept."

I found parallels with Neo-Platonism: evil is simply the absence of good in the lowly place we occupy in the continuum. Many contemporary writers have come to the conclusion that this world is, in actual fact, hell.

❦

Dr. Manna invited us to his village, Garbalia, thirty-five kilometres from Calcutta, for a weekend. The road to it was strewn with potholes, and like most others disastrous to cars—Ambassadors, made in India. They're very sturdy and always include a driver, who is cheap, but travelling by car is expensive because of the exorbitant price of gasoline. The cars are also exorbitant: a lakh in rupees—in our equivalent about $100,000. Parts are hard to come by, so men in their back rooms manufacture them, and this must work successfully because the cars continue their heroic battles with the roads. One driver asked hopefully if he couldn't come to Canada to be our chauffeur. Walter told him he could drive himself, and then added that even I could drive. The man was astonished.

On the way, we saw a building being constructed entirely by women. Everything is done by hand in East India: we saw no bulldozers, cranes, cement mixers, power saws, or extension ladders. These women used a structure of saplings stripped of bark mounting to the top of four storeys. They passed heavy baskets of bricks up in a human chain, working fast (far faster than men we'd seen in the city), and rhythmically.

Dr. Manna was waiting for us on his verandah. A garden struggled with the heat around a white-tiled house. The inside consisted of a living room, dining room, and dormitory with three immense beds, their mosquito netting drawn back. A bearer, a cook, and a young girl looked after the place and had prepared fruit and delicate Indian foods. When we were in the garden, children crept to its edge to stare at us. It may have been the first time they'd seen white-skinned people: they whispered to each other and then became bolder, daring to come from behind bushes. Walter turned around to look at them, and a little boy burst into terrified tears.

Dr. Manna had a meeting to attend, so his brother, Mr. Manna, a pedagogue, and various cousins or friends — all men — showed us around. This is their village, based on a baronial system, where most of the extended family lives in the original large house. Later Dr. Manna told us that when he is spiritually ready, when he has evolved to a purer state, but not until then, he will return to his village to die.

It was important to his brother that we reach a vantage point to see the sunset, but before that there were shrines and artisans to visit. We walked along, Mr. Manna talking and beaming, delighted to show off his village. We'd heard funeral music earlier, and on our way passed the burning ground. Young men were standing around a large fire, occasionally throwing wood into the flames. It takes four hours and much wood to burn a body, despite its being anointed with *ghee*. Later the ashes would be collected and thrown into the Ganges. The corpse — that of an old man — was plainly visible through the flames and was sitting up slightly. The time could not have come to break the skull. There was no sense of mourning: that would come later, and for days, with many restrictions placed on the family. Indian women don't attend cremations because, the men told us, they would weep and carry on, and since the spirit is simply returning to its place of origin and preparing to be reborn there's no need to lament. There was no restriction on our being there. I was surprised, having been told by my mother that no one in the family, man or woman, could attend her father's cremation.

We went on to gaily decorated shrines. In this village, Durga, one of the incarnations of Shiva's consort, is the aspect in which the great Goddess of India is worshipped. She appears in several forms: as Shakti, the Mother Goddess who embodies the female energy of the gods, and as Sati, who immolated herself in sacrificial fires because her family snubbed her husband. Reincarnated, she took the form of Parvati, "Daughter of the Mountains," whose story is the most charming. The gods, during their war against a demon, Taraka, needed Shiva to father a son who, according to prophecies, alone could destroy their enemy. Shiva, however, was undergoing a great penance and spent his time in meditation, clothed in ashes and live snakes. He was immune to the charms of women. The gods directed an unwilling Kama, the god of love who carries a bow of sugarcane strung with murmuring bees, to shoot his shafts of scented flowers at Shiva so he would fall in love with Parvati, the beautiful devotee who stayed close to him and tended to his needs, of which he was oblivious. Kama, despite his stealth, failed and was shrivelled to ashes when Shiva, observing him and annoyed at the interruption, opened his third eye: an eye so filled with God-energy that no one could look upon it and live.

Finally Parvati succeeded in enrapturing the god through devotion and meditation. Their son, Subramanya, destroyed Taraka, and Shiva had mercy on Kama. He resurrected him, but in invisible form: the human race needs the love god's arrows to survive.

Shiva's consort has one further aspect: Kali, one of the three principle deities in the Hindu pantheon.

Depicted as Durga, she is the goddess of power and rage, the destroyer of Mahisha, the buffalo demon who tormented gods and men. In her shrine in Garbalia, she rides on a lion. Her symbol is the fish. In seven of her eight hands she carries weapons with which to fight evil; her eighth is outstretched, palm up, in blessing. We stared at her, fascinated, and for the first time, even though I'd read much of the literature on God as a woman, had seen Judy Chicago's "Dinner Party," and attended a witches' midsummer sabbat—in which countless goddesses are invoked—I responded to the concept of the Goddess. It was a surprise, but then India is filled with surprises. At the time, I knew little about Hindu iconography—it takes time to sort out the numerous gods and goddesses and their stories, which in any case consistently vary. In the Western world the Goddess had appeared artificial; in India, she's never been denied, is a living part of the culture, and I found my heart going out to her, but said nothing to Jenny or Walter.

After the shrines, we were taken to the artisans' houses. By this time, more and more people were following us: first the children, who were then gradually joined by their fathers. Originally they hung back, but then came closer. In one shop, artisans were carving the intricate white pith headdresses worn by grooms during the marriage ceremony; in another, working with hemp. But it was the potters who interested us most. The men work on wheels spun by hand, throwing *chatties* ranging from small ones for tea to large ones for water and storage. Now Walter dared admit that he, too, was a potter. They were delighted. They showed him the type of clay they use, their simple tools (much like his own), and their kilns, shaped like beehives and fired with cow dung.

Despite their balance and harmony, potters' cheap wares—"just mud"—are thrown away after use. Dung is in short supply and is becoming expensive, and ubiquitous plastic is making its way to India. Who wants an ordinary mud pot if one can have a bright yellow bucket that lasts for years? Soon these cheerful men squatting in front of their wheels will be unemployed, and collectors will prowl around looking for what is now of so little value.

The goddess replicas certain of the potters make will hopefully not be replaced, not that they wouldn't be if this were feasible, but because after their festival they're taken, with dancing and music, to a river or tank where they return to their original form. We were in Garbalia just before the festival to Sarasvati: the goddess of learning and wisdom. She's depicted with the swan, reputed to be able to take milk out of water and therefore purity out of impurity: thus she creates the real from the unreal and produces wisdom out of the nothingness of the phenomenal world.

The Sarasvati effigies in Gabarlia are lined up in a double row on the verandah of the pottery once they're completed. They are cast clay images built over straw, hardened in the sun and then painted with white saris and gold diadems. Finally, they're given long black hemp hair and a clay swan.

When we went to Shantiniketan a day or two later, we saw many Sarasvatis. They were life-size, some of painted clay, some in real saris, and some constructed of small, white, intricately patterned shells. The goddess, sitting in a shrine decorated with lights and marigolds, held a sitar while a phonograph or ghetto-blaster played loud music—abrasive to Western ears—in front of her. After the week of celebration, she was taken by dancing people to the local tank where she was submerged. An architect we met said this was quite the wrong procedure: the goddess signifies learning, and who desires to learn for only one week? In his home, she was kept intact all year.

In Garbalia, after all our peregrinations we finally fulfilled our quest to see the sunset. By this time two or three hundred people—but few women—were following us. Sometimes children dared to touch us. They were marvelling at Walter's size, Jenny's blonde hair, my blue eyes. We were experiencing what it's like to be royalty: intriguing for a day; appalling for a lifetime.

The sunset was as impressive as it was supposed to be, and when we returned the town was dark. The villagers still used oil lamps, but we noticed a single shop had electricity. It had been brought in—Dr. Manna's house also had it—but the ordinary people were too poor to afford it.

Garbalia, with its thatched houses and pool set in trees, was blessedly quiet after Calcutta, but that evening the silence was enlivened by children's voices. Dr. Manna had invited them to his verandah to give us a concert. Twenty or thirty came. They sang songs by Tagore, and then a girl with a particularly true voice sang while others danced. When they'd finished, he gave them each a sweet, and afterwards they "wiped the dust from our shoes." This, a sign of respect, consists of touching a hand to the recipient's foot and then placing the hand on the giver's forehead. It's a graceful movement, a sweet tribute.

When we returned to Canada, I asked Barid Manna, Dr. Manna's son, if the village still operates in the old ways, if it's still structured on a caste system, and if some of the people are still untouchables—chiefly those who remove the night soil. I knew untouchability was illegal and that children of untouchables could now go to school and escape their ancestral calling provided they'd never practiced it. He said the system was the same; nothing can be changed rapidly. From what I'd read— not to do directly with this village—it's the women who go surreptitiously into homes to clean up excrement while the men take their swine into the fields to devour it. It had been the sweeper, the gentle *bhangi* in my father's household, who'd been my particular friend over fifty years before—but fifty years is nothing in the social history of India.

Chapter Ten

*T*HE POSITION OF WOMEN
in India bears little relationship to the idealized concept of the female, the Goddess, as the embodiment of active creative energy whereas the male deity, the God, is passive and cannot function without her. Shiva, in one of his highest forms, is androgenous: man/woman sharing spiritual power. The mother is revered and worshipped as the powerful Mother Goddess. The earth that supports all life is Mother India; the sacred river, from which water is carried throughout the country, is Mother Ganges; the chief deity in Calcutta is Kali.

Even so, in the old hierarchical system women were far from equals with men—in classical plays, they were lumped with slaves and not permitted to speak the holy Sanskrit language—and for most the situation in general has changed little over the centuries.

Kalyan Pal and his wife are Brahmos, advocates of an enlightened Hinduism which has stressed women's education and fought against untouchability. Mrs. Pal works in the Writers' Building. When I first heard of this building I was naïve enough to think it was actually for writers. In fact, it's an enormous structure originally used by copyists for the East India Company and now for government offices. Kalyan has a chemical distribution company. They live together as equals: there's no question of the wife waiting hand and foot on her husband and then taking a back seat.

This is not general. Despite their education and the reality that many women, like the High Court Judge we watched in the Law Courts, hold responsible positions in politics, universities, the medical field, and other professions, we were told that in the home the old system prevails: the man is god and the woman supposed to be his devotee. Angry feminists claim that the Bengali woman, particularly, has no identity of her own, that she's defined by the bedroom, kitchen, and courtyard, by her husband, the space she occupies, and the labour room—still the worst room in the house: she's supposed to take small steps, small mouthfuls, and to keep her eyes and voice lowered. She is the breeder, the nurturer, the milk cow, and across India advertisements stress the comforts, dress, and desires of the son and husband. If a woman is included, she's depicted as beautiful and submissive and is often situated compositionally beneath male members of the family. In a nineteenth-century painting, the wife is portrayed drinking water from the toe of her husband. Feminists suggest there's little metaphorical change today.

An Irish woman, met by chance in the Great Eastern Hotel, spoke about a friend, a university lecturer, who told her, "We rebel against everything—arranged marriages, dowry payments, the position of the women in the household—but we can't do anything and never will be able to. Society is living but we are dying."

Her view is reinforced by an article written by Madhu Kishwar[13] in which she cites the story of Dr. Shakuntala Arora, a lecturer in Hindi, who died of burns in 1982 after a ten-year marriage to another college instructor. Dr. Arora was constantly harassed for money by her husband and in-laws and was permitted to keep only 100 rupees ($10.00) of her earnings. Kicked in the stomach by her husband just before her second delivery, she was neglected and abused. Two days before her death, she was beaten and dragged out of the house in front of the neighbours, who did nothing: "It would be simplistic to interpret the violence as resulting from excessive greed. The beatings were part of a larger design to humiliate her, destroy her sense of self. The deadly power [her husband] could exercise over her life arose not from her economic dependence on him but because her family and social circle could not provide her with the assurance that a dignified life without marriage was possible."

Kishwar produces many similar cases, some to do with poor tribal women who are totally dependent on their husbands even if it is they who do the work and keep the family together; in other incidents, women who were successful, well-salaried before marriage, lost all rights—including their savings—after. If a woman, no matter how well educated or connected, is told by her mother-in-law that she must "live with" her husband's brother as well as with him, or told by her husband she must "go out" with his friends and tolerate his affairs she has little choice but to comply. Her only hope is for her own family to come to her aid and this seldom happens: marriage, with its social, religious, and economic values, is regarded so highly that parents will go to any lengths to persuade a son-in-law, no matter how abusive, to keep

13 *The Illustrated Weekly of India* (Sept. 1989).

142

their daughter. Kishwar quotes a woman: "I told my son-in-law that I was ready to eat his shit if only he could keep my daughter. In my family, divorce is unknown." She and others claim that dowry deaths, at last claiming attention, are the tip of the iceberg: a cause the courts and press have overstated as the only way to gain attention. If there is no obvious motive (dowry) for violence, judges prefer to believe the woman committed suicide. The dictates of the *Ramayana* are still powerful: "She should never enjoy independence; though [her husband] should have no good points at all, the virtuous wife should ever worship her lord as a god."

Recently Amnesty International reported that in a single year it noted over a thousand rapes—of course, a tiny percentage only is admitted—and 4,600 live burnings of women in India. One case of abuse received international attention: an eighteen-year-old blind girl was raped by her employer and his son and impregnated. Both men were freed of charges; she was convicted of adultery, fined, and sentenced to fifteen lashes and three years in jail.

Caste complicates the situation, although here the man is equally "at fault." In 1990, a fifteen-year-old girl fell in love with a boy beneath her in caste: she, the boy, and his friend who helped in the affair—all adolescents—were hanged.

This is not first-hand information—we had limited opportunity to talk to women. But we did notice that in one household where we were meeting a famous artist who was also a university lecturer, a woman in the room was not introduced and was ignored. At first we assumed she was a servant of some kind, but finally understood this was his wife. She barely spoke, and when she did it was to comment on how great a man her husband was. It finally emerged, as an aside and a joke, that she was more highly qualified academically than he was.

However, none of this had anything to do with the women we met in Calcutta through the Tagore family, also Brahmos: lively, highly educated, and sophisticated, they took charge of their own affairs. The same was true when we later reached Dehra Dun and were taken around by Brigadier-General Bakhshi and his niece, an out-going and charming girl who had her own accounting business. Walter asked her about arranged marriages and if one had not been arranged for her. She laughed and said, "Well, they paraded some of these men in front of me, but I wasn't interested." When asked if she didn't worry about not being married, she said she sometimes did if she thought about it so it was better not to think about it. However, she lived and worked at home. Unmarried, it was virtually impossible to be independent.

In the same city, we met the wife of Arun Kapur, a teacher at the Doon School attended by boys, including Rajiv Gandhi, of élite families. She is a psychologist, is liberated (the only woman we saw smoking in India; an act of defiance which outraged her parents who called her a whore), and told us something of the horrendous dowry problems women were encountering. She also talked of barriers to women's independence, saying that her unmarried sister, at twenty-six, was a professional who longed to live independently, but this was not possible.

These people belong to the élite. Among the general public, there's still an assumption, and it starts at birth, that women are not as valuable as men. Fewer girls than boys survive, not because they're loved less, but because a boy is automatically given the best food, attention, and medical care: he will carry on the family name, will support his parents in their old age, and will perform the last rites at cremation. A girl is not only lost to her parents once she moves into her husband's family home, but is also a financial liability. According to Heise, of the Worldwatch Institute,[14] in India women use amniocentesis as a sex identification test. Clinics, until this was recently outlawed, advertised that it was better to spend $45.00 (Canadian) on extruding a female foetus than to spend $4500.00 in years to come on a dowry. Upon examination of 8000 foetuses in six Bombay clinics, scientists found 7999 were female. A different kind of infanticide is taking place from that of the period when my mother found her "thrown away" baby and was told by my father not to be surprised at the numbers of "stillborn" Gurkha girls. Statistically, there are now 22,000,000 "missing" females in the Indian population.

All over India we noticed boys working hard. They are endlessly cheerful, expecting to contribute all they can to the family. But girls, apart from the very poor, disappear at puberty. They're confined to the family house or court where they learn to be perfect wives: they tend the babies, cook, and clean—not money-making ventures. They also weigh heavily on the consciences of their fathers, of all classes and castes except the most enlightened, who incur shame in the present and karmic penalties in the future if they don't find them husbands, most of whose families demand steep dowries.

[14] Report, 1989.

Dr. Manna's cousin—probably a distant one—was part of the entourage which showed us around Garbalia. He was a tall, thin, distraught man, who had suffered the misfortune of producing six daughters, all now of marriageable age. He said, "I am not permitted to sleep at night." He was expected to pay dowries of between 60,000 rupees and 70,000 rupees for each of them: "One I can manage, but the rest, it is impossible."

Dr. Manna told us no one in his immediate family had ever asked for a dowry but that it's still common practice despite its illegality. Depending on whom we spoke to, we were told it's the growing middle class, infected by Western materialism, which demands heavy payments, while the poor do not, or that it's the poor who drive fathers to the wall while the custom is dying out among the middle class. The former appears more likely. Mrs. Kapur, in Dehra Dun, told us India has very few psychologists (people can't afford them), but they are desperately needed to help settle middle-class quarrels which may lead to dowry deaths: these disputes generally relate to television sets, refrigerators, cars, and other modern toys.

No one we spoke to about life under the Raj mentioned violence against women or dowry deaths. The only written account to hint something was amiss was in *Mother India* by Katherine Mayo who was accused by Vivakananda, the great religious teacher, of acting like a drain inspector.

Today there's an official attempt to do something about these deaths. While we were in Calcutta, the police were attempting to bring to trial two villainous-looking men, a father and son, accused of murdering the son's wife. We also read of radical women's groups, set up in the late seventies and early eighties, which have been formed to give help in cases of death, rape, suicide, and battering. An article in *The Hindustan Times* quoted a speaker for one of these groups: "No woman can stop violence by becoming diplomatic. There is no rationality or pattern in this violence. It has nothing to do with caste or class or education. Men are just conditioned into believing they have the right to, indeed they should subjugate women. If a man uses force for this purpose, why then it's his . . . right to chastisement."

The murder cases are not easy to prove since the usual method is to douse the woman with kerosene and then set her on fire, with the husband and in-laws insisting her sari caught alight while she was cooking. The women's advocates claim that usually the police are slow to investigate and are bribed by the husband's family, but investigations are taking place. *The Globe and Mail*[15] gives the following account (extracted), taken from an Indian paper:

> Arveen Rana's parents were torn with indecision last summer when they got her desperate pleas for freedom. They wanted to help their daughter, but marriage is a powerful institution in India, and there is little place in high society for a divorcée with a year-old child.
>
> "Papa, don't throw me away like this," began Ms. Rana's last request to come home. "Each day it gets unbearable here. They don't like anything about me. They want me to change in every single manner. They want a puppet, not me. I feel like a prisoner, Papa."
>
> Six weeks ago, Ms. Rana was found hanging from a ceiling fan in the palatial New Delhi home of her husband's parents. Her father immediately charged that she had been murdered. Her in-laws insisted that she had committed suicide, but they abruptly absconded when police began to investigate.
>
> The Rana case is one of the more publicized of India's many thousand annual "dowry deaths," but its essential elements are identical to those in the unnoticed deaths of far less affluent brides.
>
> "The Singhs (Ms. Rana's parents) had offered a Maruti sedan," says Kailash Rekhi, vice-president of the Women's Vigilance Association, which is investigating the case. "But her in-laws wanted something more expensive. They demanded a Tatamobile. The Singhs refused, and that's when the in-laws really began making life hell for Arveen."
>
> By official count, that sort of domestic hell results in a young woman's death five times every day. Activist groups say the toll is much higher, perhaps as many as 10 unreported deaths for every one entered in police records.
>
> In November, four daughters of a Kerala policeman hanged themselves in a mass suicide rather than bankrupt their parents with dowry payments [even though these payments are illegal].

❧

Families appear to be very loving. On trains and in buses, fathers hold and caress children, and we never heard squabbling. Divorce is almost unheard of, but occasionally it does occur. In Pondicherry, Jenny met a beautiful and cultured divorcée, who asked if she minded sharing her

[15] January 28, 1989.

table. The family room was full and a woman could not sit alone in the common dining room. This woman said she had no part in Hindu society, where she is relegated to a position below that of widows. Ironically, she'd hoped to join the ashram founded by Sri Aurobindo whose work was carried on by "The Mother," a French woman, much revered although herself divorced, but was not admitted. Neither could she return to her father's house: a divorced woman is too great a family failure.

Widows in India still constitute a generous part of the population: recent statistics state there are 23,000,000 of them. They are presumably still the little white ghosts of former times, although in some parts of the country remarriage is possible.

Suttee, extraordinarily enough, is making a comeback despite its illegality. It has only ever taken place in the north and in high-caste families. Chitralikha, of the Tagore family, gave us a different reason for the custom than that women, perfect wives, took the same course as Sati; she said that after a calamitous defeat of Hindus, their wives entered the flames rather than be raped and enslaved.

However it started, in Rajasthan some women are choosing this ghastly death. In the 1980s, a young girl who voluntarily entered the fire was escorted through a crowd of five thousand people by a bodyguard of men who separated her from male relatives with swords. When interviewed after the event, her mother, who had not been there since it was a cremation, said her daughter had chosen wisely and being "possessed" had felt no pain — despite bystanders saying the girl, who was later deified, shrieked with agony. The following year, in commemoration of her action, hundreds of thousands gathered to worship her: perhaps she took a tempting alternative to living out her life as a widow.

One of the images that stands out most clearly in my mind is of a painting by a modern artist in the Birla Gallery in Calcutta. It portrayed a wealthy Moslem smiling with self-congratulation. He had a woman seated on either side and two more behind him. They were covered by heavy black *burqqas* with mesh eye-holes; only their feet, shod in elegant high heels, and their wrists and hands wearing gold watches and expensive rings, were exposed. They were his wives, his possessions.

Later we were to see many women encapsulated, some in black, some in ochre, others in exquisite white garments which dropped in pleats from the crowns of their heads to their feet. Their mystery naturally invokes excitement. In Nainital, Walter was moved to unknown emotions by a passing woman who had slim ankles and small feet in high heels—all he could see of her. He said he'd never come across anything so sexually stimulating. Some women, particularly in Rajasthan, simply cover their faces with a veil. If this is out of place, the woman faces a wall and, holding her baby on her hip with one hand, adjusts the veil with the other. Today, the *burqqa* has become a status symbol, and as women at the top free themselves from it, others adopt it. The heavy material hampers movement, obstructs breathing, is a prime cause of TB, and makes the woman faceless.

Education is free in Bengal and taken so seriously that children are streamed at the age of three, but 60 per cent drop out at a very young age in order to help their families. Nevertheless, many women as well as men are well educated but again the ironies of India, where so much that is attempted appears to lead to further difficulties, surface. Once married, a woman may not pursue or use her education if her husband objects. Also, it's education that has spawned a whole generation of women who seem to be endemically discontented. Agehananda Bharati refers to these middle-class women as having a "cosmic sulk." He suggests it stems from their now knowing how badly they've been treated in the past. Others, with more sympathy, say it's because they have no power. Along with financial security, they may have all the gadgets they want but no freedom. The women of the poor, with their windswept lives and lack of expectations, appear to be so much happier, although at Kalighat, the great white temple to the Goddess on the banks of the Hooghly, we were almost attacked by women beggars in threadbare saris desperate for a few coins. It was the only place we found people who were perhaps starving.

And yes, there are still *devadasis*—brides of God. We asked Danny, the film-maker, about them. He said they are there to raise money for the temples and in exchange are promised burning on the banks of the Ganges when they die. Jenny suggested this may appear to be a secure life for a girl, particularly with the additional bonus of merit accrued through a sacred cremation.

We watched many wedding parties in Calcutta, but it wasn't until we reached Varanasi that we saw the most extraordinary of all. Outside our hotel, a band was playing in front of a gaily decorated *tonga*, the horse a mass of marigolds. An awning was stretched over the groom's seat, and while we waited he emerged in his wedding silk and high, carved headgear and got in, accompanied by a small boy who was probably his

148

brother. We'd noticed, lined up along the road, twelve large and heavy heart-shaped metal structures on pedestals. Once the procession was to begin, these were heaved up by coolies, men and women, who put them on their heads. They were connected to each other by cables. Finally the whole lot took off, in the lead a man setting off fireworks, next the musicians, then a mobile generator pushed by more men, after that the hearts which burst into lights—sometimes white, sometimes yellow, sometimes red. The groom brought up the rear. His friends danced inside the oval formed by the lighted hearts which were set to flicker on and off in time with the music.

There had been much chatting and shuffling around before the procession took off. At first, we thought this was simply the usual Indian way—all the time in the world—but then remembered the groom's party had to arrive at the right moment according to the horoscope. In the epic *Ramayana*, Rama and Sita have endless difficulties in their marriage because it didn't take place at the propitious instant. The gods wished Rama to kill a demon who was bothering them, and they distracted his attention at the appropriate moment: had his marriage been divinely happy, he would have been content to sit at home doing nothing more than tasting endless bliss.

We saw the bride and her party only once. By chance, we entered one of the temples in South India when a wedding was taking place. The very young bride and groom were sitting side by side surrounded by flowers—marigolds and jasmine with their heavy, sweet perfumes. The women wore their hair in long pigtails decorated with bougainvillaea. We were given small packets of seeds, no doubt signifying fertility, to eat. The little bride did not look happy. She probably wasn't, but in any case apparently isn't supposed to look it. The only explanation we were given for her downcast face is that since she's moving out of her family home, her mother might be jealous if she appears joyful or takes any interest in the occasion.

The vast majority of marriages are still arranged, with long columns in the daily papers listing requirements. Occasionally in the would-be groom's advertisement no dowry is requested: for example, "NO DOWRY, preferably Kshatri, slim, Graduate, very fair [mandatory for good looks], beautiful, respectable, sharp featured, 26-30, wanted for well-settled businessman, 190 cm., fair, handsome." More often nothing is said about dowry, an understanding that it's required, but much about horoscope readings. The man's family often desires a woman educated in the same field as their son. For instance, if he's a medical student or graduate, they want a female medical student. When we asked friends about this, they laughed and said the family was advertising for somebody who would bring in an income. Many of these advertisements ask for a "beautiful, homely girl," a stunning Indian-English contradiction.

Some women still consider arranged marriages preferable to love matches. One of them, a Loretta Convent graduate, told us they are far more romantic: you see your groom when he raises the tinsel from his face and he sees you when you raise your veil. Expectations being what they are, if the family has done a good job in selecting the mate for a son or daughter, probably as many happy marriages result as in the West. If the family has not looked into the matter carefully, a bride may find herself married to a man who is simple-minded and impotent—Mrs. Kapur told us of such a case—but she can do nothing about it once the ceremony has taken place. Even if an extraordinary mistake is made, such as the veiled bride being married to the wrong groom, and this has been known to occur, once the ceremony is completed, there's no going back.

How much change in the position of women has taken place between the period of British India and the present? More women are much better educated and some of their problems, once hidden, are coming out into the open. In this, there's little difference between East and West. After being in India for even a short time, one simply feels that life goes on: vital, brilliant, beautiful, amusing, difficult, filled with pain, and terrible. We live in the phenomenal world, distorted by Kali, and in Indian cosmology, we live in her epoch, *Kaliyuga*: "In *Kaliyuga* righteousness, virtue, and goodness completely disappear. . . . Anger, distress, hunger, and fear prevail, and rulers behave like highwaymen, seizing power and riches in various ways."[16]

[16] R. K. Narayan, *Gods, Demons, and Others.*

Chapter Eleven

*M*Y FATHER HAD A PAIR of cuff links which he claimed had been a gift to his uncle, Colin MacKay, from Rabindranath Tagore, whose private secretary he'd once been. I don't know if they really had been Tagore's, but I do know that when I was in my teens I saved my lunch money and bought translations of Tagore's books. Today they appear dated and facile, but then I devoured the gentle mysticism which is also a hallmark of his paintings, found in galleries and museums all over Calcutta, where he's admired as Shakespeare is in England. Poet, artist, and musician, he was the first Indian to win the Nobel Prize and the only one ever to win it in literature. Also, he was a freedom fighter, founder of a private university, and member of an aristocratic family, most of whom were talented in multiple directions.

Rabindranath's grandfather made a fortune in banking and shipping. He was a flashy man who travelled with kings, including Edward VII, and held parties with hundreds of guests. During these celebrations he gave every woman a cashmere shawl, intricately woven from the undercoat of the Kashmir goat and even then extremely expensive. Today they are museum pieces. This Tagore was so extravagant he died leaving huge debts which his eldest son paid off. Rabindranath himself was not a wealthy man but had enormous energy and was determined to build a liberal arts university at Shantiniketan, outside Calcutta, where his father had had a vision of happy and dedicated students while sitting under a "holy" tree. He succeeded, travelling across the world to raise money, and called it Sriniketan: "abode of grace and plenty."

We were extremely lucky to meet his great-niece, Chitralikha, who now lives on Vancouver Island, before we went to India, and even luckier in that she was in Calcutta when we were. She was staying with her brother, Siddharthe, whose flat is in a building which had once been Whiteways Laidlaw, the Harrod's of India. Jenny remembered it clearly as an elegant structure with a great glass dome. Now it's been turned into flats and offices and from the outside appears to be a deserted warehouse with collapsing stone and twisted iron. The magnificent glass dome that once filled the building with light has been sliced into sections, and we found bits of it only because Jenny was sure it existed somewhere. It's so black with dirt, it's unrecognizable.

The Tagores' flat was cheerful and unpretentious. It was filled with antiques collected by their father, Subho Tagore, the artist and poet, now dead, who has been called the last of the renaissance men. Soon after we arrived, it transpired that two days later Chitralikha and Siddharthe were opening a private exhibit of their father's collection in their apartment. Cheerful men were scurrying around demolishing walls, cleaning, and repainting. Paint was scattered everywhere. A young man was squatting on the floor with an ancient typewriter, attempting with one finger to type out cards giving the medium and provenance of the objects. All this knowledge was in Siddarthe's head: he knew exactly what each piece was made of and where it came from, but to transcribe while crawling under ladders, over lumber, and around pots of paint in his attempt to find and display these treasures was impossible. He finally said, "I lack experience," and insisted everything stop while, with typical Bengali hospitality and optimism regarding time, he entertained his guests. We were urged to sit down, drink whisky, and pass a leisurely hour or two.

In the meantime others dropped in to talk, observe the chaos, and debate over what should be done with glass cases holding, we were told, inkpots. The cases covered an entire wall and were so encrusted with dust we couldn't see inside them. The pots were originally to be a major part of the exhibit, but now the Tagores decided to cover the cases with drapes because of lack of time. We asked if we couldn't start scrubbing. Everyone appeared to be astonished, particularly the workmen who were being given vague orders while we were being entertained. One of the women, also visiting from Canada, laughed and told us she'd suggested to Subho twenty-five years before that the inkwells needed refurbishing, but he'd absolutely refused — he wanted them left as they were.

Finally, filled with enthusiasm and whisky, Jenny, Walter, and I insisted that if we were given water and rags we could surely do something. Servants fetched buckets, opened cases, and we moved into a brilliant world of gold, blue and green enamel, of coloured glass and cut crystal. We had no idea what was going to emerge until we scrubbed surfaces. One pot had been used by Napoleon, others by equally impressive individuals. The servants caught fire and started to clean the cases: their backs and dividers turned out to be mirrors, so that finally over a hundred inkwells twinkled with their reflections, lighting up the whole room.

The Tagores—this was during the period I was a famous poet—had invited intellectuals they thought we should meet to the opening. When we arrived, all was miraculously in order except for the identification tags—the typist had given up—but, used to the Western custom of giving our hosts some leeway, we came about half an hour after the show was to open. Everyone else had come two hours early and most had left, concluding we'd moved on in our travelling. We felt rude, unhappily aware that time means different things to different people and we'd made our first *faux pas*. But our hosts were unperturbed—only disappointed we'd not met their friends.

Siddarthe told Walter he was astonished at the contemporary world where there seemed to be so little interest in the arts. In the society he'd grown up in, they'd been the focal point of existence.

Later we visited the "university for poets" that Rabindranath Tagore had founded in Shantiniketan. He'd refused fees, competitive pressures, marks. Students sat under trees where they discussed art, literature, and metaphysics with their teachers. Now it has been taken over by the government, and while we were there was under investigation (an endemic procedure) for fraud. The fees are still nominal—only thirty rupees a year—but the philosophy and energy have evaporated; the university is no longer the fulfilment of a dream, but an institution with political and competitive pressures as well as difficulties upon completion of a degree. While we sat under the trees, a young girl approached us, saying she wanted to work in Canada or the States because it was impossible for her to set up a studio in India: she didn't have the money necessary to appear before a judge to get a permit or to go through other bureaucratic hurdles in order to start her work.

Except around Tagore's own former compound, where a museum has been established, the grounds are dusty and barren. However, his houses remain and give an indication of the kind of man he was. First he started with a humble one, which is what he wanted, but when he needed more space he built onto it. He couldn't bear the pretentious building that resulted, so he built another small one, and finally ended up with four houses. One of mud—cool and pleasant—is the house that Gandhi chose when he visited. He and Tagore were fast friends and respected each other but also disagreed, chiefly because Gandhi thought there should be more discipline in the university. The idealistic presence of the two men still hovers in the Spartan mud house, whereas so much they fought and worked for has been only half-realized, diminished in an imperfect world. As I wandered around the compound, I thought of my great-uncle, a gentle and generous man, and wondered if his ghost also inhabits Sriniketan, the university for poets.

Possibly there will be a resurrection. Chitralikha and her husband are negotiating to buy land in Shantiniketan. They hope, with Siddarthe, to revive the idealism of their forebears. They may succeed; they belong to a renaissance family.

Chapter
Twelve

I COULDN'T HAVE STARTED
my quest in a better place than Calcutta. Its energy and ability to
function in the face of extreme overcrowding and poverty, its great
temples, its love of liberalism and the arts, its hospitable people with
their willingness to share their knowledge, all bolstered our confidence
and opened our hearts. At the same time, its chaotic enthusiasm was
stripping away layers of conditioning: schoolgirl judgements; the Prot-
estant ethic (subconsciously there) that God looks kindly on those who
work hard and gives them success; the belief that life is fair; but, above
all, that those who are materially dispossessed are necessarily miserable.
Jenny had already been stripped, almost to the bone. I was, perhaps, a
skin lighter.

Not all, of course, was positive. A great deal was negative, but was
generally tolerated in a way that was different from our way: we were
constantly told, but often with humorous acceptance, of the endemic
corruption—of the fact, for example, that in India almost every professional, including university professors, buys his or her position: entry
depends more on financial assets than on qualifications. Danny told us
many business people simply accept the system. They say, unabashed,
"Why should we care? We use it. It's the way to get things done." He said
the Congress Party is trying to create a larger middle class—those who
earn about 2000 rupees a month—as they then have a vested interest in
the *status quo* and will keep the party in power. But it's this class that
operates within the system of open corruption, so presumably the larger
it gets, the more corruption there will be. The poor simply suffer from it,
with no expectations of anything else. Even so, the society works and
sometimes works with unexpected efficiency, at least in small things: we
always got our films developed on time, our laundry carefully washed
and ironed, the clothes we ordered well made and ready when we
expected them. No one tried to cheat us or steal from us.

Unlike our premise that money can cure all social ills, Dr. Manna
believes the Western world could pour millions into Calcutta and it

would make no difference. Only the people who live there can change things. It's a matter of education. As an example, he talked about the lepers. Leprosy is easily curable if it's caught in the early stages, yet India is filled with lepers. The attitude towards it is much like our own in the Middle Ages: it's unclean, a punishment, and anyone who develops it is cast out of the family, sometimes violently. Since the family is the basic unit, and often the world outside it unknown, this is an appalling catastrophe. As a result, those who contract the disease hide it until it's too late and its victims eventually lose their noses, hands and feet, even entire limbs. The only cure lies in a change of attitude. But even this painful and disfiguring disease doesn't destroy a buoyant optimism. Jenny had visited a hospice run by a Catholic priest in the south where she'd met a woman with no nose who wanted a new sari so "she could be beautiful."

Men we spoke to recognize all these difficulties, but their main concern is that there are just too many people, most of whom are too poor to pay taxes for the upkeep of their city and for social services. No doubt, if Jenny and I could see Calcutta as it was when my grandparents lived their charmed lives, or later when her parents were there, we wouldn't recognize it. It had been inhabited even then by the rich and the poor, but was nevertheless a splendid place, and we, insulated as we would have been, would not have seen below the surface.

⋅⋅⋅

Walter and I flew to Madras, where my grandmother, Mary, had been born and my great-grandfather had practiced medicine. I should have looked up records, have found out more about the city, but I didn't. I was losing interest in these ancestors. India itself was taking over and we were, we'd been told, going to find its true nature in the south, where we would still, in any case, be in their general territory. Because of changed social and historical circumstances (the chief one being that we could do what we liked), little of what we were to experience could have been experienced by them.

We stayed only one night in Madras and, ironically, considering my family's past in that city, in one of the worst hotels we encountered. Our Lonely Planet Guide had praised Broadlands as the "nicest hotel in India." The resultant publicity must have gone to the heads of those who ran it.

We noticed the rickshaw-*wallah* looked surprised when we directed him, but thought nothing of it. On our arrival, an English couple of about our own age, carrying backpacks, were on their way out, smiling broadly and telling us what a great place it was. We never discovered if they really believed this and it was we who were hopelessly unable to cope, or if they wanted us to suffer as they had. The "friendly and unassuming staff" paid us no attention beyond giving us a tiny room with no windows, a filthy bathroom with a broken sink and no hot water, a single drinking glass coated in grime.

So much for Madras. We decided to hire a motorized rickshaw and go on: after our night in Broadlands, we couldn't face the buses and there was no train from Madras to Mahabalipuram, our next stop. This was our first experience, often to be repeated for shorter runs, with these motorized rickshaw *wallahs*. Two men always came along, usually a young man and his brother. They were invariably good friends, took all obstacles with amusement, and talked to each other ceaselessly. They crammed us into the back of the little vehicle with our suitcases—an impossibility until it's done—and then went off at the highest speed possible, which is not high. These two found us a wonderful resort.

Mahabilapuram, like Madras, is in the state of Tamil Nadu, and we noticed many differences from Bengal, perhaps because it doesn't have an idealistic Communist government. It's much cleaner, better organized, not so crowded, and has an excellent chain of government hotels where we could stay for about 60 rupees ($6.00) a night. Children surrounded us everywhere, as they had in Bengal, but here they asked for pens or coins as souvenirs, not money. They touched us tentatively, shook hands, shouted "Hullo" and "Good-bye," and then burst out laughing. If we moved from one bus to another, a group of them would show us the way, climb on board, and surround us until we moved off. If we stopped to take photographs, people were delighted and wanted us to take more. Extremely curious, if we looked at our map, they crowded around to look with us. If we smiled, they smiled back, delighted. We were strange to them—visiting Gullivers—but they never made us feel like freaks. I particularly attracted the children and was later told it was because I had white hair and blue eyes. At the time, I wondered if it was because this had once been a matriarchal society and they thought they were actually seeing some ancient goddess. In one temple, a beautifully dressed little girl, her hair decorated with flowers, stared at me as if I were some extraordinary and exotic animal. She finally touched me, stretching her arm out carefully, not daring to come close. Encouraged by her mother, she whispered, "Where you from?"—where could such strange people live? In another, a poor and again lovely child who was alone followed us like a shadow at a discreet distance. When we stopped outside for coffee, we noticed her again about ten feet away. Finally she had the courage to give me a "holy" picture. She wanted something personal, a souvenir, but I had nothing, and to her disappointment could give her only a couple of rupees.

In one place we had a disaster: we left a hotel in a hurry and forgot to pack our toilet paper, a cause for considerable lamentation; Jenny had learned to use water, like the Indians, and to eat with her fingers, but we were slow to master these skills. While we rode in a bicycle rickshaw to the bus, we looked out desperately for a shop which we thought might possibly stock such a luxury. Finally Walter went in to one and enquired, embarrassed because the other customers were so entertained at his request. After some doubts, the proprietor climbed a ladder to a high shelf, found a roll, dusted it off, and said, grinning: "Top shelf; top quality."

White, humped bullocks appeared everywhere in Tamil Nadu: sleek and as well groomed as Nandin, Shiva's mount, who is depicted in life-size statues throughout the temples and shrines. Their horns, lying back along their necks, are stained various colours—usually blue or yellow. They pull most of the carts, moving slowly and steadily. Sometimes their drivers live in the carts—or at least sleep in them. I wanted to photograph a team, and Walter said while I was taking a shot, he watched the people around me. One twirled his finger about his head, indicating I was crazy; they naturally saw nothing exceptional in these animals. We also encountered our first elephants; two, chained by their feet, workers for Vishnu, were in the temples. They're trained to take a coin in their trunks, give it to their keepers, and then bless the donor with a pat on the head. Intricately decorated with paint, they get unutterably bored, developing skin diseases. One was moodily swinging his trunk back and forth, his only exercise until he was taken out during the hours the temple was closed in the afternoon. He'd been with his *mahout* for twenty years and obeyed every small order.

The personal hygiene in Tamil Nadu is about the same as in Bengal. Men urinate, squatting down, into the drains or against the walls. Thoughtfully, they obey occasional requests, notices saying, "Please do not urinate against this wall." If we walked in the mornings down the long, sandy beach in front of our hotel outside Mahabalipuram, we discovered small mounds of excrement about ten feet from each other in a straight line waiting for the sea to come and wash them away. It was easy to imagine people squatting, staring at the waves, as they performed their morning duty.

We did, in time, have a problem with food. It became boring beyond belief. We ate rice and heavily cooked vegetables, unable to find any *dal* or curd. The chicken, considered a delicacy, was expensive and pathetically scrawny. On one occasion early on, to our delight we found a bar (unusual in this area), drank beer, and then went to dinner. Few of the items on the extensive menu were available because they were for lunch; later we discovered that at lunch nothing on the menu existed because it was for dinner; and later still, we found this was the usual thing. That evening, we ordered chicken, roast potatoes, and carrots. When our plates came, they had something on them that might have been squash. It wasn't until we started to eat that we realized this was the chicken— recognized by the bone. We never identified the potatoes.

In our hotel one night, Walter looked thoughtfully at our nearly empty jug of water with a disinfectant tablet in it, and asked wistfully, "Have we got enough money to do our teeth?" Exhausted, we became hysterical.

At one point, we hired a taxi to take us from one town to another in Tamil Nadu. Generally we avoided doing so because of the cost and because once in a taxi we were separated from the people we wanted to meet. Also, when we arrived we were walking targets: news travels quickly and all over the town men would say, "Oh, come by car, you did," and prices instantly shot up.

This time it was worth it. We drove some distance, from Mahabalipuram to Chidambaram, with a humorous driver who owned his own car. He'd picked up some English and spoke in the peremptory way of Indians with limited knowledge of the language: "Come, come. Sit, sit. Just now we are now going."

He talked, like others, of general corruption. When we told him we thought Tamil Nadu seemed much better off than Bengal with its load of refugees, he said, "Of the good state of the government, I will not speak," and went on to tell us that if a government official had problems with his car, he, as a mechanic, had to fix it free of charge. He also said the roads are contracted out to those who build them by covering the earth bed with large, rough-cut stones which are cheaper than small ones. As a result, he has to drive very slowly or the stones will jump up and injure his car. Their size also causes the surface to break up almost immediately. We came to a village of three or four houses where, for some curious reason, a huge statue, which causes many accidents, sits in the middle of the thoroughfare. He sighed: "These are the politicals."

In the villages, the road was always thick with traffic. Our driver drove in and out and through it while we tried not to look at what was going on. In a traffic jam, he slammed his brakes on a hair's breadth from bullocks pulling a cart: they were unperturbed and so was he: "These are the brake inspectors."

Waterways are choked with the blue water hyacinth, beautiful to look at but disastrous to the concourse and impossible to eradicate. But we enjoyed them, and the palm, date, and ebony trees; the tamarinds; the bullocks with bougainvillaea wrapped around their painted horns; the meandering cows which we were told go home at night by themselves to be milked; the small delicate goats. The village houses, of mud with thatched roofs, are nestled into trees and spaced around shrines with red colonnades and corrugated tin roofs. The village water tank builds itself in the depression made by taking mud for the homes. Walls are plastered with cow patties, a valuable commodity collected still warm by women using bare hands.

Our driver was also critical—but not angry—over the use of the highway (if one could call it that) as a threshing machine. Piles of rice are spread along the roadways for buses and cars to drive over. He said this was dangerous because tires slip on the dry stalks and collide with large stones left behind by farmers who use them for threshing be-tween passing cars. Women were sifting through the grain, sorting out stalks—used for roofs and fires—from edible portions. They reminded me of Keats' exquisite lines about Ruth when "sick for home, / She stood in tears amid the alien corn." But these women were not alien. They'd probably never left their villages.

We also passed what was called a salt factory. It wasn't really a factory. It consisted of a gigantic marsh where white-dusted people—over three thousand, many of them women—looked like ants. The salt is raked into small, conical piles in long rows after being dried and is then collected into huge stacks and covered with thatch. Finally it's packed into sacks transported on the heads of the workers. In intense heat, people were drying, raking, packing, and transporting this heavy, caus-tic substance: a scene out of an ancient world.

The Shore Temple Beach Resort, where by lucky chance we stayed while in Mahabalipuram, is the kind of place one hears about but seldom finds. For 140 rupees a night, we had a modern cottage with an immaculate bedroom and bathroom and a fan that worked, on a magnificent beach. We were told we shouldn't swim, it was too dangerous, but we did, and it was superb.

Admittedly, various creatures—beatles, ants, mosquitoes—also inhabited our room, but we were learning to share our space as the Indians do. The most entertaining of these are the wall lizards, called, depending on where one is, tiktikis, chipkalis, geckoes. They lie flat on the walls and make friendly knocking and chirruping noises. At first, we thought the sounds came from birds, and looked for them, but finally discovered it originated with these engaging little creatures. There's a story attached to them, another perfect wife tale.

Kana was an exceptionally intelligent woman, excellent at casting horoscopes. Consequently, her father-in-law, a minister of the king, was revered for his fruitful advice. But he had an enemy who discovered the source of his wisdom and went to the king with the object of dishonouring the minister. The king, even though he didn't wish to believe him, decided to check and sent for Kana who, unwilling to shame her father-in-law, refused to come before him. The king had her dragged to his court, but before he could do so, she cut out her tongue so she couldn't be forced to answer his questions. In this way she saved her father-in-law from embarrassment and turned the wall lizard into an indicator of truth: it swallowed a piece of the tongue, so now, whenever it cries "tik-tik" ("right right") after someone's words, they never fail to come true.

It must have been a wall lizard our *mali* cut into two pieces so long ago, telling me it was alive and unhurt.

The skies are filled with vultures and kites, the trees sometimes with parrots and monkeys, the streets with *pi* dogs, the beach and temple areas with men and small children trying to sell necklaces made out of sea stones, seeds, carved wood, glass beads. It's hard to escape them, they're so desperate, with the men being particularly persistent, telling us that if only we would buy something they could then go home at last: their day's work done. Walter became so enraged over trying to fit even a seashell into our two cases, he was unwilling to walk along the beach: once we bought something, I refused to discard it. In Mahabilapuram, a little girl came up to me with strings of necklaces over her forearm. They were constructed out of polished apple seeds interspersed with white, blue, or green seeds from other plants. I didn't dare buy them, but she desperately kept coming down—offering me more and more for the same price. In the end, I bought four necklaces for 5 rupees and later estimated the labour that had gone into them. I had 2400 apple seeds and 400 coloured seeds (both treated first) strung in intricate patterns on fine thread, for fifty cents. Tamil Nadu appears to be flourishing, but abject poverty still exists.

We were surprised at the number of Indians we were meeting who now lived in Canada and were back visiting. One of these, in Mahabalipuram, was a lively man, an entomologist who taught at the University of Manitoba. With the sense of humour we encountered everywhere, he shook his head wistfully, saying, "They never get it quite right." We'd already discovered this in, for example, the restaurants, and would go on discovering it. At our splendid resort, the *mali* who spent countless hours raking the gravel in front of the hotel into complicated patterns left the back wooded area filled with refuse. Guests walked by it every day.

The entomologist, Dr. Sinha, recipient of the Gold Medal from the Royal Society of Canada (he refused to believe this honour at first because there was no political motive behind it), son of a medical doctor, told us that when he first emigrated he made his way by washing dishes. He was married to a Canadian girl "off the farm." She was charming, an Evangelical Christian who was able to live happily with her husband, a committed Hindu. But, as usual, we didn't see much of her; it was invariably the man who was there to do the talking.

The conversation soon drifted to religion, and he told us he was not interested in all the gods and goddesses in the Hindu pantheon, but in the essence, in which all religions are the same: the longing of the human heart for the unity of the *Atman* (the divinity within man) with the Brahma (the ultimate creator). The only way to reach this union is through non-attachment, without self-interest in what one does. He said he used to give a voluntary course in Winnipeg on Hinduism but stopped because it was too successful: "I have to ask myself always, what is your motive? If the motive is incorrect, if it adds to the ego, what you do must be abandoned. So often it's the important people—the PhDs —who are obsessed with the fruit of their actions. You know Ramakrishna: he says self-important people fly high above the earth like

vultures, but their minds are on the carrion below—material better-
ment and what they can gain."

Dr. Sinha had idiosyncratic views on the British in India: "At one
stage they were very good. They sent out Orientalists, great scholars
from Oxford, who translated Sanskrit and contributed to knowledge
about ancient India. But then the 'fishing fleet' arrived and the Raj
settled down to domestic life. This changed things for the worse. They
built railways and hospitals and a great administrative service, but the
excitement of discovery was gone."

As an intellectual, he regretted the death of scholarship but admitted to practical advantages—chiefly the elimination of corruption. I
thought of the memsahibs, many of whom had at one time belonged to
the fishing fleet, who struggled with dirt, disease, and death in attempting to turn their pockets of the country into English suburbs. I also
thought of current films denigrating what had been accomplished,
flawed though it was, and of the puerile humour, common in our
country, "Well, he was in *Injuh*—one of those chappies, wot?" Pro- or
anti-imperialism is one thing; ignorance another.

Possibly we were getting closer to some kind of truth regarding the
past, although truth is never definitive. When we later visited Madurai
and a museum containing Gandhi's blood-stained shirt, his brief, tender
letters, and illustrations of events during the British occupation, I was
stunned by the violence that had taken place during the time my family
had been in the country. I'd heard mythic stories about the Black Hole
of Calcutta, which had actually been a small affair, when the Bengalis
"didn't get things quite right." I'd never heard of the sickening atrocities
on both sides during the so-called Indian Mutiny, or of the massacre
which took place in retaliation, when caste was broken by stuffing men
with beef and pork before hanging them and by smearing others with
blood before blowing them from field guns.

Dr. Sinha, although he didn't mention it specifically, was attempting
to live by the tenets of the *Bhagavad Gita*, and we were in the town where
the huge wall sculpture depicting Arjuna, hero of the *Mahabarata*
(which contains the *Gita*) is located.

Arjuna is conducting a "penance" to obtain a boon—a weapon,
which he receives—from Shiva. This deadly weapon, like our own,
once given may never be returned. Arjuna's tutelary deity is Krishna, an
incarnation of Vishnu, supreme God in some accounts. In the *Gita*,
Krishna acts as Arjuna's charioteer. He instructs his devotee before a

great battle in which Arjuna must, unwilling as he is, kill his kinsmen. Krishna tells him their deaths don't matter: the soul (the *Atman*) never dies. What is important is that a man fulfil the task imposed upon him by the gods and by his karma: Arjuna is a warrior, a *kshatriya*, and as such must follow his *dharma*, acting without self-interest, desire for gain, attachment to sense-objects, or to lustful anxiety and anxious lust:

> He who does the task
> Dictated by duty,
> Caring nothing
> He is a yogi,
> A true sannyasin.
> But he who follows
> His vow to the letter
> By mere refraining:
> . . .
> Making excuse
> For avoidance of labour,
> He is no yogi,
> No true sannyasin.[17]

Krishna urges Arjuna to fulfil his destiny, and by extension the destiny of mankind: to follow, with disinterested action and steadfast execution, one's *dharma* and to recognize the *Atman* within.

Vishnu has only man's interests at heart and has incarnated himself many times, in various forms, when mankind has needed him: "Whenever the Sacred law fails, and evil raises its head, / I take embodied birth. . . . I am born from age to age."

Krishna is our equivalent to Christ as an incarnation of God but, unlike the Christian concept of a celibate, suffering deity, he is also the pipe player, the pastoral lover, the desirer of the peasant girl Radha with whom he sports eternally. A particularly engaging story tells us that a young man approached him, saying, "Great Krishna, you have thousands of beautiful wives, allow me one for just this night." Krishna, generous as always, concurred. The lover went at dark to the lady he desired and found Krishna already there, so, somewhat embarrassed, he went to another, only to find Krishna ahead of him. Again he moved on, but the god was always before him: thus love is everywhere, waiting to be recognized.

---

[17] Trans. by Prabhavananda and Isherwood.

"Arjuna's Penance" (we would use the word "vigil") lay for many years, like the nearby shore temples, under water. Two of these temples have been recovered, four are still submerged. We were told that if we could get a boat and go out, we would see them clearly under the waves: elephants and Nandins and small white buildings now inhabited by fishes.

Carved in rock, all the cosmos comes to watch Arjuna at his penance. The Ganges rushes from its source in the Himalayas. At the base of the bas-relief, ordinary life goes on: free-standing sculptures of men milking cows which nuzzle their calves, of elephants and their young marching forward, all life-size. Over thirty feet high and eighty feet long, this monument dates from the seventh century.

Meanwhile, down the beach a nuclear plant—much admired by our taxi driver—generates its twentieth-century electricity. Possibly Krishna would approve. It's giving people light: a godly attribute if used wisely, without, of course, self-interest on the part of governments or multinationals.

❦

All over Tamil Nadu, Dravidian *gopurams* (gateways) guard the central shrines—some with solid gold roofs—set in multiple-walled enclosures holding courtyards, tanks, and "thousand-pillared halls." These are actually supposed to have 999 pillars (they vary) all of which are enormous and elaborately carved with real and mythical beasts. They represent the petals of the lotus on which Shiva dances his cosmic dance of destruction and regeneration: when his left foot is raised he is happy; when his right foot, he's angry.

These temple compounds may cover up to eight hundred and sixty-five acres and are as impressive as our cathedrals. Their *gopurams*, pyramidal structures covered with carved stone gods, goddesses, mythical animals, may reach over a hundred and fifty feet in height. The enclosures are filled with holy men, beggars, devotees. In one, saris were drying beside the vast tank holding sacred water, a gift from Shiva intended for ritual immersion, and our guide talked contemptuously about the profanity of soap and toothpaste—recent luxuries.

I remember being taken to a temple only once as a child. Jenny also remembers a single visit, and, oddly, we both recall how unwilling we were to take off our shoes. We must have been well inculcated with the horrors of hookworm. There was no question now of not removing them and of walking on blistering stone while a boy earned his money by watching over these invaluable commodities.

After the first few days of visiting temples, Walter and I made a pact to give no more alms: we felt we required no more merit, and if we gave to one, we were surrounded by a crowd of others. But while I was limping through a *gopuram* in Madurai, not far from the tip of India, by myself, avoiding eyes and outstretched hands, I was stopped by a beggar.

She put a hand on my arm and I tried to shake her off, but she forced me to look at her. She was heavy for a poor woman: she was also outrageously alive, and she barred my way, the guardian of the gate extracting a fee.

The woman had one eye which, direct and demanding, looked into my two. There was nothing of the beggar in her: she was a challenger, defying me to ignore her. The living eye blazed with vitality; the empty socket was wide open. I could see for at least two inches inside it to the naked skull. She was life and death, the Black Goddess Kali who creates in one aspect and destroys in another.

Her living eye held a world blazing with colour: coupling and generation and growth; peacocks and angel fish; bougainvillaea and rose trees; grass and clouds and a setting or rising sun; children, proud men and women, gods and goddesses; slugs and worms making their patient way across or through the earth; micro-organisms endlessly destroying and converting all that lives and dies.

Her empty socket indicated the shadow, the necessary adjunct for all that beauty, the ash in the *ghats* that makes way for and is a part of the whole spectrum starting once again.

I saw India for the first time. No reading or talking to others had conveyed to me the reality of Kali with her undeviating recognition of the real, as this woman did, who took her coin proudly, and with indifference.

❧❧❧

In Chidambaram, still in Tamil Nadu, a woman who in any other country would have been a noted beauty gave me another gift. She sat stringing garlands of jasmine under the wheel of one of the chariots used for taking the gods on their annual holiday. The stone effigies, far larger than lifesize, are bathed and dressed each day, but on that occasion they are taken from their shrines to the nearest tank or river where they're bathed and then permitted a week off. Their carved, ebony chariots are immense and require three thousand men to drag them to their destination.

The wheel stretched high above the woman who smiled at us as we passed and offered me a sweet-scented leaf. Used to *baksheesh*, I found a rupee for her — she earned possibly half a dozen a day — but she waved it away. I was ashamed; she wasn't a beggar, and still ashamed, I waved and smiled at her from our bus. She waved and smiled back.

Nataraji, the great temple to dancing Shiva, is in Chidambaram. This is the only temple where non-Hindus are allowed into the inner sanctum to watch the fire-ceremony. It didn't take place, naturally, on the evening it was supposed to, but we stayed on to see it. Our tiny, deft, and attentive guide, Anandam, took us into the packed and claustrophobic sanctum. Walter, polite and aware of his size, stood against a wall, but I edged into the centre. Continual talking sounded like water going down a river bed. Do these people find us very quiet, I wondered? Do they think we hate each other because we are so silent?

A child tried to get out. His mother and another woman started to fight with each other, angrily punching and slapping, overwrought with the occasion. Their saris, the flowers in their hair, suffered in the struggle. Anandam, a shadow, slipped through and tried to pull me away; Walter sternly called me to leave. But I wouldn't. We'd waited too long — not just the extra day, but an extra four hours because the ceremony was so late.

Loud resonant bells, small tinkling bells, rhythmic knocking — wild, deafening and hypnotic — stopped the scuffle and the ceremony, unchanged for five thousand years, began.

Silver gates open and people gasp. Inside them, the chief priest and lesser priests, carrying candelabra and balls of fire on plates, walk rhythmically around the *lingam* — signifying control and fertility — through which Shiva is worshipped. Made of crystal, encased in silver, it's washed in holy water and then in milk, honey, and coconut oil. The liquid flows into the *yoni* in which the *lingam* is set, and devotees push and struggle to catch it in their hands, wiping it over their faces and through their hair. The priests carrying the holy flames step down from the shrine and go through the crowd so worshippers may run their hands through the fire and again anoint themselves, gasping each time.

They then hold their hands in salutation at their foreheads and bow before Shiva, the Dancer of the Cosmos.

Burning camphor oil obscures the sacred area and wafts out over the crowd, distorting images and perfuming the air.

❧

The next day a well-dressed man came up to me in this temple and asked if I were alone. I pointed out Walter, who was some distance away. He then said, "This is a very dangerous town," and walked away. I had no idea what his reaction would have been had I been alone. We never felt threatened, but we did find Chidandaram an intense city, unlike the others we visited.

❧

Anandam, our guide, invited us to a meal at his house, where we sat on the immaculate floor and tried to eat neatly with our fingers off banana leaves while his mother served us excellent food and the entire family silently observed us. He was at the station to say good-bye when we left and still regularly sends us ash and holy pictures from his temple. We certainly over-tipped him, but he was worth it. In any case, everyone bargains for double what you offer—no amount is ever specified. We later estimated we'd paid his extended family's rent—which he considered exorbitant—for two months. His optimistic letters hope for more.

Chapter
Thirteen

*W*E WERE TO GO NORTH
again, to the state of Orissa, where we planned to rendezvous with Jenny
in Puri, one of the holiest cities (one gets used to this) in India, situated
on the Bay of Bengal. My maternal grandfather, Charles Gregory, had
laid the last five miles of rail into it years before I was born.

Before going there, we were caught in one of the Indian festivals. We
seldom knew when these were to take place and they, along with strikes,
often caught us unawares: banks and travel organizations are closed,
hotels crowded. Unless we had American money to exchange on the
black market, we were stuck. The first time this occurred we were in
Tanjore, ancient capital of the Chola kings, resplendent with Dravidian
temples and therefore with pilgrims. For the night, we could find only
one tiny room with a *charpoi*. Walter was forced, very unhappily, to sleep
with stray bugs on the floor, stubbornly refusing to trade with me even
though, as he occasionally pointed out furiously, this was my journey,
not his.

Once the country was operating again, we started off, passing
through Hyderabad, "city of pearls," and there found a hotel run by
Arabs who, unlike the Hindus, were formal, cool, and business-like:
they demanded foreign currency (legally mandatory but always, except
here, ignored) at a poor exchange rate. In this chiefly Moslem city, with
its palatial mosque, Mecca Masjid, capable of holding 10,000 worshippers—all, of course, men—and its new, exquisite Hindu temple, we
saw our first desperately exhausted children scouring the streets for
scraps of paper. Dirty, trailing enormous sacks behind them, they
staggered with the weight, or sat sadly on the curbs. They paid us no
attention, grimly getting on with the work. Equally depressing, in the
splendid zoo we watched a white lioness who had born most of the other
lions in the enclosure and were told she'd soon be dead: she was too old,
her usefulness ended, so she was now not given enough food and would
starve to death.

Constant contrasts are, of course, what India is noted for: street after street of shops selling precious stones and pearls (my father had bought a pearl for his sister, Rona, in one of them), magnificent buildings, but also children working like automatons; a refusal to kill animals juxtaposed with indifference to their suffering; *pujas*—the *tikka*, signifying blessing, was constantly applied by insistent priests over my "third eye"—blending with political rallies; an ironic dependence on English and reverence for British customs in a people who had hated the British: among the many slogans scrawled on walls, the most common is "English ever, Hindi never." Riots have broken out over the attempted imposition of Hindi, theoretically the official language but spoken by only a minority of the population. Other slogans, contrasting with the reliance on English and interspersed with the ubiquitous "Please do not urinate against this wall," call for further rumination: "Kick out the Padres, get rid of the Bishops"; "We despise colonial and medieval education"; "We demand justice. Uproot [so and so]": democracy at work in a country that's largely illiterate.

In Puri, a sprawling city of 75,000, we stayed at the South Eastern Railway Hotel. I'd assumed it was where Charles Gregory had lived when he'd laid the railway, but found he'd completed his earthworks and bridges too early—the hotel was not built until 1925: a pity, because he would have enjoyed the South Eastern, a Raj hotel (our first), with spacious verandahs covered in bougainvillaea, high-ceilinged rooms, mosquito netting, bathrooms with enormous old-fashioned tubs (a huge luxury) and towel racks, reading lights (we love to read in bed but it had become obvious Indians don't), ping-pong tables, an army of servants, five-course meals, and, best of all, English marmalade. Walter instantly developed diarrhoea so he could sit on the verandah drinking gin and tonic and reading his book without being forced to look at more temples or go swimming off the wide, sandy beach. As it turned out, he was wise.

Jenny and I went swimming. A fisherman built of steel and wearing a conical straw hat (his identification) insisted (for a fee, naturally) on going into the waves with us, holding us each by the hand. Our guide book had scorned these self-elected life guards, saying they were useless. Believing it, and thinking in any case I didn't need him, I relinquished his hand, was somersaulted ruthlessly through churning water and caught in the undercurrent. We recovered each other's hold although he was still also clinging heroically to Jenny, but the damage had been done.

My eardrum was broken and ear infected. At the time I felt nothing, but in a few days started to go deaf—an experience which turned out to be invaluable in a country where so many are maimed in one way or another.

Puri, with its single wide business street crammed with the usual traffic of people, vehicles, and animals, has no doubt changed little since Charles and my grandmother, Louise, were there. Certainly the fishing village of tiny thatched huts up the beach, where little boys run around naked, small girls carry fifty-pound baskets of fish on their heads, and fishing craft are three logs tied together with rope in more or less boat fashion, must be unaltered. The occasional generosity of the very poor must be the same: a woman tried to give me a large fish and couldn't understand why I didn't take it—I couldn't explain I had nowhere to cook.

The chief difference between then and now, and of course this was true of everywhere we went, lay in our freedom to be a part of those around us, not separated by colour or caste.

We had a bicycle rickshaw-*wallah*, Jagannath Reddy, who waited for us outside the hotel from six in the morning and looked after us well into the evening. Intelligent, energetic, responsible, he could be trusted implicitly. I wanted to find out more about the history of the city and asked him to take me to the Ramakrishna library: a useless exercise because on arrival we were told a ceremony was about to begin (the usual thing) and it was to shut at that very moment. Jagannath then took me to a government library which closed early and where nobody was helpful, but I was finally given the name and address of a "very learned man," Padmashree Sadashib Sastri, an instructor at the Jagannath Temple. My rickshaw-*wallah* said he would try to find the *pandit*'s house, but the address was very skimpy.

It was growing dark as he biked into a warren of back streets, pulling me behind him. Children in alleyways jumped out at us shrieking with laughter, dogs packed and barked, chickens scattered, oil lamps appeared in houses but the streets were unlighted. I clung onto my bag, thinking of the jewellery in it I'd bought hoping it would pay our way back to India (it didn't), and to my camera.

We finally found the house. A man answered the door, and I asked to go in. Told to remove my shoes, I was led into a back room where the rotund *pandit* was sitting, lotus position, on a cushion. Naked except for an ochre *dhoti* on his hips and a rosary around his neck, he was decorated with the symbol of Vishnu on his forehead. He was instructing a student and was astonished, unable to imagine how we'd found him. I couldn't imagine myself. He told me to write down my questions and return the next day, which I did, taking Jenny with me.

The *pandit* could no doubt speak many languages, but English was not one of them. While we struggled to make ourselves understood, and we did obtain some information, we were constantly interrupted by men coming and going and grew intolerably bored. Through a window, we could see the rickshaw *wallah* and he could see us. At one point, he flashed an amused smile, and I was sure he'd picked up on what was going on although he could hear nothing. He, simply waiting, was not bored at all. I wondered why he didn't read (he was not illiterate; he even wrote a little English) or at least do something during his endless standing about. Jenny said later, "When I first came to India, I whipped out my book if I had to wait somewhere, but then I got into their habit of doing absolutely nothing. It's a gift."

One night, alone, pulled in a rickshaw by this man on his silent bicycle, with enormous stars low in the sky, a small breeze coming off the sea, perfumes of night flowers catching the senses, with the Jagannath temple raised against infinite space, I felt as close to perfect harmony as one ever may be in an imperfect world.

Jagannath is "Lord of the Universe." His temple, its tower topped with the flag and wheel of Vishnu, is open to Hindus of all castes (but to no non-Hindus) so draws many pilgrims. He is served by 7000 brahmans; his seventy-eight kitchens prepare food on the aroma of which he survives; after he's inhaled it, his devotees consume it. He lives in the temple with his brother, Balabhadra, and sister, Subhadra. On their annual holiday, they're pulled in a *rath* by 4000 men to the "Garden House" for their week's holiday.

Our *pandit*—there are some doubts here, since we understood each other so inadequately—told us that Jagannath with his sister and brother correspond to the Christian trinity and that Christ had visited Puri, one reason for the city's extreme holiness, with another being its former role as a repository for Buddha's tooth, now in Sri Lanka. There also appeared to be some connection with the Book of Genesis.

Outside the city, down a mud road, a temple to Shiva stands beside a large tank. One festival evening, Jagannath Reddy took Jenny and me as far as he could along this road and then, instructing us to watch our handbags, he waited with his rickshaw: Shiva was not his god. In the eerie half-light we held hands, buffeted and squeezed, afraid we'd lose each other. Booths lining the route sold food, cheap mementos, the odd replica of the Virgin. We tried to avoid human and animal excrement. Two friendly students struggled to talk to us: "Auntie, we are reading your Shakespeare—a great poet. And that John Donne. Now him we prefer above all others."

Like other Indians, they addressed us by one or more of many possible variations: Mama, Mummy, Mother, Auntie, Misses, Madam, Memsahib, and sometimes Sir. Walter was generally referred to as Sir, but could also be Mister, Poppa, Uncle, and occasionally Sahib. We are all considered to be very old.

Christ, Buddha, Jagannath, Shiva, Vishnu, the Virgin were not all of the various deities. Our rickshaw man suggested we go to Konarak, about twenty miles from Puri, to the temple of the Sun God, Surya. Built in the thirteenth century, it's known as the "Black Pagoda" in contrast to Jagannath Temple which is white. Both served as navigational landmarks, with sailors believing the black temple, filled with iron, pulled their craft to shore and wrecked them: many, indeed, were lost. "Black" also echoed the somewhat infamous reputation the temple acquired when it was unearthed in 1904: not only its extraordinary size and beauty were revealed, but also its erotica depicting positions from the *Kama Sutra*. Scholars don't agree on the intent behind these bas-reliefs and sculptures. Some suggest they illustrate vegetative deities and invoke fertility—although at Khajuraho, another temple complex, some figures masturbate or engage strenuously with animals such as horses while women pretend to hide their horrified eyes. Others surmise they're connected with the sexual mysticism of medieval Indian thought and are found in tantric centres. Still others suggest they represent the *devadasis* in action or constitute a "how-to" manual. In any case, the guides love to point them out, watching covertly to see what one's reaction will be, especially to the more athletic and orgiastic groups of figures.

Surya, like the Greek and Sumerian gods, Helios and Shamash, drives an immense and dazzling chariot, its rays catching the cosmos in their net, across the day-time sky. His temple, built in the form of this chariot (its twenty-four sculpted stone wheels are each ten feet in diameter) was once pulled by seven giant horses, parts of which, along with mammoth free-standing mythic animals, remain. The whole appeared far longer than a football field. We were silent, overawed by the imagination that could conceive and execute such a monument.

I thought of my grandparents and wondered if they'd seen it during the British excavations in 1904 when Charles was working on the railway. Would Louise possibly have visited the site of copulating dryads: she who, if she rode horses, would have done so sidesaddle?

Despite the magnificence of its temples and the comfort of its hotel, the lasting impression we took away from Puri was of our rickshaw *wallah*. He transported us tirelessly and ran errands such as finding us hash, legal there, but which in the end we didn't dare to smoke. Jagannath Reddy was about thirty. One day when he was pulling us, Jenny inquired about his business. He'd never asked for anything extra, unlike many of the guides and bearers, and obviously didn't expect it, so he didn't have expectations in mind when he told his story. He supported his wife, mother, son, and sister, for whose dowry he was responsible. Their food alone cost a hundred rupees a month. He had to pay fifteen rupees a day rent for his rickshaw in good weather and bad, in season and out. He was paid little for his labour, being merely a beast of burden: for dragging two people three miles he would get about six rupees — less if his passengers were Indians. He told us regretfully he'd pulled an Italian family around for a month, and they'd promised to send him a down payment so he could buy his own rickshaw. Every day for five months, he'd been watching for the money which never arrived. What he most regretted was not having a "rainy" coat for the monsoon period. Jenny muttered something about leaving or sending him one.

We consulted and put money together before leaving, and when he took us to the station, I gave him an envelope with 500 rupees in it: his down payment. After opening the envelope, he ran to catch us, stunned, and kept shaking our hands, promising to send a photograph of himself with the rickshaw to Canada, so we would know he'd spent the money correctly. He did, writing a little sadly about the "rainy" coat. I sent him the rupees we had left — enough to buy his family food for four months — and promised a coat if we heard he'd received them. He never did. We both wrote several times, but he never got my letters and no doubt finally decided we'd forgotten him. Perhaps the Italian family had the same experience.

Chapter
Fourteen

*B*EFORE WE LEFT PURI, Jenny thanked the sub-manager of the hotel, saying she was very pleased, that this was the best hotel we'd come across in India.

He said, "We have to work well, Madam. It's our duty, we are paid to do it."

"People can be paid to do things but don't always do them nicely."

"Oh, well, you see, we can't always be running to the temple. Worshipping by work, we call this."

This worship may account for so much of the goodwill offered to us. No matter how humble or demanding an occupation, if it's looked upon as a form of prayer there's nothing degrading in it. Hardship is accepted, no doubt in the hope that the next incarnation will be more prosperous. For example, the porters are often small men, but the weights they cart defy description. We watched one of them carrying a loaded tin trunk on his head: every muscle in his body trembled with the effort. Others will carry up to five pieces, three piled on the head and one in each hand; they're paid by the piece and beg to take handbags and cameras, wanting to drape them around their necks, as well as everything else. They would find the right ticket office for us, the train, compartment, place to buy food, coffee, or dreadful Indian tea.

These porters pick their way through the crowds and at night over the sleepers, some in family groups, who spread out a cotton cloth on the station floor and then curl up on it, bundles of possessions, if they have any, beside them. They sleep through the cries of vendors, shunting and blasting engines, rumbling carts, high-pitched whistles. Hungry *pi* dogs haunt the stations: passive, nervous, they slink into corners. When we came across a puppy with every bone in its body exposed, to the amusement of those watching, I bought a packet of biscuits—all I could get—for it. It was so terrified, it barely approached the broken pieces on the ground.

Having got hold of railway sleeping bags (not an easy feat), we caught the night train back to Calcutta for a brief visit. By this time, my ear was aching and I was growing deaf, so when we arrived I went to see Dr. Prager, the English street-doctor. He said he could do little without a surgery but gave me a prescription for antibiotic eardrops: as it turned out, they were not the right thing for a perforated drum, but of course he didn't know what the trouble was.

By the time we caught an evening train to Varanasi (formerly Benares), I'd started to withdraw into my own world. Looking back, I'm astonished that I wasn't more concerned about my growing deafness and can only suppose I was emotionally overloaded or had become as fatalistic as the Indians. Quite calmly, looking out of the window, I considered sending a wire to tell my university I wouldn't be able to teach in the summer. As the train drew out, a young man moved along the platform on his hands and knees, dragging his useless legs behind him, and I knew I was becoming part of the world around me with all its dreadful deformities. Like the sleepers on the platform, I was deaf to cries and whistles and shunting trains, to the effort involved in conversation. Instead, I could simply look, or sleep, or read and move into my private centre.

In a railway kiosk holding trivial books, I'd been lucky enough to come across a volume of *Speaking of Siva*,[18] translated from one of the Dravidian languages by A. K. Ramanujan. Passionate, subjective, they were written in the twelfth century by four saints, *Virasaivas* (those who sing hymns to Lord Shiva), as part of the *bhakti* movement, which protested against reliance on empty tradition and ritual. The poets were wandering mendicants, mystics. One, Mahadeviyakka, a young woman (she died when scarcely in her twenties), betrothed herself as a small child to a specific form of Shiva, Cennemallikarjuna or the Lovely Lord White as Jasmine, to whom she addressed all her poems. In love with God, a rebel who discarded her clothing and wrapped herself in her hair, "her struggle was with her condition, as body, as woman, as social being tyrannized by social roles, as a human confined to a place in time" (Ramanujan).

While reading of her despairing search for her Lord, I recalled the naked woman my father had seen during a festival on the banks of the Ganges in Varanasi, where we were now going. Living in my interior world made it more possible for me to enter her interior world. In some of her poems, Mahadeviyakka writes of Shiva as her illicit lover ("I will

[18] Also spelled Shiva.

176

. . . go cuckold my husband"), the highest form of love in India because the most dangerous, at other times as her husband, but generally as the one who has been lost to her through countless incarnations:

Not one, not two, not three or four,
but through eighty-four hundred thousand vaginas
have I come,
    I have come
through unlikely worlds,
    guzzled on
pleasure and pain.
    Whatever be
all previous lives,
    show me mercy
this one day,
    O Lord
    white as jasmine.

Her singleness of vision, her aching need to unite the *Atman* with the Brahma, her laying bare the lonely journey, taken up so often in trivialities, upon which we are all embarked, humbled our own searching.

When we reached Varanasi, we found a doctor, Ram Gopal Tandon, whose desk was piled with books and who not only knew the *bhakti* poets but was also willing to explain some of the terminology to me. There was no question, with Ram, of going through a clinic in an allotted time: after the second visit, he suggested I come after his other patients had finished so he could talk to me of Hinduism and I could instruct him in Christianity—a task for which I felt ill-equipped. I taught him nothing, but I learned from him, as from others, that Hinduism is monotheistic and non-credal; it doesn't expect the individual to accept dogma, but to recognize God through meditation and to learn "I am Thou."

On our arrival in Varanasi, Walter had been determined to find a doctor with "chambers." He'd asked at the station information desk for a hotel with a resident doctor—an unlikely request. With the usual Indian desire to help, the attendant sent us to a small guest house owned by Ram Raj Meha, a large, gentle man, who put me into a rickshaw, showed me how to brace myself in case of an accident (no one else had thought of doing this), and went with me to a specialist, talking while we crawled forward about the pollution covering the earth. I could only catch fragments of his voice, couldn't clearly hear the cries of the vendors, the bells of the rickshaws: it was like being in a cell underwater, part of a rushing river made up of people flowing down the wide street. I'd become so aware of deformities, of lepers' fingerless hands, of children with unformed legs dragging themselves along the side of the road, that a transference was taking place: my own hands tingled when I saw their hands, my feet were physically discomforted when I watched a boy pulling his patient way along a wall.

Dr. Ram Tandon practiced in a tiny room up a narrow, twisting staircase. He had an ancient audiometer. He said he hoped he could help me—I'd lost seventy-five per cent of my hearing; his "hoped" was unnerving, but I said nothing. With antibiotics and nose drops, a cure began which he said would take a month. He was exactly right. He told me of a drug, Nootropil, successful in some cases in treating sensory-neural hearing loss but said it had to be taken under the care of a doctor in Canada. In Canada, no one had heard of it, and a specialist was contemptuous (an Indian doctor!), suggesting I'd never had a perforated drum: an example of Western arrogance.

After we had left India, Dr. Tandon sent me a scholarly edition of the *Bhagavadgita* and wrote to me:

> You must have felt that practicing as a specialist in a country like India and then a city like Varanasi with minimal amount of money and equipment, it is not easy to do lots of scientific work. I think you can understand, but at the same time we have to keep a positive approach, along with humanity and confidence, to all the negativity we have around us, and that is why we and our patients are happy to each other.

> One thing which the experts forget is that the human body is not the scientific facts only; it is much beyond that, and science is one thing that keeps changing every day. A thing which was taken as fact 100 years back, you can laugh at, and things for which we are confident today will be of no value after 100 years so the fact is not science. Being a human being and your survival is the only fact. This may sound a little funny to you but I feel this way. . . .

> I wish I could meet you again and talk to you. You are welcome again and again. Convey my good wishes to your charming husband. You can come and stay with us. We have small house with lots of love for you. My wife and daughter and son will be happy with you.

178

We were stuck in Varanasi because of my medical treatment. Walter had some bad days. First there was a guide who attached himself to us even though we didn't want him and insisted we had no money. He said that was all right; he didn't want any money. This impressed Jenny and me, but not Walter. The man eased us along to a silk shop (the last place Walter, who felt he was being conned, and was, wanted to go) owned, he claimed, by his brother. Walter left in a towering rage while Jenny and I bought expensive saris and silver-embroidered stoles on our Visas.

It was true we had no money. The banks were unwilling to cash travellers' cheques: they were being forged by some Westerners while others claimed to have lost them when they hadn't, so received the money twice. Not knowing this, Walter had undertaken to go to a bank. First he tried one where he had to wait nearly an hour. Then nervous tellers examined documents and told him they'd never before seen Cook's travellers' cheques; he would have to see someone else. Finally he made his way to the Andrha Bank, which always took cheques, and saw a large sign saying "We do not cash travellers' cheques." In a ferment, he walked out into the traffic—so solid an acrobat could have walked on the tops of vehicles—and was run into twice by rickshaws. The second time, his watch flew off. Passersby were horrified and ran to pick it up, but he was so angry he wouldn't thank them. When we met again, he said, "I'm going to get you well and we're leaving this fucking country."

Our landlord said it was not a propitious time for us.

We went out again, anyway. Walter, so much taller than most Indians, was just the right height to have the end of a metal bar on a vendor's heavy cart catch him in the eye. Fortunately he was wearing glasses. They were knocked off in the melee. Bleeding and astonished, he stopped to staunch the blood. The sullen vendor pushed his cart away as quickly as possible while I stormed after him, shouting, "Apologize at once. You could at least say you're sorry."

The man, going faster and faster through the crowd while I chased him, finally muttered, "Sorry."

"Not to me, you idiot. To my husband. Go back and tell him."

He pushed on grimly.

"I'll get the police. You have to apologize. You might have put his eye out." I looked around wildly, asking the gathering crowd where the police were, but no one spoke English. Then I saw, about four feet away, two policemen sitting on a bench casually watching what was happening. They also spoke no English. Demented, I tried to tell them the man should say he was sorry. They did nothing, looking at me passively until I shouted, "Tourists." That they understood and jumped up eagerly to search for the culprit who had disappeared.

Walter said sadly, "They all thought you were mad. I did, too."

Ram Gopal, amused, looked after Walter's eye. Our marvellous hotelier, deaf in one ear himself through slight brain damage sustained after falling sixty feet out of a window as a small child (a fall cushioned because he landed on other children) pacified us by cashing a cheque at the top rate. He never told us what had happened to the children he'd landed on.

That night Walter, his eye bandaged, looked through my notes and said if it weren't for him, I'd have no humour in my book. That's not quite true. We took a bus tour to Sarnath, the holy city where Sakyamuni (the Buddha) first preached his message of the middle way to Nirvana. In Sarnath, a Bo tree, said to be a travelling transplant from the original under which Sakyamuni attained enlightenment, grows. We barely arrived at it when I began to feel appallingly ill. Jenny and Walter continued the tour, but I took a motorized rickshaw back to our hotel and after much vomiting and diarrhoea fell into bed.

During the course of many people's lives, they have the fantasy of acquiring a devoted bearer: one who is attentive, smiling, honest, willing to do anything. We had such a bearer in our guest house. However, he had one weakness: he seldom knocked. It's not the custom. He would scurry in at all hours, and this time he came in while I lay prostrate, my back towards him, determined to have nothing to do with him. Apparently he was carrying clean clothes. As soon as he saw my back, he said, "Madam, *dhobi* wash. Count."

"Take them away."

"No, no, Madam. Count. Five pieces."

Struggling into a sitting position, I counted. I'd thought there were six pieces, having counted socks as two, so our numbers didn't tally, but I didn't care. "Yes."

"Seven rupees."

I scrabbled around in my purse but could find only a hundred rupee note, a tattered, filthy one at that. I thrust it at him. His face fell, "Oh. Nothing?"

"No. Nothing. Go to office and get change. Ask in office. Don't come back."

I fell asleep. Some fifteen minutes later he was there again, this time with a great bang on the door. He was triumphant. "Seven rupees *dhobi*. Count, Madam."

"Keep it."

"No, Madam. Count."

He stood over me while I counted out the change—ninety-three rupees. It was a slow business, but he was going to prove his honesty down to the last tattered paper, even if I had to get up and vomit during the transaction.

On their way back, Jenny and Walter became entangled in a wedding. Their rickshaw-*wallah* managed to run into the electric wires joining the light bearers together. Men inside the wires were dressed in suits and were jiving. Decorated elephants and palanquins and several bands were taking part. It took some time for the rickshaw to free itself, and they wondered if the propitious moment had passed. However, the procession went on to a main *ghat* where guests made their *pujas* and then got into a boat and crossed to the other side of the Ganges. A bystander told them the festivities would take three days, after which the bride and groom would become "man and wife in one bed."

❧

There are eighteen *ghats* in Varanasi, most for ritual bathing, some for burning. Behind them are endless temples, chiefly in muted colours which blend together, and ashrams. On this long strip of peaceful water, people say their *pujas*, submerge themselves, give their offerings of flowers and candles in small baskets to Mother Ganges, and holy men meditate. Masseurs ply their trade. Jenny and I tried one—very thorough; knuckles, toes, tummy buttons—who had a chit: "He has great respect for women." Piles of wood are stacked by the burning *ghats* and always four or five fires burn with men gathered around them. Stretcher bearers carry shrouded bodies down the warren of pathways, too narrow for rickshaws, between the temples. After the burning, the chief mourner spends ten days meditating and praying by the river. This is considered an educational process.

At sunrise, a soft light falls across the water, singing and music come from the temples, people bathe, fires are lighted, and beyond the *ghats* the *dhobis* are already doing the washing. Cows, bullocks, goats, and donkeys rummage everywhere. If cows make their way into tiny shops or houses through open doors, they are backed out by frustrated owners. Women pick up cow dung, forming it into patties. In the Durga Temple, monkeys pick lice off each other and occasionally attack people, whipping glasses off or biting.

A little later, women gather in temple compounds to listen all day to holy men propounding the scriptures or to worship in the great temple to Shiva. Boys start playing cricket, a passion in India (Walter's stock went up immeasurably when he said his name was Dexter, apparently that of a famous cricketer); too poor to have equipment, they play with pieces of kindling taken from the burning piles as ball and bat. Little girls never play with them; they amuse themselves by drawing in the dust. They have no toys; they don't need them.

All this cannot have changed in any way since my father, and possibly my grandfathers and great-grandfathers, had stood where we were standing. But there will be a change, and an unromantic one. The burning takes a great deal of wood, a commodity growing ever scarcer, so there are plans to bring in electric crematoriums.

Not all bodies are burned. While we stood staring at the small boats going back and forth on the river, we saw two enormous vultures perched on and eating a body floating past us. A man close by told us that holy men, lepers, and children under five are not burned but are put, wrapped in white cloths for male and orange for female, into the Ganges. Holy men, he said, do not wish to be burned: they want their bodies to provide food for others. The rotten bodies of lepers smell too hideously in the flames: there's no smell of decay or putrefaction in Varanasi. Children, if they die so young, have learned nothing so are reborn instantly, thus not needing the ceremony. Later we discovered the bodies of indigents without money for burial are also thrown into the river.

Going down one of the many long series of steps leading to the Ganges, we came across an old woman angrily poking at a puppy with her foot. The puppy was trying to suckle from its mother—a panting bag of bones. It was very hot. Over twenty puppies lay in a mound. There were two bitches which must have whelped at the same time. People were simply walking around them. Involuntarily, I said to the woman, "Oh, don't."

Furious, she picked up the puppy and thrust it at me, saying, I presumed, "Then take it." I remembered that other woman who'd wanted to give me the fish. What could I do with a dying puppy?

Thoughtlessly, we took the same route the next day. The bitch had managed to crawl some distance away from the puppies. One, stronger than the others, had crawled after her for three or four yards and then died. The mother was dead. Further down the steps we found the second bitch, also dead. The mass of puppies in their heap were still alive, panting. We didn't get milk for them. We didn't do anything. We could at best only prolong the agony. Surrounded by those whose precarious lives hinged always between living and dying, we were changing.

An educated guide told us he came across many young Americans who, it seemed to him, were empty within. He was astonished that already, so young, they were using sleeping pills, taking dope, appeared to be lost. Religion and the family are the most important things in India, he said, and both give a sure footing. Our hotelier, Ram Raj Meha, suggested without judgement that a problem in the West appears to be we have no ritual. He added that he thought neither the East nor the West is in a good situation: "We have too little and you have too much. We are both suffering. It's hard to manage too much. Our people, if they can eat, they are happy. That is all they expect, so they do not clamour and make themselves miserable wanting more."

Jenny had not stayed with us in the guest house, but had taken a cheap room right in a *ghat*. With an earth floor, it had no furniture except a *charpoi*. Her landlord told her he had problems because his room was so cheap. People stayed there (particularly, he said, the French) who were sometimes rude and not clean. A brahman, he felt he lived with them after they'd gone since this was his family home and his shrine. Shiva, placed in a corner of Jenny's room, added to its attraction for her.

Early each morning she would go down, dressed in her nightgown covered with a blouse, to the women's small section of the Ganges where she went into the water with those who had already arrived with their baskets of *puja* goodies. They immersed themselves, fully dressed, three or four times, ran water through their hands, lifted them to the rising sun, and prayed. They gave her flowers to sprinkle on the water and were disturbed when she didn't appear one day; they'd been waiting for her.

Ram Raj wanted to give us several books he had lent us when we left. We took one, *In the Image of Man*, an expensive volume on Indian art. I take it from its place next to the *Bhagavad Gita*, Ram Gopal's gift, and look through its images. Those who do not have much, may be so generous.

Chapter Fifteen

*F*ROM VARANASI WE MOVED ON, travelling north-east, to Nainital, a honeymoon haven where brides and grooms gaze at each other with liquid eyes, ignoring everyone else. Their marriages, one would think, are made in heaven, even though quite possibly until a week or so earlier they'd never seen each other.

Here Jessie, my father's cousin, had delivered her first baby and had never forgotten the weeping child who was terrified of returning to her husband. And here—a cool hill station—Jenny had gone to school during the Second World War.

Getting there was a nightmare. To begin with, we couldn't locate the man in charge of railway sleeping bags—he was hidden away, fast asleep—and when we finally did, he said there were none. Jenny, furious, told him she'd rented bags all over India, why not in Varanasi, particularly when we were paying an outrageous price for tourist first-class tickets? He was unperturbed: "Madam, we are not having any here."

She and Walter went to the left luggage, and she couldn't find her suitcase until she realized that an ancient muddy brown object was hers: it had been a pristine blue. In the restaurant, only two of some fifty lunch possibilities written on a board and optimistically pointed out to us by the waiter, were available: curd, which I wisely ate, and curry—a kind of unwise soup—chosen by Jenny and Walter.

The outlook improved when we found we were travelling with an entertaining surgeon on the government business of sterilizing people. He was enthusiastic about cutting down the birth rate, but said wistfully that since India is a democracy, people have to be educated, not forced, to undergo the operation. He had small success with men. Women were more amenable because drugs and food are paid for their existing children if they undergo the government-financed operation.

While we were travelling, a demonstration accompanied us with men waving banners, chanting antiphonally, and shouting slogans as they climbed on and off at each station. The doctor told us they were railway workers and Walter, somewhat bitter after recent experiences, said, "I suppose they want more money."

"Of course, more money but not more work. It is their democratic right." The doctor obviously thought democracy was the least successful of governments.

He insisted on ordering us train food for dinner, saying it would be dreadful but better than nothing. The procedure is to order at one station and then pick up the tinfoil wrapped food at the next. Ominously, he didn't eat any himself. We felt we had to, as he'd been so generous and sat opposite us, enquiring about its edibility. It was as dreadful as he'd claimed.

At about one o'clock in the morning, we left the train at Bareilly, thinking we could find beds in the retiring rooms which exist in the stations. However, these were full. Jenny, pulling herself to her full height and behaving with memsahib fortitude, asked, "Then where is the upper-class ladies' waiting room?"

We were pointed far down the station and struggled with our luggage. It was too late for porters. Walter wanted to find a hotel for the five hours between trains, but we, thrifty to the end, thought that was ridiculous. In the waiting room, Jenny and I found a heavy woman asleep on the only available couch. I took the single *charpoi* and Jenny a wooden bench. She woke up to find a man staring at her and sat up in a rage: "This is the *ladies'* room." But he was merely a husband trying to settle his wife and children beside her on the floor. She drifted off again. When she woke up, she found a small boy getting sick all over her.

In the morning, filthy and exhausted, we discovered the woman on the couch was the attendant. Grumpily, she found water for us to wash in and then stood waiting for a tip. We hesitated—she'd had such a good night's rest—but then with the usual Western guilt gave her a couple of rupees. She held her open hand out with the coins in it, rigid with scorn. A warm glow rushing though me, I said to Jenny "How amazing. She's too proud to take anything." As it turned out, she thought the tip too small and was demanding more. We exploded, telling her she should have given us the couch, but she declined to understand a word.

More travel, and we arrived at another station where the train stopped with our carriage far down the track. We climbed down steep steps with our, by this time perfectly bloody, luggage which had naturally expanded greatly during our travelling, and staggered along beside the train. Miraculously, halfway to the station, porters appeared, took the cases, and led Walter to a bus depot where we were to get tickets to Nainital. The single wicket selling those particular tickets was closed, the seller having wandered off, and no one else would sell him any: they had no change, that was not their wicket, not their responsibility. He was beginning to feel wretchedly ill — not surprising after the last two meals — and wouldn't even discuss his night, it had been so grim. He still talks about how mean-minded we were over a hotel.

The porters put us without tickets onto a bus crammed with people and luggage; there was no question of limiting what it could carry. Jenny found a seat where she could see out of a window and was told for some obscure reason she had to move. She staunchly refused, becoming more and more Raj-like the less she looked the part: bedraggled hair, filthy clothes, smelling of vomit, she sat proudly, face averted. Later we understood the problem must have been that she was sitting next to a man, apparently not the thing for a woman to do in India: the driver wanted us to sit together — an impossibility. Meantime, Walter and I lurched to the back of the bus and inched into a place in the last seat which was without springs. Every time the bus went over a bump, we hit the roof. I thought briefly of the spacious carriage, the shy and apologetic women my family had travelled with so long ago.

Halfway up a vertical hill, the driver stopped to let the engine cool down. We sat unable to move — the aisle was crammed — until Walter, looking agonized, said, "I think I'd better get off."

"You can't."

A few minutes later, the driver fortunately opened a large window behind us. Walter turned to me: "Where's the toilet paper?"

"In the suitcase."

It was impossible to get at the case.

"Why isn't it in your bag?" he asked furiously.

"It's never been in my bag." I was equally furious. "How can it be? I can't get a huge roll in as well as my camera, tape recorder, cigarettes, make up, comb, pen, notebook, glasses, nasal spray, aspirin, handkerchief, and God knows what else."

He stared at me in wild despair. "Well, what's the use then?"

Use or not, he had to leave. He crawled over luggage, over the back of the seat, and through the window. A group of men told him to go up a ravine with others. He hurried, urged on: "No, no, Uncle, not yet."

Finally he found a clearing, recognizing the right place when he trod in faeces. An anxious young Sikh said, "You've found it. No problem."

Afterwards Walter had to throw away his underwear, sidle around crab-like to hide his back. The men were sympathetic, showed him where he could wash, tried to help him. They, too, have this problem, as we'd already discovered in a variety of latrines so filthy there's no spot in which to put one's feet while squatting over a hole.

When he squeezed back on the bus, instead of swearing to leave the country at the first possible moment, he said weakly, "They were so nice. They didn't laugh at me. But I can't stand up."

At Nainital, we were besieged by a crowd of noisy porters ringing the bus to a depth of about twenty feet. They were holding out metal disks. In a daze, I took one through the window, not knowing what it was for. It actually meant he was now our porter, but in the meantime Walter had found another. Disappointed but not angry—not a propitious day—the man walked away to wait for the next load.

Jenny talked enthusiastically about the gem of a hotel—once a manor house—we found in Nainital. I was not so sure and was even less sure when we were presented with our bill. The hotelier modelled himself after the Raj British. Lofty, relaxed, he dressed in a sports' jacket (imported), gloves, a woven Scottish hat, and, covering all, a huge, grey cashmere coat with a cape. He ate English breakfasts, including porridge and marmalade, and sat in front of a glowing grate reading the paper or watching cricket on television. It was very cold. The house, with its high ceilings, was heated by small fires. We were sympathetically urged to have the bearer light one—night, morning, and in between—in our bedroom. In our thin clothes we were freezing and didn't discover until we left that each fire cost us forty rupees, the price of some of the hotels we'd stayed in. We were also billed for every cup of tea or glass of lime fizz generously urged on us and for the service; the latter meant nothing—we were well primed to tip on leaving.

Hovering over the small flames, we were envious of our host's wonderful coat. At night our bearer, who told us proudly he'd worked for the British and his grandfather had been bearer to Mountbatten, put hot-water bottles in our beds; in the morning, he woke us up, pulling back the curtains: "*Chota hazri*, Sahib. Memsahib, *chota hazri*. The sun, it is shining. Kippers you eat for breakfast." The proprietor, the real sahib, had English friends who came out every year to visit him.

They sent him seeds for his English garden: stocks, pansies, violets, delphiniums.

Nainital is a fragment of England as it was fifty years ago. The only difference we could discover is that its nest of boarding schools is inhabited by Indian rather than British children: blazers, crests, polished shoes, grey flannels or tunics, caps or hats depending on sex. The parsonage is still called "The Parsonage" but is now a girls' school. The Hallet school, Jenny's, had been co-educational, but is now an exclusive boys' school run on house lines. The large Anglican church still stands but is locked up in the off-season; grass grows out of its Norman tower. The spire on the Catholic church where Jenny was confirmed, and where she had a temper tantrum over wearing a veil, rises over the town. She said the Capital cinema and the roller skating rink, built on the lakeside mall surrounded by Himalayan foothills, are unchanged. The houses have English names: Balmoral (Jenny's old home, now surrounded by new buildings and much the worse for wear), Primrose Cottage, Dudley Grove, Seven Oaks, Stafford House. But she said the hills have been denuded of trees since her time and buildings have multiplied outrageously.

Small men with tiny pack ponies and donkeys, laden with immense stones for building, block the vertical brick streets. The people look as if they are Nepalese; they wear jackets, caps and scarves, hand-woven shawls. Down by the lake, we found a Tibetan refugee self-help area — this, of course, would not have been there when the British were — consisting of small shops. I wanted to buy a brass and silver teapot like the ones my Aunt Gwen had inherited, acquired some eighty years before from camel caravans. An old Tibetan had one, but its chain was unlinked. He said he could mend it, but when he took a closer look, he found the pot itself was cracked and warned me not to buy it. A young man sold me some tiny whale-bone carvings he said his father had brought from China.

"Are they very old?"

"Not so old, not so new."

The people were honest and easy-going, but many said they made little money and worried about their children's education. Even so, the usual phrase, "No problem," we heard all over India was endlessly repeated, and indeed there usually was no problem, and if there were some way was found to handle it.

We made friends with an English birder, Roger, who was staying at our hotel. He told us of one way a problem was resolved. He'd had an exceptionally difficult time trying to cash travellers' cheques. After going through the usual business of waiting in line for over an hour, filling in a book demanding his name, occupation, age, sex, height, and passport number, he'd been given a numbered disk which meant he could proceed to the next barrier to get his money. While he again waited patiently—India enforces patience—a problem arose: the man who had to sign the book in authorization had locked it up in a desk and gone off with the key. After much confabulation, a clerk left and re-entered the bank with a huge crowbar. Roger, still on his bench, thought—they can't be going to pry it open with that! That's exactly what they did, demolishing the desk in the process. He forgot his frustration and started to laugh, feeling ashamed of himself when one of the men rebuked him gently: "Do not laugh, Sir. To help you we are doing our best."

Roger told us he showed slides at home after his regular birding expeditions; the Nainital area has over three hundred species, including vultures and eagles with up to eight-foot wingspans. During one of his journeys, he'd landed up and taken slides at high flood time in Agra where the Ganges meets the Jumna. Many corpses—and no doubt also dead dogs and pigs; we'd seen them at Varanasi—had been washed ashore where dogs were crunching bones and vultures tearing rotten flesh. His audience was horrified. We weren't. As he talked we were resting in a serene grassy area surrounded by early roses, peach and cherry blossom, speedwell, violets and periwinkle. Terraces stretched up the steep incline behind us where people and donkeys struggled to build pockets of earth for growing food. Life continued its circular course, and what happened to the body after death seemed quite irrelevant.

He also told us that when he was last in India, six years before, people were starving. He talked of a dead beggar by the side of the road, who'd been too weak to buy food with the scattered paise passersby had thrown to him: no one had picked them up.

I went to the municipal office and found the record of Jessie's baby, Mark, born 7/7/22 in the Ramsey hospital, and of Pauline Brandon's baby, June, born 12/2/23. The stillborn babies were marked in red ink: there were many of them, almost all British, and all but one were boys. A miserable reminder of the exiles' lives.

When we left Nainital, the hotelier's son drove us to the early morning bus, passing the governor's residence on the way. He said, "It has, yes, three hundred and sixty-five rooms. He is staying there one week in the year. The Prime Minister and the President for one week. Otherwise it is empty. The gardens, they are beautiful and expensive but we cannot see them. The gates are locked."

⋅৽ৡৡ৵⋅

Coming down the terrifying descent with its corkscrew curves and immense drops on our way to the Jim Corbet National Park, where we planned to stay, we were also travelling through the Indian spring: into pale red acacia-like trees with their sweet early leaves, red-blossomed plum trees, large yellow celandines, white jasmine with its intoxicating perfume, powder-blue flowers covering the hillside. For the first time in India I saw the deodars my father loved, the ponderosa pine, cedar, berberis. Spectacular gibbon monkeys appeared and everywhere there were tiny terraces growing wheat or oats. Eucalyptus trees reminded me of my father who put the leaves in his bath. Brilliant kingfishers illuminated child memories. The egrets I didn't remember, but I did recall the anthills that had once astonished me, six and seven feet tall built out of arid earth, they'd towered over me. We passed dried-up river beds: home.

Intriguing signs pointed the way to the park: "Visit Jim Corbet National Park: a place for trumpted and song." A man on the bus talked about Jim Corbet, calling him "a veritable hero."

Corbet was an Irishman born and brought up in Nainital. Coming from humble beginnings (his father was a postmaster), he first worked as a government clerk. The world wars gave him his opportunity. He was a superb hunter and military man, and for one of these wars he raised 4000 men, ending up as a colonel. Corbet was much loved by the Indians because he went after man-eating tigers—one had killed over four hundred people—but he admired and respected the animals, few of which attack people. He called the tiger "a great-hearted gentleman" and pointed out, long before preservation became a common concern, that it had to be protected: its extermination would be a terrible loss. Loving India, he became a citizen and gave all the royalties from his six books, co-authored with his sister (exceptionally attractive people, neither married), to the blind. The park named for him is a tiger preserve; a sign at its gate quotes Blake: "What immortal hand or eye dare frame thy fearful symmetry."

Trees the Indians call "dakh" fill the park. They must be flame trees—brilliant dark red blossoms large as magnolias appear before the leaves: pyramids of flame filled with singing birds.

It is hard to get rooms in the park, it's so popular, and if you do get in you can stay for only three days. We'd booked ahead, but the keepers had no record of our doing so. However, they did have one spare unit and offered to put in an extra bed for Jenny. Their computation was a puzzle: "Extra bed, 60 rupees. You take it, I advise, because in any case you pay the 60 rupees."

The park is extensive and superbly run. Hoping for a glimpse of a tiger in its natural habitat was as close as I'd ever get to that childhood Raj hunt. There were other differences: cement mounting platforms about fifteen feet high instead of rope ladders with which to climb the elephant; *machans* without railings but with carved wooden posts to cling to; savannah-like expanses covered with grass twenty feet high rather than jungle; a stucco room instead of a tent; dining in a Spartan building rather than in a clearing waited on by *khidmatgars*; patient *mahouts* looking for tiger-pugs, but no beaters.

It was blessedly silent: no transistors, no night photography, no driving after dark. Solitary wandering off—as I had, looking for four-leaf clovers—is theoretically not permitted. Several accidents had recently occurred. A guide staring up at birds had trodden on the tail of a tiger and been demolished; the year before, two Danish birders had been killed and a *mahout* attacked while collecting grass; he'd been saved by his elephant, but was badly mauled. The park attendants simply warned us, however, and then left us alone. Their fatalism had become obvious to an enraged Englishman who said his car had broken down halfway into the park the night before; no jeep had set out in rescue—perhaps because of its noise—but a man carrying a gun and another a torch and stick. The tourist and his party had to walk twelve miles carting their gear through the darkness, hearing in the morning they'd walked right past a place where a tiger had been seen a few minutes earlier.

I had no memory of the tranquillity one experiences when moving across the earth on an elephant which sweeps the long grasses aside noiselessly while passing wild boar, deer, antelope, and brilliant birds: hawks (osprey-like hoverers), birds with red iridescent breasts and turquoise-blue wings, others pure red or yellow, wild peacocks, small, crisply demarcated black and white bundles of feathers swinging close beside us on grass stems. And everywhere, that pungent wild plant with pink, blue, and purple florets with the odour which had haunted me for years. The huge elephant feet trod on it, extracting that half-remembered child world.

The sun set, a red-orange ball: the mountains beyond the yellowing grass a deep purple, the clouds a plum-purple lined with gold; while it slid down the sky, the full moon shone through shreds of cloud in the east. Our old *mahout* hacked, his chest heaving. Soon he would die, but soon we would all die, and this would still be here. Personal desires, ambitions, worldly accomplishments became ludicrous.

The next day we had a younger *mahout.* He took us to watering holes, forded a river, followed tiger-pugs. Our elephant, with prehensile feet, balanced on rounded river stones. We went up and down mounds, hanging onto the posts. When the elephant stopped to have a dump, the *mahout* said, amused: "Bathroom." When it peed, he patiently waited out the waterfall. We ran into a herd of wild tuskers with the adults forming a laager around their young. One ancient animal with an injured back leg turned towards us, her front leg raised: she was protecting a newly born calf. The herd and our elephant froze; the *mahout* whispered to us to do the same or she would charge. We were aware of syringa perfume coming from small white flowers on thick rope vines. In the end, we silently backed off.

The rolling motion, the quiet, was not broken by a single tiger sighting.

Walter said, "It's not surprising the Indians love their country. The British must have, too, many of them. Jim Corbet loved it. When I go home, I'm not going to work so hard. I'm going to canoe and take time to look around and live like an Indian."

He changed his mind about living like an Indian the next day when we travelled on by bus to Ramnigar, a wretched town where we had to transfer. The three of us sat miserably, dying of heat and dust, in the only available place—a bench outside a makeshift shop located in the middle of the road. Behind us a man cooked *samosas* over a blasting fire. Buses swirled around the stand, barely avoiding our luggage, coating everything with dry powder. Walter and I ate bananas and oranges, the sweet juice pouring down our throats. Jenny, cast-iron stomach, ate everything, including the *samosas* we'd been warned to avoid.

We were heading for Dehra Dun, my childhood home, but first we had an eight-hour drive to Hardwar, some claim a city even holier than Varanasi or Puri because this is where the Ganges leaves the Himalayas and comes down into the plains. It's so holy, in fact, that one cannot buy a beer within a twenty-mile radius and so strictly vegetarian that not even eggs are available. When we arrived in the evening, we didn't care about the eggs but were filled with an irrepressible longing for beer. We'd been subsisting on warm bottled water and oranges. Besides that, we were so exhausted, we were becoming subject to subterfuge and bad temper.

On the bus, we'd managed to get an aisle seat for Walter. In a seat for three, he and I took up the whole space, hoping to look like three, which in fact we did—he's the size of two average Indians. I'd lost all my democratic, anti-colonial principles: wasn't it possible I'd be recognized as a daughter of the Raj and be permitted to travel with a modicum of comfort? Of course, neither bulk nor past counted. We had only two heads. When a large woman and her daughter got on, several people eagerly pointed out the third seat. Walter stood up—not strictly speaking; his head would have gone through the roof—to allow her the inside seat so he could keep the aisle. Without thanks, she sat down and gestured her daughter beside her. Walter looked puzzled, but Jenny and I started objecting vociferously—"One only"—and eventually the daughter, a calf following a cow, stood up, but was not allowed to sit by a man in the couple of inches of space that was found. We didn't care. Walter sat down and the woman promptly went to sleep, her head on his shoulder. At each corner, it lurched over onto me. Two women in white *burqqas* with tiny mesh eye-holes looked like ghosts. The aisle overflowed with people, puppies, bags, suitcases, chickens in baskets. It was stifling.

We travelled very slowly, passing hundreds of bullock carts pulling gigantic loads of stripped branches which looked dried out. The whole caravan appeared to have been on the go for some time: blankets and *chatties* of water hung from the carts. Tiny children and old men travelled on top of the wood. Smaller loaded carts were pulled by men on bicycles, some even by men on foot. We passed exhausted bullocks, their legs splayed out as a team leaned one against the other. Occasionally three or four travelled abreast, taking up the entire road and had to be manoeuvred aside with much honking. At least five carts with their unfortunate beasts had turned over in the ditches. We never discovered what it was all about.

In Hardwar, we had a grungy room with a stinking toilet, but the next day, a lovely cool one, we went down to the *ghats*, waded in the flowing water—blessed Ganges—and bought little baskets of flowers for a few rupees from a smiling woman. They had lighted candles in them and were to float theoretically to the Bay of Bengal. Jenny and I sent them off while Walter watched us, embarrassed to make an offering but his good humour restored by the softness of the place.

Chapter Sixteen

WE ARRIVED IN DEHRA DUN on the eve of the *Holi* festival. Young boys were already celebrating by going around spurting balloons filled with coloured water at people. Walter just missed being drenched: missed fortunately because it's hard to get out. Orange and pink dye is rubbed into people's faces, red powder into their hair. I remembered my mother's disgust over this festival, her saying the powder represented menstrual blood. No one else said this. An exuberant country celebration, its basis goes back in legend to a woman who was the jealous stepmother of a boy child. She wanted to kill him and told her servants to build a fire into which she planned to push him. Before she could do so, her shawl caught in the flames and she was incinerated. This woman is considered to have been a demon, the symbol of evil (and if it had been a girl child? Many were immolated in suttee) so originally the day started out as a happy occasion with people decorating each others' foreheads and hugging. But we were told that now the streets are filled with hooligans who throw oil and tar as well as powders. Our hotelier begged us not to go out until the next afternoon —bonfires and merriment would last all night and into the morning. It's a festival for boys and men; women and girls stay clear of the streets.

It's also a day for riots. Indians are volatile people and, patient as they are all year, *Holi* has become a day to let go.

We understood our hotelier's concern when we read the papers after the festival was over. In Puri, a boy threw red powder as a joke over a policeman, who became angry. A crowd collected and backed the boy; other police arrived and fired on it, wounding and killing people. In Calcutta some youths entered a refugee camp and threw powder onto a girl whose family objected. By the time the riot ended, a hundred hovels had been burned and people stabbed.

Shortly afterwards, Jenny met an English girl who was still in a state of shock. She'd arrived in Varanasi on the feast of *Holi*: "She'd been warned by some educated Indians not to put on her best clothes and to be careful, but even so she went out in a miniskirt. When she got out at the station, Varanasi was like a ghost town, no one was in sight, there were few rickshaw-*wallahs* and the ones who were there refused to take her. Finally a man volunteered, but when she got into the rickshaw a crowd of young men appeared, surrounded her, and smeared her breasts and crotch with colour. She was terrified. The ageing rickshaw-*wallah* said, 'Madam, you are in great danger' and proceeded to peddle as fast as he could. The crowd got bigger and the rickshaw man more and more worried. Going through a narrow street, a man on a motorbike cut them off, shouting, 'Jump on, Madam, you are in great danger,' and the girl thought, well, this is it, I'm going to be raped, and was petrified that she might be in more danger from this man than from the others. However, he took her to a police station. She thanked him hysterically, and he said, 'It is my duty, Madam. You are a guest in my country and I must protect you.'

"The police chief gave her a jeep and an armed escort of six men. They took her to the *ghats* and put her on a boat with four of them accompanying her until they reached her hotel. When I met her, she couldn't bear any Indian men going near her, but I said perhaps she should think of all those who helped her rather than the mob hysteria she'd experienced. Maybe they'd been drinking *bangla* or smoking hash. We both agreed that often Western women behave badly, and she was paying the price for it."

On *Holi* the streets are spattered with red juice looking like blood.

❦

Dehra Dun is an unprepossessing city now, not the small village it was when my family lived in the area. In the interim, the minister in charge of oil and gas decided this was a good place to set up his ministry. With the usual Indian philosophy — no problem — he brought in, overnight, 40,000 people, without providing accommodation or amenities. It now has a population of a quarter million. The resultant chaos combined with government money is the reason, we were told, its inhabitants are uncharacteristically aggressive. It's more difficult to walk the streets than it is in Calcutta and almost impossible to cross them. The only creatures who gain any respect from the traffic are the cows. Drivers are indifferent to pedestrians, including tourists: they back into them, sideswipe them, blow horns on top of them. We had to walk in the ditch or get run over.

But Birpur, the subdivision where the cantonment area is located, is cool and lovely, with large houses, tree-lined streets, scented gardens with climbing roses trained into circular waterfalls of flowers, and with the Forestry Institute, once run by Lionel Brandon's stepfather, Chief Forester of the Indian Empire. No doubt this was the area in which the minister lived.

It's also the location for the prestigious Doon School. Through a student in one of the United World Colleges which is set in Canada, we'd been given addresses; carrying the black and white snapshot I'd taken with me of my childhood home, we made our way up to the school to meet Arun Kapur, a house master.

With huge grounds, gardens, playing fields, impressive buildings, including an outdoor theatre, swimming pool, squash courts, the school houses boys in whites playing cricket and boys in uniform, two of whom showed us around. Surprisingly, these boys who were being trained to run the country claimed they didn't speak Hindi, the official language. We were later told this wasn't true, but in any case, they spoke excellent English, their usual language. Arun Kapur's stone house, covered in creepers, with its large rooms, high ceilings, western furniture, could have been in Devon. The low-voiced, formally dressed parents visiting him could have been the parents of boys at a superior English public school. We were treated with great courtesy, given scotch to drink, told we would be introduced to a Brigadier-General Bakhshi who could with luck get us into the cantonments, out of bounds to visitors. Dehra Dun, as a military centre, is in a vulnerable position: close to China, with which India was on uneasy terms over Tibet and its refugees pouring over the Indian border, and to the Punjab, at that moment making anti-government political connections with Sri Lanka. India was also on the verge of another possible war with Pakistan.

Arun Kapur thought he knew of a house at the end of a road with a large banyan tree surrounded by a platform in the garden (my chief identification), but he couldn't take us there.

He did take us to meet a historian who was writing on Mussoorie, the hill station outside Dehra Dun, who could possibly tell me something about my grandfather's house. He did give us information which turned out later to be incorrect, but something else he said made an impression: "It is true you belong here, like others who are returning in search of their past roots. But you and they will be the last. Your children, they will not be interested. They will be different."

Jenny had been told much the same thing by another man, a brahman priest. She'd said, "You must be rather surprised at this middle-aged matron coming back."

He'd answered her: "Not at all. Necessary it is for your development. Mother India, she is calling you back. You have been nurtured further by having eaten her food, drunk her water, breathed her air, learned important things in your life—you belong here. You are welcomed home."

We met General Bakhshi, who was willing to help us, but in the meantime he had to attend two funerals so we had a week to wait. I asked him if the Dehra Dun Club still existed and if he knew where it was. He said, "Of course. I was member and president for many years, but now I do not enjoy it so have resigned. At one time it was black tie—no longer. I prefer the Mess. All over the world, money is in the wrong hands today."

I felt instantly at home with him. He could have been my father or one of my uncles: the same military bearing, moustache, vocal expressions. He introduced us to Mrs. Roy, the widow of another general, a beautiful, light-hearted woman, who said, when I told her I was dismayed at not picking up Hindustani, the language I'd grown up speaking, "I wish to God we still spoke it. Then we all understood each other. Now there's so much trouble at the imposition of Hindi. Eighty per cent of the people don't know it so can't get jobs. It leads to riots." I hadn't known the language, a mixture of Hindi and Urdu, had disappeared. Others say it hasn't. In fact, I was beginning to pick up a few Hindi words.

She joked about the traffic: "There's no need for birth control here—the three-wheelers and buses are so rough."

After we left them, Walter said, puzzled, "But aren't they English?"

Both work as volunteers at Raphael, a Ryder Cheshire Centre for the relief of suffering. General Bakhshi is the director, and the place draws him, he says, "Like a bee to honey." The centre has a romantic history. It's a continuing wedding present to each other from Group Captain Leonard Cheshire, VC, and his wife, Lady Sue Ryder. Cheshire, a bomber pilot during the war, a horrified observer of the Nagasaki bombing, wanted to do something constructive when it all ended. He had little money but did have a plan: he would draw people together and inspire them to open homes for incurables. He must be a charismatic man because he succeeded and now Cheshire Homes exist over most of the world. Sue Ryder, who worked with survivors from the concentration camps, was equally committed and established Sue Ryder Homes, chiefly in eastern Europe.

Mrs. Roy showed us around. We went to the leper colony, where the inhabitants card, spin, weave, cut kindling, garden. They have to be careful with tools, because they can feel nothing—their nerve ends have ceased to function: they may cut off a hand or foot without knowing it. Leprosy takes a long time to develop, so families keep their children with them until they are five and then they're moved to "The Little White House," where they're housed and educated. Even so, the stigma of leprosy remains. It's particularly hard for girls who have no support system when they leave, find it hard to get jobs, and cannot live by themselves. Mrs. Roy said, "A woman alone is too vulnerable, even if she's educated."

The Centre also looks after the chronically ill, retarded or demented children, and those who have TB, widespread in India. Tiny children, orphans dying alone on the earth floors of huts, had been brought in: some to live, others found too late. A young, pregnant bride, Kunta, hated by her in-laws for the disease and further complications, had been thrown out of her home to die a wanderer when she was brought to Raphael.

While Mrs. Roy was showing us around, the children were being fed. One little girl had to be shut outside by herself—a crying, distraught waif—because she ran around snatching food off plates if she ate with the others: a scrap of life, impossible to love.

Most of the money to run Raphael comes from donations. An Australian prisoner, known as Wally, had persuaded his fellows inmates to donate on a regular basis. After twenty-seven years in jail, he was released and changed his name. Funds dried up. The centre lost touch with him, but Mrs. Roy said they're still waiting for him to turn up because he'd said one day he would be there. We wondered if they would know him: "Oh, no, he won't want his past to be known, so we won't know who he is when he comes. But I don't think he's come yet."

Despite shortages of water, electricity (it's constantly cut off, as in other cities), housing, staff, and enough trained personnel, Raphael— once a tent town—flourishes. General Bakhshi says, "Money always comes. Once, a wonderful thing, a Dutch woman sent me 20,000 pounds. No letter. Just a cheque. Now we have a mobile TB clinic and it goes all over the state."

Young Western girls work as volunteers. Their visas restrict them to three months, barely time to become acclimatized. Most of them are thrown untrained into this culture, and they have to get used, among other things, to caste. With Western attitudes, they may become rebellious, may say: "The cook must eat with me. I am used to a democratic system." This is impossible, of course, for the cook.

We were also confused by caste. In our hotel, the Relax, considered a rather high-class establishment, the hot-water system had broken down (two years later, when we went back, it had still broken down). It took an hour or more for someone to bring a couple of buckets to the room so we could wash effectively. When we returned from Raphael, Walter impatiently took our buckets to get the water himself. The head man was very upset: Walter was the wrong caste to be carrying buckets of water. Or perhaps he was merely performing someone else's "duty." On both our visits to Dehra Dun the manager said in astonishment, "No hot water?" as if this were indeed unusual. The first time we believed him.

A note on my tape says: "Sitting on toilet in marble bathroom. No hot water. No cigarettes. Three more days. Might as well go to bed."

General Bakhshi had drawn us a map from the hotel to the Dehra Dun Club. We walked through dirty, congested streets, hating the town more and more, wishing we could leave. This was supposed to be a highlight, but by the time the second funeral had delayed us again, we wondered if we would ever see the house I'd travelled halfway around the world to find. But the Club, of course, had also to be part of the expedition.

It was almost unchanged except that it was now for Indians, not British. Men in white were playing tennis. Two squatting *malis*, using small scythes to cut grass (we saw no mowing machines in India), worked in the garden which the secretary told us was once a parking lot; this seemed unlikely—so few people had had cars. The splendid entrance, the long verandah with arches, potted plants, and wicker chairs, was unaltered. I remembered the night my father, now dead, had taken me out during a party to show me the rain battering down at one end while the other end was bright with stars. I remembered my hand in his large one.

The secretary, whose duty it obviously was—he was far from enthusiastic—took us around. An ageing man, world-weary, he showed us one room after the other: "Now this is the billiard room and it was always the billiard room. Now this is the card room, but we have to have another card room, so many people they play cards. This was the ladies' card room because ladies played cards separately from the men but now they don't. This was the library and is still the library. And this was the bar and is still the bar." Most of the rooms were curtained and dim. The people in them—the new élite, so unlike the curious, friendly poor—paid us not the slightest attention. We might have been ghosts.

I told our guide I wanted to see the ballroom. It was silent and empty, not nearly as large as I'd thought, and was filled with rows of chairs. The stage where I'd once been presented with bouquets of flowers turned out to be minute. I knew exactly where I wanted to go: to the back of the room. Sure enough, the cloakroom, where my mother had left me during a fancy dress party for which I'd been dressed as a paperboy, was there and was unchanged. Standing in it, I thought I could smell the coats in which I'd buried my face.

The whole place was a little run down, even though its members have money. Perhaps after a time, one simply doesn't notice flaking paint, worn floors. In the library, a man was oiling panels so there is some attempt to keep the building up.

We were offered lime juice, drank it in the bar, and were still ignored.

There were magazines there. I picked up a copy of *Time*, Indian edition. It had a long article on Jimmy Swaggart in South America preaching to immense crowds, telling them Roman Catholicism is a cult; Catholics are not Christians. He spoke glowingly of Pinochet and his "beautiful wife." Bigoted, right-wing evangelism, North American trumpeting in the last place one would expect to find it. An article discussed John Huston directing "The Dead," a short story I'd taught many times. And then, even more extraordinary, an account of drinking tea at the Empress Hotel in Victoria, my Canadian city. It was old publicity stuff, so far from the truth I wondered if the writer had ever been there: English dowagers, ladies in gloves and hats who drank tea while listening to a small orchestra but who avoided the hotel when tourists were in town. They didn't care for all that brashness.

We were tourists being avoided in another town, in the club where my mother had met my father, and where she'd poured, or not poured, tea after tennis matches. Time warps, synchronicity. The world-weary boredom of the secretary, who hadn't had enough interest to drink a juice with us, devoured both Walter and me.

For some obscure reason, weighing scales stood on the verandah. I'd lost fifteen pounds. My hip and breast bones were bare of flesh. Not only weight was melting away: like Jenny, layers of my skin were being stripped from me.

❧

Rishikesh, made famous by the Beatles and the Maharishi, is not far from Dehra Dun. Once the English yogi whose alms' bowl and rosary had long stood on my father's mantelpiece had meditated there, and it was there, a quiet place, my parents had visited him. We took a bus and arrived in a crowded, traffic-thick town. The tourist office was locked, but eventually a man grumpily opened it. He'd obviously been asleep in the dark interior, but he cheered up and told us to take a boat across the river. Three-wheelers rushed up, demanding ten rupees. We were lordly: "Too much." A man in a *tonga* came up with a fare for six, and then all burst out laughing because they were undercutting each other. A second *tonga* appeared for four. We took it, its battered horse pulling us over the stone streets, and then transferred to a boat which transported us across the river to a street of shrines and ashrams on the other side. Once again, we were with laughing people.

It was very hot. In a small shrine garish pictures decorated the entrance hall. They meant little to us. Another visitor approached: "You are understanding?"

"Not really."

"From *Bhagavad.* Life of Krishna."

In difficult English, he pointed out one frame after another. I knew a little about Krishna, sometimes considered the supreme God, sometimes as one fairly low in the hierarchy, certainly Arjuna's charioteer, and certainly lover of the peasant girl, Radha. An attractive god, he's often painted blue of skin, playing a reed pipe. I'd never heard of the illustrated episodes depicting the ambitious uncle who, after killing the six little boys born before him, tried to kill him at birth. His mother spirited him away and replaced him with a girl. The uncle, to be safe, killed her anyway. Krishna, however, like Jesus whose parents fled from Herod, was saved. His subsequent adventures were not unlike various biblical stories except for his pastoral dalliance with a *gopi.*

Walking past commercial ashrams, we had an unexpected encounter with two people, their faces heavily made-up (unusual in India), their bodies clothed in red, gold-embroidered saris. They were sitting on a platform belonging to a fruit vendor and called out to us. To our surprise, their voices were low pitched and they recited obscenities in English. We stopped, embarrassed, and then went on, supposing these must be male prostitutes, perhaps attached to a temple. In actual fact, they must have been *hijras*.

The *hijra* caste is the only one that a person is not born into. Boys with female characteristics are adopted into it. They are supposed to be, and still claim to be, radically castrated, although Agehananda Bharati thinks this is no longer so. Theoretically, in any case, they're neither men nor women and may be challenged to verify the fact by lifting a sari to mothers who pay them for their services in celebrations for new babies. A *hijra* dances, mimes pregnancy, birth, and motherhood, taking on the sins committed in past incarnations by the newborn. He/ she also has the task of tossing obscene imprecations at passersby. The agonizing castration is (or was) performed by tying a strong thread or horsehair around the genitals, pulling it ever tighter, and then slicing everything off with a sharp razor.

The *hijras* didn't scorn us; they were merely fulfilling their function.

Perhaps for everybody, not just the Indians, the Himalayas and the Ganges have assumed mythic importance: one the home of gods and of hermits with transcendental powers, the other the Mother, the sustainer of life. At Rishikesh, the commercialism becomes unimportant. In places the huge river flowed swiftly, but in others she'd dried up, and we could walk on her bed of smooth, rounded stones. I picked up one, pure white, glittering, and put it in my bag: a blessing.

On the way back, we travelled on a boat so crowded with pilgrims that I couldn't sit in the shell but perched on the bow above a mass of faces. These people were from Rajasthan and were visiting the holy places, travelling over India in an ancient bus with wooden seats. Most were farmers. Walter told them, speaking through their guide, that he'd also come off the farm, and they were amazed. Farmers in India are very poor—how could this sahib who'd come so far have ever lived on a farm? They were so enthusiastic the guide asked us if we wouldn't like to join them, he could fit us in, we would see all the most important places. But we were still on our own pilgrimage.

We had another invitation. I sat next to a government accountant from Delhi on the bus back. He cradled a jar of holy water on his lap while he asked about Canada. What really interested him was what happened to our old people. Did they live with their families? Who looked after them if they got sick? How often did we see our children? Did we all live together? Did we get along with our brothers and sisters? I told him about nuclear families and broken homes. He said, "We are not having those specific problems," and invited us to stay with him when we reached Delhi.

Chapter Seventeen

*W*E DID FIND THE HOUSE. General Bakhshi and his niece arrived one morning in a jeep on the dot, as we'd been warned in a note, at nine hundred hours.

It was at the end of a road — the road Dawn and I had ridden along daily as children. The hedge around the garden had gone; in fact, the whole garden had disappeared leaving dried-up expanses of uncut grass, but the ancient banyan tree surrounded by the stone platform on which we used to tricycle still stood. The row of eucalyptus trees with their clean, sharp smell remained, but not the long bed of yellow roses. The river, a tributary of the Ganges, ran by it, not dried up as I recalled but with a stream of water. On the hill across the river, where there'd been a couple of white-washed huts, in one of which my mother's servants had found the dying baby, a full village stood. On the other side of the road, there was a farm, and beyond it the 9th Gurkha Mess to which we'd been allowed to walk when the grass had been short, not hiding snakes.

The long verandah, part of which had now been enclosed, where I'd once sat talking to the sweeper, was the same. The thatched roof had gone, replaced by corrugated red tin: noise would explode from it during a monsoon downpour or hail storm. The servants' quarters at the base of the hill had been cut in half: the general told us it was no longer the thing to have many servants — they'd become extremely expensive since oil had been brought in and people could get government jobs: "And why not? They are no longer dependent on the whims of others."

The stables were there, but were no longer used as stables: one of the real differences in India was that we saw no one riding except in former hill stations where Indian tourists, slumped in the saddle, sat on docile hill ponies as they meandered around a lake or up a hill. Fifty years before, riding a horse well had been mandatory, and people had taken immense pride in good horses and equipment. They'd also been a chief means of transport. When my parents left India, they took all their riding paraphernalia with them.

I knew where all the rooms were: drawing room where my mother wrote letters; dining room where I'd once interrupted a dinner party; my parents' bedroom where a doctor had tried to insert a catheter into me; the nursery with the grungy cement bathroom which now had running water. I'd never seen, as far as I remembered, the guest room where my grandmother, Mary Murray, sometimes stayed: now it was the only furnished room in the house: two neat, made-up beds. They looked as if they'd never been used.

Walter and General Bakhshi were patient while I looked around the deserted, almost empty house, peopling it in my imagination. The drawing room with its now dead fireplace sparked a memory of three men in uniform throwing my sister from one to the other and refusing to throw me, without intention making me feel unwanted. One was the man who demonstrated Chinese tortures on me as entertainment. I had liked him. I wondered if the other had been Gerry Crampton. I'd been told his story by my mother after she'd been to see the film, *Gandhi*. She'd been very excited, her voice filled with conspiratorial energy. I recalled its exact tones in the silence of the room where she'd once entertained her friends: "D'you remember the part when General Dyer gave the order to shoot in Jallianwala Bagh—you know, the Amritsar massacre—and the man asked if he could give a warning first and Dyer said no, they'd already been warned?"

"Yes."

"That was Gerry Crampton. He was a friend of ours and was often at the house in Dehra Dun. Do you remember him? Well, he gave that order to his Gurkhas. Nobody ever talked about it in the Mess, but Robin told me privately. It ruined his whole life."

The massacre took place on Baisakha Day, one of the most important of the Sikh festivals. In 1919, because of spreading unrest, the British had published a decree prohibiting meetings. Even so, pilgrims from the countryside, most of whom had never heard of the prohibition, poured into Jallianwala Bagh, an area surrounded by high walls with a single narrow entrance, in the holy city of Amritsar. While they were celebrating their festival, Brigadier-General Dyer marched with fifty riflemen down the narrow ally, positioned his troops, and through a subordinate gave the order to fire on the festive crowd trapped inside; the numbers given for those killed vary from five hundred to two thousand.

As it happened, a contingent of Gurkhas, armed only with kukris and officered, according to my mother, by a man still in his teens who'd just arrived from Sandhurst, had been passing through on its way to Dehra Dun. The officer had been told to disembark from the train with his men and to march them to Jallianwala Bagh, where, knowing nothing of the circumstances, they were sent to reinforce General Dyer and were therefore involved in the massacre.

In one respect, at least, my mother was mistaken; family myth-making had taken over. The Gurkhas didn't carry guns so couldn't have done the shooting and it seems likely that the man who transferred the order was the only other Englishman present, an NCO. However, the rest of her story appears entirely feasible: that Gerry Crampton, a novice of eighteen or nineteen, was either party to or privy to the act of mowing down hundreds, perhaps thousands, of men, women and babies by a firing squad. This was his introduction to India. She claimed the experience was so terrible to him that it was never mentioned. This, at the time the usual way of treating traumatic events, meant he could never come to terms with his appalling images by talking about them. My aunts, Irene and Gwen, when I had asked them about this said they didn't know the story, but, yes, of course they knew Gerry Crampton. They told me, when I asked them what kind of man he was before I mentioned Amritsar, that he was one of those people who is already old when barely out of school. They also said that had he objected or refused to give the order (presupposing he did give it), he would have been court-martialled and dishonourably discharged, a hopeless outcome in an era when so few choices of profession were available and when to be so disgraced meant the end of career, friendships, social life, and financial security.

Had any of the riflemen refused, he would have been strapped across the barrel of a machine gun and annihilated. My aunts pointed out, as a matter of fact, that if a man chose to go into the army, he chose to obey orders.

For a moment a violent history filled the empty room. Gerry Crampton may not have been one of the men I specifically recalled, but he had certainly been there. When I rejoined General Bakhshi, I only said, "It was nice when the fire was lighted. My mother had photographs along the mantelpiece."

The house was in good shape, not princely but adequate, with high ceilings, white walls, stone floors. General Bakhshi was excited at having found it and patient, insisting we take many photographs. It had been empty for some time, he told us, but would now be made into an officers' Mess. A garden would be planted.

It was the garden I missed: the perfumes, the sweetpeas and roses, the voices of men and women sitting drinking beer under the banyan tree which now had dried grasses growing through its stone platform. I missed the people—Asha with her sad face, the sweeper, the three-fingered man. They would have died long ago—few people live to an old age in India.

I found a sprig of that ubiquitous shrub with its strong, pungent odour which had haunted me all my years. I broke off a stalk and took it to General Bakhshi: "What is its name?"

"It grows everywhere. We call it lantana."

He took us to the Mess, Second Battalion, 9th Gurkha, explaining that most of the officers had once been his cadets, the reason he could take us into the cantonments at all. We asked if he had been one of the first officers after Independence, and he told us that Indian officers had been trained since 1924, but had not been accepted into Gurkha regiments until the British left. Sadly, he said that in the Messes some of the British officers had been "ungentlemanly," had smashed china, glass, and furniture before leaving: "Those were not good sorts. Not the Ninth, though. Some were good, some not. The Ninth was a wealthy battalion and still is."

I'd seen photographs of the interior of the Mess: silver on the dining table, wine glasses for each course, damask cloth and napkins. None of that remained although the building and grounds were handsome. The animal heads on the walls had all been removed.

I wanted to "adopt" a child at Raphael in memory of my father. We were given a little boy called Ajit but when we returned to Dehra Dun two years later, we were first directed to the wrong Ajit: there were two of them. This one was in a classroom and jumped up when he was identified. A Gurkha, six or seven years old, he stood so straight and was so thin he was swaybacked: shoulders back, chest out, chin in, he saluted. I wanted to put my arms around him, but how could I affront such splendid dignity? His forefathers had served in my father's regiment, had refused to eat chocolate because they might enjoy it.

⊷§⊷

Jenny and Walter at a tourist guest
house, Shantiniken, West Bengal.

Poverty and lack of space produces
two-strata shops! Calcutta.

Artuna's Penance,
Mahabalipuram.

Goporam, typical of
Dravidian architecture.

Varanasi, formerly Benares, with cremation *Ghats* at the edge of the Ganges.

Mother and child at a fishing village, Puri.

Tibetan trader, Nainital.

Our former house, *Bide-a-Wee.* Compare with page fifty-one!

Tibetan monk, Mussoorie.

Amber Palace outside Jaipur.

Painted housefronts, Shekhavati area.

Gulam's son in *Shikara*, Dal Lake.

Back waterway in Srinagar.

Rona and interior of houseboat.

Fellow traveller, photographer
Dale Windrem, New Delhi.

Pottery and pulchritude, New Delhi.

Rangdum Gompa, Zanskar.

Karsha Gompa, Padum.

Khajuraho.

A Pathan in Darra on
the North-West Frontier.

North-West Frontier Military Police,
Peshawar.

Peshawar market women wearing
burkas (*burqqas*).

We were running short of travellers' cheques and had twice asked at the Relax Hotel — just to make certain — if they took Visa. Certainly, they did. I thought Walter was fussing: a Visa identification was pasted to the entrance. When we went to pay the bill to the manager's son, who appeared to run the establishment, he was aghast. Often people who do not speak good English won't admit it, and they want to please. This had obviously been the case. He'd never seen a Visa before, only a Diner's card. Walter showed him the replication on the door. At that point the owner — a *pukka sahib*, who appeared to spend his time betting on something or other — appeared and told his son to get it scratched off. Two years later on our second visit it was still there.

This time, Walter patiently told them the Andhra bank would honour the card. They claimed there was not an Andhra bank in town. We gave them travellers' cheques from our thin supply and 100 rupees to distribute in tips. Some tips we'd already given, but some not.

The son came to our bedroom while we were packing up. There was a problem. The staff were all fighting over the tip, he didn't know what to do, wouldn't Sir please distribute it himself?

"How many are there?"

"Fifteen."

"Have all fifteen come through this room?"

"Certainly, Sir. They all are wishing for ten rupees each."

"Too much," Walter decided. We looked around the small room, wondering what on earth fifteen people had done in it. It was so dark, it was impossible to tell if it had been cleaned at all. A window designed for light had been covered by a heavy curtain with a large, roughly torn hole in it to make way for an air conditioner that didn't function. If the wretchedly dim electric light was turned on, the TV didn't work. Walter finally said, "We haven't even seen these people. How about seven each — that makes a hundred and five rupees."

The son was laughing and apologetic but also agitated. "I give you fifteen five-rupee notes, Sahib, and you do it. Five each one." He'd brought some currency with him and started sorting it. A clutch of anxious men — fifteen of them — waited at the door. Walter started to distribute the money.

One man, who looked Chinese, snarled and threw his bill on the floor. Walter, enraged, looked at the manager's son, and both agreed the men should get nothing. The young man had said several times, "Not necessary, Sir, to give anything. Easier."

Furious, we closed the bedroom door. We went to the restaurant and had lunch, walking past any servants on the way with dignity. We returned to our room and despite a clutch of offers carried our own bags downstairs. Nothing. The manager's son had meantime been put into a terrible position. The staff blamed him for the evaporation of 100 rupees. They said they would take anything if he would reason with us. The head waiter — a calm man — appeared and said he would distribute the money: "No problem." We gave it to him.

The Indians don't tip. We had not needed to, but felt miserly if we didn't. We'd been if anything overly generous in the amount. We were pretty sure that in any case a service charge would be added to the account. It was. When he paid the bill, Walter asked if the extra really went to the staff. The manager laughed, unashamed. "Not at all, Sir. Going it is straight into the boss's pocket."

The staff all gathered around us and salaamed when we left.

❦

This was the area in which my father, Robin, had undertaken the task of paying compensation to farmers whose holdings had been damaged by military manoeuvres, so I decided to go through his papers again, jammed into my case, before going on to Mussoorie, the hill station outside Dehra Dun.

He had written that these manoeuvres generally took place in February, just when the crops were appearing. The usual method had been to call together Indian overseers to discover what damage had been claimed in their areas and then allow them to make adjustments. But in using this manner of compensation, little money ended up in the hands of the actual sufferers, who made no fuss because they were abjectly philosophical over the issue: "The peasants expect nothing and acquiesce thankfully in anything they may get. They appreciate the attempt at fairness, and I expect each hopes in his heart that one day he may perhaps be the man to control the distribution."

He took my mother with him, and both were intrigued with the possibility of actually delivering into each owner's hands the equivalent of his loss. They had a week, which meant moving their camp each night over a not large area. First they obtained information on the average return per *ser* per *biga* (kilograms and acres) of the crops in the district and then converted these into rupees and annas. Each evening they held a *durbar* with the land owners. These men were always pleased with their awards; so much so, that Robin realized he was overvaluing, particularly with regard to the mustard fields:

> On our fourth day, an eager farmer led me to his field of mustard, half of which had been destroyed by fire. He claimed someone had thrown a cigarette into it. I enquired at what hour the soldiers had crossed his land. He replied at nine in the morning. This tallied with my records. I promised to return the next day to settle his case.
>
> Next day I kept my appointment at nine o'clock. I told him I would compensate him well for the whole of his field if he would set fire to the unburnt portion by throwing lighted cigarettes into the crop. He took up the challenge very half-heartedly, declaring his cigarettes were too valuable. I gave him a box full of matches. He returned them and walked away crestfallen. At nine, his field was still wet with dew. Even in the evening, he must have used much oil to get it burning.

The time of day Robin and Enid enjoyed most was sunset when the farmers arrived in the local village with their families, including their children, and squatted in groups on the ground while the scribe checked the acquittance roll. Robin wrote that the air creaked with the Persian irrigation wheel—a monotonous, endless sound—operated by bullocks treading their tedious circle. Women and girls collected around the well and gossiped while they filled their *chatties* and then helped each other to lift the heavy pots onto the cloth pads on their heads. Since there is no night life in Indian villages, the families would withdraw with many thanks after receiving their compensation, and soon the fragrance from wood fires and cooking would fill the air. Enid and Robin would themselves withdraw to their own tent where their bearer would have a steaming-hot meal ready for them.

Robin claims that in the end they achieved a complete and exact compensation for the area, but admits he was flummoxed by an Afridi,[19] who complained that his mango tree had been cut down. It didn't seem likely he would have done this himself, as the whole village would have known it.

> However, it was rather difficult to understand why any of the troops would have cut it down. One had to accept his explanation. The tree was in a narrow space between houses, and he said a column of troops on the march had got bunched up there. A gun became wedged against the tree. The mule

[19] A member of a North-West Frontier tribe.

transport of following sappers and miners crowded behind and could be neither backed up nor cleared from the track. The whole column was held up. The quickest remedy had been to hack the tree down with tools carried in the panniers of the mules, an action of moments.

Robin said that by the time he had finished with the silver-tongued Afridi, who claimed the tree had been his life's work, a really first-class Saharanpur mango that was to pay his daughter's dowry, he was in a cold sweat. He finally gave him fifty rupees, whereas few farmers were getting more than ten or fifteen. Even so, he heard from his astute bearer that the villagers were mostly delighted with their awards, which gave him a pretty good idea as to what generally happened to the compensation monies in that much manoeuvred district because he was shocked at how much remained.

These were in silver—heavy and bulky. There were stringent regulations regarding the transport of government funds, which even in the cantonments travelled with an armed escort. In the end, he and Enid camouflaged the silver in the cheapest roll of tentage with protruding iron pegs to account for the weight. Enid sat next to the driver of the bus in which they left, and after her complaint that the seat was too high, Robin nonchalantly threw her the roll on which to place her feet.

Their problems, however, were not resolved. Their young Sikh driver, on the strength of having recently qualified as a coachman, had clinched a lucrative marriage contract. All this had gone to his head, and with his hand on the horn he tore through the streets, showing off his vehicle. By the time they were toiling in bottom gear up the pass of the foothills, the engine coughed and stopped. The driver opened the bonnet and looked astonished, saying there was not a drop of gas in the carburettor or the tank.

After much advice from everyone and with Enid at the wheel, the passengers pushed the huge bus over the crest of the hill and it coasted some miles before again coming to a stop. Fortunately, another Sikh driver happened by and gave them his tin of extra fuel. However, the engine had a gravity-feed pressure tank, and if the small amount of donated gas were poured into the tank it would immediately disappear into the works. At this point, Enid came into her own: she suggested it might be possible to syphon the gas straight into the carburetter:

> We forced our Sikh to suck it, very unwillingly, through a tube and the engine caught at once while I, from an insecure perch, held the cowling and

my wife steered. The other passengers thought this *bahut achcha bandobast* (a splendid plan), and in this grotesque manner we negotiated the last few miles with the money bags safe in the tenting.

Robin's account of patient peasants who expect nothing, of corrupt overseers, of amusing, silver-tongued strangers, and of mad drivers parallelled our own experiences, particularly later in Kashmir. In its basic elements, surely India has changed little.

Chapter
Eighteen

*W*E WENT TO MUSSOORIE, outside Dehra Dun, then, and again more successfully, two years later. There, as well as in Dehra Dun, scrawled messages on walls and fences advocated action over Tibet: "The Sino-Indian border is a myth"; "Free Tibet: Tibet belongs to the Tibetans"; "Tibet today, India tomorrow"; "Free countries unite to help Tibet." The West has largely ignored Tibet. India can't afford to. With their strong faces and colourful clothes, refugees have formed settlements and set up stalls all over the northern areas.

We went up by bus at night over the, as usual, terrifying road. In the Gregorys' time a bullock cart track existed as far as Rajpur, a village, and from there on, only horses, caravans of donkeys, people on foot or carried in *dooleys* by other people on foot, could traverse the steep path clinging to the cliffs and gorges. That part of the journey took about four hours on a horse. For the most part, coolies carried the building materials, the furniture, glass, china, cutlery, cooking implements, clothes, baths, toilets, food—fresh and preserved—up to the top, often hidden in mists.

Mussoorie was then an English preserve: a cool, fresh, uncontaminated Shangri-la with its huge trees, its two hotels—one partly owned by my grandfather, Charles Gregory—its churches, and its small exclusive shops built along the Mall, again owned in part by the Gregory family.

Those who knew it from earlier times agreed it had once been a beautiful place but was now ruined. General Bakhshi said he wouldn't go up. He'd recently been invited for lunch: "I said no, I would not go to that damn place in daytime. All the trees have gone. Dreadful hotels, very vulgar, everywhere. I said I'd only go to dinner, when it's dark and I can't see what they've made of it. Well, I did. A damn good dinner, excellent wines, but I'll never go again."

Our hotelier said much the same thing: "The British, when here, much better then. Great old trees. Now these people, they do not even keep up the graveyard. Just a place for tourists."

Mussoorie actually reminded us of Banff or Whistler in Canada. High in the mountains, the little village was gaily lighted and people were shopping for food, curios, and handwoven shawls. At night, in the cool mountain air with huge stars and small shops, it was enchanting. We followed a man through a dark back street to a hotel and came out on a cliffside looking towards the Himalayas. In the morning, we had our first unobstructed view of range after range, stunningly beautiful with snow amber-pink in the early light.

We'd landed up in a clean, inexpensive hotel, owned by a Mr. Mallak, who tried to help us find the house my grandfather built. After many enquiries, we found the wrong house but on our next journey we located the right one.

Mr. Mallak talked to us about the Indian temperament. He claimed Indians are unlike any other people in the world because they believe in God and in fate. Fate, he said, may be considered the same as karma. Anything that occurs is either good karma or bad karma so an individual seldom resents lack of achievement or other people's success. He said Indians ask for little more than one decent meal a day—then they are lucky; if they are ill or are cheated, they put it down to bad luck, rather than to poor living conditions or to the man who cheated them. If people try to rouse them—Communist or Marxist groups—they have little success. It's difficult to form unions, for example. Most Indians can't comprehend the new point of view: they have rotten karma or good karma, and that's that. He was talking, of course, about the poor, still eighty-five per cent of the population.

We found him to be, like others, disillusioned: "You give your life for your country. You love it. You are electing your government. They are all corrupt. How can you be proud of a government that is corrupt?"

His view on the destruction of the environment was the same as the general's, but Bakhshi was more philosophical: "One good thing— these people who've never had a holiday, can now have a holiday. That is the middle class. They go to the hill stations and eat fruit and acquire a taste for it. That is good—healthy."

Mussoorie sprawls along a mountain ridge. Many of its roadways are very steep, and cars are not permitted into the town itself, so the only means of locomotion is by foot or in a type of ridiculously heavy rickshaw pulled in front by two men and pushed at the back by another two. On our first visit, we had good and bad karma. Bad because we took one of these vehicles, were charged outrageously, and then left to find our way "round the corner" where we were told the municipal office was located. The corner turned out to be a couple of miles of hard walking. When we got there the records could only be unlocked on a Saturday, after we were due to leave. We were also unlucky in that after much walking we found the wrong house—the one the historian had indicated. But we did, of course, find the Mall where my grandfather had built the shops and the hotel, an unsuccessful venture: we still use cutlery he'd been given as some recompense for what he was owed.

Our good karma arrived when we ran into a Tibetan Buddhist monk. I'd had an unacknowledged hope that in our travels we'd find an enlightened soul, one who "knew" in Ram Dass's term. This man, strongly built, using a walking stick, carrying a rosary and a book, wearing a plum-coloured robe and shawl, was the nearest I was to come to such a person.

Walter and I carried on the briefest of conversations with him—not really a conversation, but an array of gestures—standing on the Mall. His face was guileless as a child's: open, smiling, unselfconscious, happy, without pretension, ambition, or evasion written into his features. Walter, who has no interest in "gurus," no belief in a previous or after life, was as impressed as I was. It was he who said, "He knows."

We saw this monk later happily pulled and pushed in one of those extraordinary rickshaws, and he waved and smiled at us. Two years later, when we finally discovered where he came from and visited his monastery, he recognized us, pointing to the place where we'd met, saying, "Road." Then I gathered up my courage and asked for a blessing, an empowerment, but he refused: perhaps he didn't understand, perhaps it was the wrong season, or perhaps he felt he was not yet high enough in the hierarchy to bestow it. He may, of course, have known I was not yet ready to receive it. It didn't matter. Neither Walter nor I will ever forget him.

❦

On our second visit to Mussoorie we were again walking along the Mall. We had a couple of days only, Walter had lost all interest in finding the right house, and I'd virtually given up. Even so, it was supposed to be somewhere below us. I was staring out over the hazy Doon Valley, when a charming voice, a woman's, asked, "Are you looking for the entrance to the Savoy Hotel?"

"No. Actually, I'm still hoping to find the house my grandfather built. You're supposed to be able to see it from here."

"Perhaps I can help you?"

I looked into her face. She was an elderly woman, but not old enough to know anything about the Gregorys.

"I don't think so. It's supposed to have been sold to a rajah, but I don't remember his name."

She said instantly, "Oh, but I know the people who own that hotel— it's a hotel now, and it's the one down there with the green roof."

It looked almost palatial, and I was doubtful. She told me it now belonged to a Mrs. Varma, a friend of hers, and I should go down and ask her about it.

At that moment a man she knew called Colin, a wiry Australian, came up to us. He'd spent most of his childhood in Dehra Dun and was also rediscovering India, but was losing his nerve and felt doubtful about going on, particularly to the south where there was an outbreak of cholera: "I've already been ill to the point of death, two weeks in a hotel alone. And then these buses. I thought I'd take one, but an Indian told me every year five or six go over the edge in these mountains. If the fall is into a ravine, nobody looks for survivors. Bodies are left there to be eaten by vultures, I suppose."

While we were talking the woman (I couldn't make out if she were English or Indian; she had a voice without Indian rhythms, a pale skin) turned furiously on some boys who were throwing firecrackers at two dogs. With that English passion for animals, she told us she kept four dogs which trapped her in Mussoorie—without them, she would go to England. She was in trouble with the authorities over these pets, but the Hindu vets wouldn't put them down: she'd been told to do it herself with poison, but she couldn't. She was stuck: an old woman who had grown up in Simla during the Raj period, a Loretta Convent graduate. Later we were told by Timpe, whom we met at the hotel, that she was Eurasian: "They have a terrible time, those people. The English abandoned them, the Indians won't accept them. Now there's talk of giving the scheduled castes (untouchables) the vote and of helping them, but nothing is done for Eurasians. They are ostracized. They belong nowhere."

Feeling slightly ridiculous, we walked down the drive to the hotel. Sure enough, it had a large black-and-white tiled verandah like the one my Aunt Gwen had described. She'd talked of listening, when she was twelve years old, to her father walking up and down it. She knew his hands would be in his pockets, his shoulders slightly hunched forward, his eyes staring at the ground in front of him as he strode back and forth. She'd often seen him like that, and had even more often heard him when she was tucked away in bed. He never deviated: he paced the same back and forth path, caged in by all he'd built—an estate filled with Victorian furniture and bric-a-brac in the foothills of the Himalayas—and all he dreamed of building.

That evening, the one she remembered specifically, was in April 1919. She'd moved into sleep to the faint pattern of the steps and when she woke again they were still there in the otherwise profound silence. By that time of year, the snow that sometimes fell until it was several feet deep—as it had the day her sister, Enid, had been born and the doctor had fallen into one of the drifts outside the house—had gone, but the night was still crisp, dry and clear. When she sat up in bed and pulled back the curtain, she could see brilliant low stars, which didn't seem in any way extraordinary to her because she'd seen them all her life, hanging like lamps over the mountains.

The night remained so clearly in her memory because the next day she'd been told by Moti, the *khidmatgar* and her particular friend, that many people had been killed in the Jallianwala Bagh and her father was very upset about it. Charles had been born in Ambala in the Punjab and had lived in India with breaks in England all his life. Like many of the British, he admired the Sikhs as handsome warrior people. He knew the site of the killing and was imaginative enough to visualize what had happened.

We hesitated on the verandah. Gwen's story still didn't prove we'd found the right house: most had verandahs and some were tiled. Going inside, we found two young men at two desks. I asked if I could look around: I thought this might be the house my grandfather had built. They became very excited and phoned a man called Raji, Mrs. Varma's son-in-law, who runs the hotel with his wife and teaches yoga. We met Timpe (a nickname) and Raji as well as the desk clerks: all young men and all glowing. They looked at me as if I were a mirage.

Raji had recently sent to Bombay for papers to do with property transactions because there was so much interest in the estate, and they'd just arrived. A couple from Australia (people who were, according to Timpe, an irreverent individual, "full of causes") were making an environmental film which included the hotel; architectural students were studying it as an example of British homes in India; botanists were interested in trees in the garden because they were unusual, or unusually large, for the location: a chestnut, a ginkgo, and a magnolia. We knew later, they must have been planted by Louise Gregory, my grandmother, directing her *malis*. But there was no sign of the wisteria my mother had said enveloped the house; when it was in flower, people (all white; Indians, except for rickshaw-*wallahs*, were not permitted onto the Mall: British apartheid) would stare down on it. Now, nobody there knew what wisteria looked like.

All this focus was recent, so to have a woman arrive whose grandfather had built their hotel appeared to them extraordinary. It seemed so to me, too, but I wasn't sure I'd found the right place until Walter noticed the doorstep: carved into the granite was its old name, "Rushbrooke." They'd thought this must be the surname of people who'd once owned it.

Raji had to leave, but first gave us the papers, which he'd not yet had time to look at. Timpe, tall, good-looking, articulate, hung over me, talking ceaselessly while we went through them. He adored the house, he said, and went on to tell us he had a BA in English, wanted to take an MFA in film in Los Angeles, had worked on musicals, plays and films, including the renowned *Salaam Bombay*. Coming from Bombay, he appeared to know everybody in India's artistic community. Between hunting through papers, he rushed us out to show us the original Art Nouveau brass work barring some of the windows, the chandeliers, which he said were there from the beginning—the hideous one in the hall consisted of huge bunches of ornate dusty grapes—the fireplaces, and a large, beautiful stone Buddha which he said came with the house. He claimed the furniture in his own room had belonged to the original owners: he hoped the table at which he wrote had once been Charles'.

We found the two deeds of sale with Charles Mais Gregory as buyer and seller. When he bought the property, it had stretched up across the Mall and included Rose Cottage on the other side, now the huge Roselynn Estate Hotel. Indeed, Mussoorie consisted of hotels, one of the major changes to take place since my family had lived there and an indication of the growing middle class in India.

Charles had sold it all to the Rajah of Rajpippla in 1925. It may have been this rajah who ended up with a dinner service for eighteen people worth a *lakh* in rupees (a huge and unlikely sum) which my mother claims was never paid. She's still bitter about it, saying every piece had her father's crest on it. Gwen said it had his initials, so who would want it? In any case, the rajah and then his widow had lived in Rushbrooke for some years and then sold it to the Varmas in Bombay, who at first had used it only in the summer; an inefficient *chaukidar* looked after it the rest of the time, the house decayed, things were stolen, the garden became a jungle. Mrs. Varma finally decided to live there year round and to turn it into Hotel Padmini Nivas. The brochure specifies the Rajpippla connection and claims luxury suites, superb cuisine, magnificent views, and yoga classes. As it turned out, we didn't have a chance to test the superb cuisine.

Timpe showed us around. An enormous bakery which he said once held five ovens had been made into guest rooms. I wondered why a family of six should have needed so much space for baking, and he said, "They probably ate a lot." He showed us the stables, now more guest rooms, and the cow barn built by Louise to give her children uncontaminated milk, now servants' quarters. The rickshaw keep, also converted into rooms, was the size of a small house. One cottage had been sold and the Varmas were engaged in a legal battle with the owners who wanted to turn it into a hotel, but the other was still theirs.

While Timpe rushed us from one place to another, I tried to reconstruct something of the life, as described by my mother and aunts on tape and through a couple of pamphlets, that had once been lived there.

Rushbrooke, at an elevation of 7000 feet, didn't look out onto the Himalayas but down over small peaks leading to the Doon Valley. Built by Charles below the town Mall just after the nineteenth century slid into the twentieth, the house was surrounded by four acres of garden. Louise was passionate about gardening. She would sit in a chair brought out and moved around by the *khidmatgar* while, stick in hand, she directed the *malis* in what she wanted them to do. Irene, her eldest daughter, said she never saw her mother handling tools, never saw her touching the earth: "I mean, you just didn't, Darling. I think she would have enjoyed planting things herself, but it would have been considered very eccentric, perhaps even bad manners or, well, the wrong thing to do."

Louise, in a dress to her ankles and a wide-brimmed straw hat tied with silk under her chin, would have ordered the *malis* in Hindustani — she'd been born in India and brought up with the language. The garden was entirely her doing. Sitting there, she must sometimes have remembered the appalling miscarriage of her first baby when, not knowing she was pregnant, she was travelling alone except for her ayah in a bullock cart, and have recalled the infant who died, and Micah, her father-in-law, an engineer who had started the family firm and who'd lived with them until he decided to return to England after retiring. He died on the way and was buried at sea. And no doubt later she worried about lack of news from Irene after her marriage and fumed at Charles's refusal to accompany her to church. If only for convention's sake, she would have liked him beside her.

Going to church on Sundays was one of the sharpest memories all three of her daughters retained. They sat with Carrie Sharp, hired as a nursery governess during a family visit to England just after Gwen's birth, in a pew separate from their mother's. They remember so clearly because of the clothes they had to wear: "ghastly" starched pinafores which scratched their throats; white, starched, and embroidered nickers; boots — worn to strengthen the ankles — with numerous buttons done up with painful buttonhooks. Chiefly, they disliked their hats from Hathaway's in England. These were white or black, silk or straw stretched over wire. They dug into the head, and if one of them fidgeted with her uncomfortable clothing, she was spanked when she got home. They would go to the morning service, sitting in their private pew, and again to a children's service at three o'clock. After that, Carrie took them for a long walk, still in Sunday clothes, gave them something to eat, and returned them to the evening service when they would stand in the vestry to listen to the sermon.

Gwen was Carrie's favourite: "her" baby, whereas she called Enid "the ayah's child." She'd chosen Gwen's name and later told her that her mother hadn't wanted her, she'd been an "accident," thus alienating her even more than usual from her parents.

Hooting with laughter as an old woman, Gwen had said, "Carrie thought an alcoholic colonel was in love with her. Really, he happened to be fond of children and would visit us in the nursery or garden — we were never allowed into the drawing or dining rooms. He liked to sit us on his knee and play finger games with us and pop chocolates into our mouths. We were only supposed to have a sweet on Sundays as a treat, but Carrie would turn a blind eye to what was going on. She thought he was visiting her. Once a week she made Enid and me sit down and write letters to him—to print them very carefully between the lines. Of course, she dictated them to us, and she always ended up with 'I hope you've been a good boy.' Can you imagine us telling an ageing, drink-sodden colonel to be a good boy? Idiot woman. And her hair! She'd spend hours at it with the curling tongs. She was heartbroken when she realized their relationship was a mirage."

Irene said, "But you know, Gwen, I think our mother needed Carrie —I mean for herself, not just as a governess."

"Yes, of course. They gossiped together, especially after church. They egged each other on, talking about the clothes the women wore and their hats and the way they sang too loudly or not at all and whether their husbands had gone to church with them, or hadn't—that kind of thing."

"You heard all that?"

"After you left, Darling, when you were at school. By that time I think they didn't notice so much when we were around. And then Carrie said terrible things about Mother behind her back. I think she secretly disliked her. She must have been very frustrated, living at the ends of the earth, looking after other people's children, being a servant and not a servant. I've sometimes thought she was interested in Daddy and that's why she said the things she did."

"Oh, Gwen, I don't think so."

"Don't you remember things like, 'You can't make a silk purse out of a sow's ear'? In any case, Carrie had a strong influence. She became Mother's associate and companion. That was the trouble of course."

Enid said, "She hated India. She used to make me sit on Daddy's knee and put my arms around his neck and beg him to take us back to England. I didn't want to leave, but I did it. And then, she always told me how ugly I was."

"She made us very manipulative, just the way she was."

"We had to be. We usually only saw Mummy and Daddy when we were in the bath, and Carrie was bathing us. Once when they were there Carrie said I was lying. I wasn't, but Mummy beat me with her hairbrush, and then Carrie beat me for arguing. And another time, Daddy came in when she was yanking my hair and I was crying. She told him I was pinching her, so I was in trouble again. After that, I decided she'd never make me cry again, and I didn't. It didn't matter how hard she beat me in the bathroom with the door shut and banged my head against the wall."

"It seems to me everything was very formal and polite," Irene said. "I don't ever remember sitting on Daddy's knee, or Mother's. We were separated from them. There were ayahs and nannies and governesses, but there was no mother. There was always a gap, a desolation. It seems to me now that's why I turned to an inner world of strangeness and isolation. It wasn't their fault. It was just the kind of life we lived."

"Do you remember Moti?" Gwen asked suddenly. "The *khidmatgar*. He was very tiny and very black and he used to wear an enormous turban and had a ferocious temper. He and the *chaukidar* had a feud and the *chaukidar*, driven to distraction, stabbed Moti. There was an enormous fuss. Moti recovered—I don't know what happened to the *chaukidar*."

"When I think about it, I chiefly remember the canaries," Irene said. "They were in cages strung all along the verandah, and when I was ill or having a rest in the afternoon, I loved to listen to them. I do wish I'd told my mother. It would have given her so much pleasure, and she was so lonely. But then, I don't remember telling her anything."

"But you did tell her and Daddy about Carrie," Enid said, "and the beatings and other things. I could never have done that. I only let you because we were in England and Carrie was miles away visiting her family and couldn't hurt me."

"It was the first holiday she'd ever had," Gwen said.

Irene said, "They were appalled and asked why nobody had ever told them before."

"How could we? They believed Carrie."

❧

Irene and Enid, having adopted Charles's belief in Spiritualism, adored their father. They remembered him as a kindly, remote man constantly reading metaphysical books and were proud of the respect his workmen had for him. Gwen said, "A number of them walked for several days to reach him and to ask him to employ them again—but my chief memory of him is as an anxious, rather unhappy man walking up and down that verandah."

According to family myth, he and his brother had run away from school in England and arrived back in India. His father, Micah, an engineer, had then said he wouldn't spend massive amounts on their education if that is how they behaved and had them tutored privately by an archbishop whose instruction didn't fit them to become engineers, as he'd hoped. Not having a degree did Charles little harm. He worked as a contractor and by the time he was twenty-two had already built a major bridge over the Brahimini River in Bengal. Twenty years later, he'd built bridges and "earth works" down the east coast into Puri, south into Madras, up into Lahore (here he was recommended as making "good *bundobust*" for work at moderate rates) where he had to import Ghilzai Pathans since he couldn't get local labour. He later returned to the area which is now Pakistan and built the New Beas Bridge—an enormous project where water had to be diverted and nine spans of 200 feet each installed. Referrals attested to his humanity and efficiency.

His success built Rushbrooke, the family home for over twenty years. When he decided to sell it after Louise's lingering and painful death from cancer, he circulated a printed brochure describing the house and its contents. Better than anything else, it gives an idea of how people lived—or at least some people, and the Gregorys never considered themselves wealthy—before the empire broke up.

With its elaborate, terraced garden, as well as the house itself, the estate had a separate kitchen attached by a covered walkway to the main building, two cottages, thirteen servants' quarters housing over twenty servants, two large godowns for storage, three good stables with *pukka* floors, and a large building halfway down the drive to house *dooleys.*

The house is described as having an entrance porch and verandah; two halls, both with white ceilings decorated with sky-blue beading and blue walls; two drawing rooms connected by a large archway and containing ventilators, a fireplace, an English stove fixed into a "very handsome carved white Agra sandstone frame, marble top, with stone work done for the Delhi Durber, 1903"; a dining room with no less than four "handsome" teakwood sideboards, a glassed china cabinet, a "telescopic" beachwood dining table with its chairs, and so on; three spacious bedrooms, each of which appears to have been a suite with dressing rooms, linen rooms, bathrooms, morning rooms, and box rooms. The house had running water (a rarity) and electric light and was filled with Victorian furniture: teak, mahogany, cane, cretonne, leather and coir (mats, jail-made); clocks, electric pendants and wall brackets of ormolu; mahogany and rosewood mantelpieces, brass fenders, fire-dogs, show cabinets, dinner wagons, cake stands, fire screens, Dresden china ornaments, screens, hanging presses, stands for ladies' gowns, gentlemen's wardrobes, ladies' dressing tables (teak and blackwood, bevelled mirrors) as well as ladies' toilet tables (black marble topped), beds with horsehair mattresses, endless occasional tables, huge Amritsar carpets, countless durries, chairs, desks, sofas, and "art" curtains. The bathrooms contained porcelain tubs from England and sanitary commodes and pans, so the sweepers would still have been kept busy.

All this, as well as the materials for building the house, must have been brought up the steep trails clinging to the mountain edge by donkeys and coolies.

The list of pictures gives a clear indication of the people who lived in that house and the period in which they lived: "Dante and Beatrice in Florence; Molier [sic] and His Troop; Burns first meeting with Scott; Shakespeare scene 'Princes in the Tower' [framed appropriately in black]; Cattle Scene; pair of Photogravures: 'Sheep'; oil paintings in gilt frames: 'Daughters of Eve' and 'River Scene'." There were also endless water colours but no mention of a reproduction of Millais' "The Knight Errant," noted on a postcard from one of Louise's aunts to be the family "crest"—certainly a misnomer. It illustrates the story of a luscious female tied to a tree by robbers after stealing her clothes and jewels. She hasn't even a modest gauze with which to cover herself as she stands, head turned away, while her rescuer, an Ellis knighted for his deed, cuts the rope with his sword. Louise may have disapproved, but she would have agreed with the note which stated: "The strikes and the Suffragettes are most disgusting, and we old dames have lived to see strange things."

The pamphlet takes eighteen closely printed pages. Even so, some things were taken away or sold separately—including Charles' library. Enid said, "I didn't know anything about books, but a man said later he would have given us what we got for the whole lot for just one book in it." A single oil painting remains: a Victorian copy of a Renaissance madonna, it had been important to Charles. Shortly before selling the house, he'd gone to a medium who had described it and then told him that when he took it off the wall it would be the end of the family. This turned out to be true. Louise had died, and a few days after the sale of the estate he followed her. Eric, his son, had no children. That painting is the sole reminder of Charles who was adored by his daughters and made a fortune (almost all lost in the crash of 1929) but does not appear to have been a happy or fulfilled man.

The three sisters almost never mentioned their mother. If they did, it would be, "They had nothing to say to each other, you know. He was abstemious and wanted to read. She liked parties and people. They were important to her. She was a social person. . . ." This was said by Irene, as if being so were extraordinary. She went on, "I believe they were not at all happy. It was a very restricted existence. Once I remember thinking, I must do something for my mother, so I persuaded her to read a book. She never had time, you know. I gave her a life of Nelson and Lady Hamilton. She not only read it, she got completely absorbed and afterwards was very angry with me. She told me I must never give her a book again because she'd wasted so much time reading this one. Who would look after the godowns if she read books?"

"She had very little education," Gwen said. "It wasn't considered important."

My mother explained to me: "The godowns were the storage areas. Every morning at five or six o'clock the cook would go to the bazaar to shop and then the food would be checked off and stored in the godown, which was underground and cool. The wife kept the keys."

Irene said, "Yes. That was the chief responsibility, I suppose."

"When Irene — do you remember, Irene? — when you married Maurice, he asked Mummy and Daddy if I could go and live with you in Meerut because he said you were too dreamy to look after the godown. So I did. I was twelve. I stayed three months."

"Did you, Enid? I forget. . . . But shouldn't you have been at school?"

"I think the war was on."

"Are you sure I couldn't look after the godown myself?"

❧

Gwen finally wrote me a letter which both amplified and contradicted what they had said:

> Daddy, as you know, suffered from diabetes, and had to retire very early, as he could not stand the heat of the Indian summers—he had two great interests . . . one religious and the other the aerial ropeway [he hoped to build between Dehra Dun and Mussoorie]. . . . He was very moral and extremely abstemious—doesn't make him sound a lot of fun, but he was naturally a nervous and serious type—a good parent, anyway.

> It's difficult to write about my mother. . . . She had great courage and a temper like a fire-cracker. We had twenty-two servants, and she spent her

life supervising them. We kept a cow and always had homemade butter. Given half a chance, she'd have enjoyed a social life, and had a sense of fun and humour—but Daddy wasn't playing, and in those days no married woman made a life of her own.

My clearest memory of my parents together, was of them sitting in deck chairs, one each side of a log fire in their bedroom in the winter—Daddy reading his Holy books and Mummy crocheting. She used to do tablecloths. Bits of linen joined together with yards of crochet.

Daddy only lived about a year after my mother died. They'd never appeared to have much in common, but when she was not there, life seemed to hold nothing for him. He was utterly lost and inconsolable. He had a large oil painting of her, which he stood on an easel and just sat and looked at.

I don't remember any close personal friends. Droppers in, so to speak. They gave two huge garden parties, one after the other—I don't know what people on day two thought. When we were small, we were allowed to be seen on these occasions—with Carrie nearby, of course. We'd be in starched white, and were only to speak if we were spoken to but usually nobody spoke to us. They did give very occasional, very formal dinner parties—we had a most elaborate dinner set, only used then. In spite of the 22 servants, Mummy washed this lot up herself.

Incidently, Mussoorie was always down market. Simla was the place to be.

And Gwen finally recalled the sense of the place: "I can see it all so clearly now. The wonderful view down to Dehra Dun. And the grandiflora magnolia—the blossoms are so very beautiful. The petals look as though they are made of vellum, and are shaped like a chalice, with yellow pistils and a faint lemon scent—there was a line of deodars on the side of the garden overlooking the Doon and a large porch at the front of the house with masses of fuschias in pots."

There were no fuschias now, and the deodars must have been cut down. The three sisters—in photographs taken at this time they look like magical children: fair, lovely, slim and laughing—are old women, widows in rest homes. They have not had easy lives. Gwen married a man in the Black Watch who never recovered from five years as a prisoner of war, Enid became obsessed with a financially insecure business she started in Canada, and Irene married Maurice Cohn. Her story illustrates how dependent women were on their fathers and husbands.

Maurice was in the Dragoon Guards. Towards the end of the Second World War, when Irene was tutoring her sisters, Enid looked at her dancing cards and kept seeing Maurice's name. Quite soon, he turned up at the house and there was an engagement party.

He'd made a point of telling Charles that he was not Jewish, pointing out that if he were, he would have an "e" in his name: "Cohen." I'd assumed that my grandfather, with his warmth towards various Indian philosophies, was not racially prejudiced, and I asked, "But would it have mattered?"

My mother and aunts were taken back. I hadn't realized they were so much people of their times that the possibility of its not mattering had never occurred to them. In fact, Maurice was Jewish, the impoverished brother of one of the wealthiest men in France. My father told me that when he visited this brother to be shown around his racing stables, they were so vast he and his host had ridden horses rather than walked, and he claimed the Paris police held up the traffic when the family was driving through, their wealth was so effectively recognized.

Irene apparently knew nothing of this. My mother said she married believing she might be pregnant because she'd allowed Maurice to kiss her. When I asked her if she'd been in love, she looked unsure and then said, "I was impressed with him. And then my mother had bought beautiful clothes and made arrangements so I felt I owed it to her to complete it."

Maurice left the Guards soon after his marriage and took Irene with him to Europe. They lived in a large flat in Paris at his brother's expense and Irene seldom saw him.

Gwen said, sixty years later, "Of course, he thought there was money. That's why he married you."

Irene didn't appear to be offended by this remark. Had she always accepted herself as being worthy of attention only if she brought a fortune with her? With her love of poetry, her self-effacing nature, her small knowledge of French, she was lost in her husband's aggressive, moneyed crowd.

Maurice left her alone with the housekeeper and a piano which she played all day, having nothing else to do. He went out in the evenings and when she asked to go with him, he told her it was impossible because a single man was always wanted, whereas if they went out together they would have to entertain in return and they couldn't afford to do so. Possibly he was being kind. Irene had never been taught to live a practical life: she would have had no idea how to entertain his friends.

236

She couldn't write home about her circumstances: there was no point, because as far as she knew there was no other life for her than to be totally dependent on the whims of her husband. Finally, after more than a year of isolation, she attracted the attention of Maurice's secretary who realized she was becoming ill, and she was sent to live with his connections in England, the Bottomleys, a kind and generous family.

Horatio Bottomley, demagogue, editor of *John Bull,* independent member of parliament, swindler, was a member of this clan. During the war, he invited subscriptions which would be clubbed together to buy five-pound Victory Bonds, with the interest to be distributed as prizes. However, the subscriptions were never invested and the 75,000 pounds he raised went into his pocket. He was an irrepressible individual. One story that circulated about him was that an acquaintance who visited him in prison and found him stitching mailbags remarked, "Ah, Bottomley, sewing?" "No," he replied, "reaping." He died a pauper.

The Gregorys connection with the family petered out after Charles sued Maurice, at his request, for Irene's divorce. It must have been a bitter ordeal: divorce was such a disgrace that for years it was never mentioned. She finally married again, a decent English officer, who had absolutely no conversation.

No doubt like many others, these three women, exiled and finally restricted each to a single room in a "residence," remembered little about their past and didn't talk about it until I pressed them for information. They felt they would be "swanking." I see them now as not unlike the little Indian widows who flitted out in their white saris and then disappeared.

♥§§♥

While Walter, Timpe, and I leaned over the balustrade of a walkway which wound around the hotel and stared across the garden, slowly being restored, at the Doon Valley, wreathed in wisps of cloud, I could visualize Louise, the three girls, Carrie Sharp, the garden parties. But Charles remained a shadowy figure, perhaps because Irene and Enid had talked many times about his visiting them with advice and consolation after his death (Gwen thought this "bloody nonsense") so he'd always had a ghostly aspect to me.

When I told Timpe my grandfather had been obsessed with metaphysics, he was delighted: that accounted, he thought, for the special atmosphere in the house. He himself meditated.

I said self-consciously, since it also applied to me, "Well, you shouldn't smoke, then." He chain-smoked.

"Oh, you move beyond all that," he said airily. "Now I should take you to see the old graveyard. Don't forget to tell your mother there are children in the house again—my aunt's grandchildren."

Chapter Nineteen

*W*E WERE BOOKED INTO another hotel but thought we could at least eat in the Padmini Nivas, so Timpe told the cook we'd be back — we saw no other guests and thought we should give warning — and rushed us off. Enormously energetic, he claimed he was a mountain climber and trekker and no doubt was. He ran everywhere. It was almost impossible to keep up with him.

It was growing dark. While we raced after him, he told us he also came from an interesting family: it had dredged Bombay and turned it into a city, his grandfather had made a fortune in gold in South Africa and had transferred it into bullion to take home with him. On the way, his ship had been caught in a monsoon and sunk. He had swum for four days and alone had survived, but he had lost all his treasure. "That was no problem," Timpe said, bounding ahead. "He still had lots of land here."

Oddly enough, considering my mother's account of my grandfather and his brother, Timpe recited a complex story about two brothers in his family who'd run away from an English boarding school. One returned to India and became a wild man, living in the mountains for seven years. The other finally returned and found him; the wild man was saved and now lives in Australia as a successful real estate agent. A popular novel, *The Pandy Brothers*, by an American living in Mussoorie, is based on the same story. Perhaps there's some truth in it all.

Timpe picked up a friend who worked in another hotel and the four of us walked some distance along a deserted road. Walter and I had no idea how far it was to the graveyard but knew we wouldn't be able to see much by the time we arrived. We had little sense of what was happening. The two men stopped at a stone bench — obviously their usual place — and Timpe's friend asked if I had a cigarette. I gave him one and in the darkness, standing behind the bench, he fiddled with it. We finally realized he was taking the tobacco out and replacing it with something else.

Timpe was wildly excited. "It's the purest in the world. You'll have some with us?"

By now we were very good friends. I was euphoric at finding the house I'd been searching for. Timpe was euphoric by nature. His friend was laughing, saying he couldn't take too much because his boss was annoyed at the way he was when he got back to work. Timpe rapidly started on another entertaining story about how he'd been thrown out of university for smoking hash. His voice altered in pitch as he insisted self-righteously he never drank alcohol, which was bad for one and clouded the mind, but that this was an elixir which elevated the senses, promoted clear thinking, excelled in deepening concentration before exams, glorified the stars. Besides all that, it was unadulterated, taken straight from the plant.

Vanity. To be accepted as equals by two lively young men, not to be regarded as ageing, gullible tourists who should be sold something or taken to museums, was heady. I took a deep drag, held it in my abdomen, used my voice as airily as Timpe did, "Oh, we smoke marijuana. I grow it in the garden," and passed the toke to Walter, who also smoked but not with quite the air of knowing just how to do it. Truth to tell, I'd not taken much marijuana and found it vastly overrated, but had grown some as an experiment.

Timpe's friend was negative: "A different thing. The leaves we don't smoke. This is resin. It's scraped off and rolled into a ball in the hands. The purest, it is."

It affected them both instantly. Their voices were high, voluble, and excited. "Look at the stars now," Timpe said.

To me, they looked exactly as they had before. Walter's voice remained unaltered. I hoped mine did too. We passed more around. I noticed the world seemed crooked and felt slightly nauseated, but assumed it was psychosomatic. "What about the graveyard?"

"Oh, it's too late now. We won't see anything. It's about three more miles to walk."

The toke glowed in the dark.

Timpe's friend said he had to return to his job. We started the interminable walk back. I had to hold on to Walter as we stumbled along the rough road, the others ahead of us, laughing exultantly.

By the time we reached the Padmini Nivas, I was feeling like death and couldn't believe people did this kind of thing for fun. I told Timpe I didn't think I was in any condition to meet his aunt, a charming and conventional person, who was waiting for us with dinner. Gaily, he insisted I was quite all right. His aunt didn't approve of his smoking, I was not to say anything, but it was not, strictly speaking, illegal.

He took us down a back entrance, leaping ahead, calling, "This way is never used."

That was obvious. Overgrown, uneven, unlighted stone steps led down a steep slope. I clung to Walter, feeling my way, the world at an extraordinary angle. We'd been quarrelling constantly under the rigours of travelling in India. I admired his patience, wondering if he wasn't tempted to simply let me collapse and to return to Canada, finished with the whole thing.

Timpe's aunt invited us to sit outside before dinner, served late in India. I admitted I was not feeling exactly well and didn't think I could eat. Concerned, she ordered ice-cream and fruit. Even that was impossible. Finally I muttered something about unaccustomed food— Timpe gesturing wildly that I was not to say anything, but from his voice she must have known what was going on—and she suggested I lie down on her bed in the master bedroom. It was a huge, silken bed in a large room with very high ceilings: the room my grandparents, circumspect pillars of society, had slept in; the room where Louise Gregory had crocheted tablecloths in front of the fire, its hearth still there, and where Charles had stared for hours at her portrait after her death; the room in which my mother and her sister Gwen had been born. Without even the strength to look around it, I tried to vomit in the luxurious attached bathroom.

Finally staggering out, I indicated to Walter that we'd have to leave, apologizing miserably for being so rude. We agreed to meet in the morning, when we'd take photographs. Timpe showed us to the gate— up the usual entrance this time, he pointed out, still laughing—and said we could get a manual rickshaw. As we stumbled away, he called out nervously, "Don't worry. Remember there's nothing to be worried about."

In the most cheerful voice I could find, I called back, "No, no," hoping I sounded as if all this were an hilarious comedy, which of course it was, but not to me.

He wailed back, "But you said you grew it."

They were the last words we heard him speak.

The town had closed up for the night. There were no rickshaws. I had had no lunch and was retching, unable to bring up anything, at one ditch after another. I was on antibiotics for a heavy cold—a collapsed lung, but we didn't know it at the time—and wondered if there could be some kind of allergic reaction with hash. Our hotel was at least a couple of miles away, up and down the vertical hills. Once we passed a curious pedestrian. I realized bitterly that he probably thought he'd come upon a ridiculously drunken European woman. Women, except in the most liberated classes, don't drink in India.

When we finally reached the hotel, my body didn't dare to lie down. The world reversed itself. At about two in the morning, we gave in and contacted a doctor. We had to tell him—and I burned with shame—what the trouble was, bringing up antibiotics, allergies, possibilities. Solemnly, he listened to my chest, looked at my eyes, and then gave me an anti-nausea pill of the kind we carried with us, saying to Walter, "She will sleep it off—a common reaction. Very strong hash. Where did you get it?"

Walter was evasive. "Oh, we met a couple of men."

There was no judgement. This man who had been dragged out of bed in the middle of the night over a stupid indulgence charged seventy rupees (five dollars) and refused to take more when Walter tried to press it on him. I finally lay down, shivering, using all the bedclothes, while Walter, to keep warm, dressed in a wool suit he'd had tailored.

The next morning I'd more or less recovered and Walter was fine, having had no reaction, ecstatic or otherwise. We went back to meet Timpe, whom we wanted to see again because he was so engaging, and to take photographs. He, Mrs. Varma, and Raji had all gone on an unexpected pilgrimage to Rishikesh. They were no doubt as embarrassed as we were.

◆⟨§⟩◆

In the Gregorys' time, the Tibetan refugee market would not have existed in Mussoorie, but the Happy Valley Tibetan Buddhist Monastery would have. I wondered if any of them had ever been to it.

Built on the side of a mountain overlooking the valley, isolated from the tourist town, immaculate and graceful, its name suited it. We visited on a soft, warm day. The sky was an immense blue behind the white *stupa,* the gaily waving prayer flags, the bank of prayer wheels which rotate with the flick of a finger, endlessly repeating the great Buddhist mantra, *om mani padma hum,* in praise of and invocation to the One Who Looks Down, the compassionate Bodhisattva, the Lord Who is

Seen Within. Literally, the mantra may be translated as *Om* (all sound and silence, everything); *mani padma* (the jewel in the heart of the lotus); and *hum*, an exhortation. It refers to the diamond hardness of indestructible existence (eternity, God) as the jewel which is within the lotus (the phenomenal world). Division into spiritual and material, into past, present, and future is a delusion. All is one and is co-existent.

Sometimes for a blessed fraction of a second, one may know this. Our petty selves with our desires, shames, agonies, and triumphs drain away.

Six monks, including our friend, were sitting lotus position in their plum-coloured robes inside a main room on a raised mat platform. A bench with silver containers on it fronted them. An enormous gong hung at one end. The monks were chanting, their voices rolling out through the double open doors and across the valley.

At first they paid us little attention. We looked around the room awkwardly, feeling out of place. Then the man at the end of the bench, with all of them smiling warmly, motioned us to sit beside him. I sat first, next to him, closed my eyes and listened. The time came for him to strike his gong—constructed of leather, suspended from a wooden bracket—rhythmically and repeatedly. Each strike reverberated through my body, each a heartbeat in common, uniting us to the cosmos.

We left quietly. For a long way, we could hear the drum and the chant filling the Void.

Chapter Twenty

*W*E HURRIED BACK FROM Mussoorie to Dehra Dun, where we'd been invited by Mady Martyn, whose late husband had been headmaster of the Doon School, to a party for "old boys" and their wives who were attending a reunion. Meeting these people, the élite of India and Pakistan, we were bound to wonder if our own élite, whom we don't know, have attitudes and expectations similar to theirs. Their chief concern at that gathering lay in their sons' education. If our political ministers, senior civil servants, wealthy businessmen, have not got their determination to expose and encourage their sons—daughters were not mentioned—to their full potential, we'll soon be left behind. Most of their boys were going, as they had, to the Doon School, originally started by an Englishman. After that, they were heading either to Oxford or Cambridge in England or to Princeton or MIT in the States. We talked to one couple who'd taken their sons to England to look over the universities, hoping they would choose one of them because of the tradition, but the boys preferred the States as being more entertaining. One of them was ready to take off, and his father said ruefully, "That's another five *lakhs*"—a fortune, but he wouldn't have considered not spending it. We felt the sons of these lively, sophisticated people couldn't fail; the world lay at their feet, as it had done and no doubt still does for the British aristocracy.

As middle-class Canadians without influence, we were not made in any way to feel outsiders, but we were. They were at the heart of things. Towards the beginning of the evening, before I recognized the situation, I talked to a woman from Pakistan and considered digging in my bag and giving her some non-refundable paper money left over from our own visit to her country (this was on our second trip to Dehra Dun), but hesitated, dimly aware that might not be the thing to do. Thank God my better sense prevailed. It turned out that she was enormously wealthy: her father had been president of the country. She probably didn't even handle small denominations. She and her husband travelled among kings and prime ministers. His grandfather had been the Akond (king) of Swat and he was still considered royalty, although his family no longer held the title. After a couple of drinks, I couldn't contain myself and quoted Edward Lear:

> Who, or why, or which, or *what* is the Akond of SWAT?
> Is he tall or short, or dark or fair?
> Does he sit on a stool or a sofa or chair, or SQUAT,
>   The Akond or Swat?

He was delighted: "That was my grandfather!"[20]

❦

The first time we went to Dehra Dun, we travelled by bus and train. Apart from financial considerations, I'd been forbidden to fly for a month because of my perforated eardrum. Getting tickets was a purgatorial endeavour. In Dehra Dun it was doubly so as we had to make various changes due to delays caused by the funerals General Bakhshi had to attend.

On the final occasion, Walter got up early to avoid the queues. The office was, predictably, closed. When we both returned, a long line of people shuffled ahead of us, and we were wild with impatience. We were even more impatient when a well-dressed man strode in, went to the counter ahead of everyone and, while buying his ticket, engaged in a long conversation with the agent, who went through various ledgers and papers, gossiping and ignoring the line in front of him. We might as well not have been there.

Walter ground his teeth and recalled Kalyan doing the same thing in Calcutta: he'd presented himself at the wicket ahead of over a hundred

---

[20] We had met Mady Martyn through her son who lives in British Columbia. A woman in her sixties, warm and charming, she was also energetic in doing all she could for her adopted country. She established a free primary school in a deprived village in the Doon Valley and as an environmentalist was instrumental in having twenty-nine limestone quarries closed. Fifteen months (March, 1991) after this party, she was murdered in her home by an intruder. She'd previously received threats, and the authorities speculate her death was caused by her involvement in the pits: the perpetrator has not been found. Her son, Dilsher Virk, a close friend of Rajiv Gandhi, received a second blow when shortly afterwards Gandhi was assassinated. Her daughter-in-law says India is changing. When she and Dilsher flew to New Delhi after Mady's death, a bomb exploded in the hotel of friends with whom they stayed, with another detonating down the street. Their friends tell them this is not uncommon: the Indian poor are growing angry and the government is in shambles.

people, saying to the agent, "I've brought you much business." The agent had wagged his head—so ubiquitous a gesture, I noticed Walter picked it up—and agreed. No one objected. While waiting in another line, Walter was so angry with a man who shoved ahead, he tapped him on the shoulder and told him to go to the back; the man had, sheepishly. Everyone else was delighted, but not prepared to do any such thing. People simply wait.

We knew at the Dehra Dun office that the agent would soon close his wicket and go off to have *tiffin*. We'd be there all day. I said, "I'll try it. I'm going up."

"You can't do that. It's so unfair."

"I don't care anymore. They've been talking for half an hour."

I positioned myself near the head of the line and when the conversation ended thrust our passes through, pointing out we were tourists and were paying top price for first-class accommodation.

"This train, it has no first class."

"All right, but we're paying for first and we want berths."

He started through ledgers with all the alacrity of a winter fly. A heavy middle-class woman, who was also thrusting her way in, pushed her hand holding money through the wicket. A long altercation ensued in Hindi as she stormed at the agent, insisting she was ahead of me although she'd not been in the queue at all. I kept hearing the word "lady" referring to me and was adamant: I was first. Walter hung back, embarrassed but unconsciously wagging his head, Bengali fashion, in agreement. The agent served me, actually moving out of his stupor. I picked up my tickets triumphantly, paying little attention to what he was saying in my still partially deaf state. The woman was furious.

"Jesus," Walter said, "what's happening to you?"

"It's India. Remember what Jenny said. You might love it, but you want to kill people."

We caught the train at eight-thirty. The second-class carriage was better than some first-class we'd encountered, but we'd been assigned seats along the train wall rather than proper berths. They were without curtains and so short the only way Walter could sleep was on his back with his knees in the air. I wouldn't be much better off. I thought dismally of people passing all night staring at me while I attempted to remain on the seat. Walter was unsympathetic, debating how he could lie down at all: "The man was trying to tell you, but you wouldn't pay attention."

We sat there unhappily, people shoving past us, when a young American, Tom, came in and took the seat beside us. We told him our situation, and he said, "There's always an inside berth. If you raise enough hell you'll get one."

Walter spoke to the conductor who answered, "Sir, my problem it is not. You must have been at the end of the line."

I interrupted. "We've paid ten times as much as anybody else. You're supposed to put places aside for tourists."

He shrugged. "What can I do? Two people, they have not yet arrived. If they do not come, you may have their beds for the night."

We watched nervously and saw two more passengers move into their private accommodation. We were exhausted in the way only travellers in India can be.

Tom leapt up and collared the conductor, "These people asked for an inside berth at the station and were told they would get it."

That, of course, was not true, and I opened my mouth but fortunately no one paid me any attention. The conductor said, reasonably, "What other people say, I cannot help."

We started to sympathize with him because Tom was so aggressive as he burst into a long speech in Hindi, pointing out, he told us afterwards, that we were old, grey-haired people (I was beginning to think we were extremely ancient myself), the kind of tourists (with money) India wanted, so what did he mean by giving us these wretched seats with no curtains? We, who would go home and tell others how thoughtlessly we were treated so no more tourists would come. The conductor went off in a rage but returned ten minutes later saying he'd rearranged other passengers and found us all amenities.

He kept repeating, "Happy now, are you?" while Walter placed the tips of his fingers together on his chest and bowed over and over again, telling the conductor how splendid an institution Indian Rail was. The man beamed with satisfaction.

Later, talking to Tom, we discovered to our mutual astonishment that we were booked into the same small private hotel in New Delhi. A Californian, disillusioned with America, he lodged with its easy-going proprietors, the Naths, on his trips out of Afghanistan where he'd made his home and conducted an export business, undeterred by the war. The Naths were also to become our friends.

When we finally got to bed, it was very hot—97 °F. I couldn't sleep but it seemed to me, irritated and envious, that Walter instantly started snoring. In the morning, he said he hadn't slept all night because children were banging against his wall and someone—he claimed it wasn't him—was snoring too loudly. The Indians have no thought for other people regarding noise: they're so used to it. At three in the morning loud general conversation begins.

Not all ticket buying and train travel was, of course, as bad as this. Some journeys were peaceful and revealing. During one of these, we sat opposite four conductors, gentle men who listened carefully to each other, talking and smiling. Some way into the journey one of them got up, went out and returned, drying his face and hands after washing. He took off his shoes, tie, and coat, and then sat lotus fashion with his arms extended to his knees, palms up, in deep meditation for an hour. No one was surprised. After meditating, he quietly rejoined the conversation.

In general, the trains are astonishing in the numbers of people they transport in reasonable comfort, but when it comes down to it, the numbers are simply too great. At one stage, we decided to take a train from Delhi to Agra, where the Taj Mahal is located, partly to see neighbouring Fatehpur Sikri, the great city built by Emperor Akbar in the sixteenth century as the capital of the Mogul Empire. Deserted soon afterwards because of difficulties with the water supply, it lies empty, splendid, perfectly preserved.

The New Delhi station was crowded with people, some of whom apparently lived there. We waited in line and after arriving at the wicket were told we had to go to a special division upstairs for foreigners. Once there, we were sent back, after again waiting, because we had to pay in foreign currency and had none. We were directed to the Northern Line in a different station. The crowds there were, if possible, greater. However, we found a slightly shorter queue at a wicket with a notice above it: Ladies Only. I lined up. Instantly, the wicket closed with the agent going off for lunch. About an hour later, I discovered I had to fill in a complex form including age, sex, and expected day of travel although we were going as soon as possible and a comparatively short distance. The more sophisticated Delhi travellers were not pushing in, and we waited patiently until a square woman barged by me, and I pointed out that there were three people ahead of her. She turned on me furiously, saying, "I am educated too."

Speechless for a moment after this *non sequitur*, I said, "Well, in that case you should have better manners."

With the two of us quivering with fury, the other women consulted each other. She said she only wanted to make enquiries and they agreed to let her. When the agent returned, she spent a long and leisurely time going over lists with him, finally walking out triumphantly, head high. Of course, I'd behaved almost as badly in Dehra Dun but was unwilling to admit it even to myself.

At last I got tickets for the next morning but, since the train was crammed, with far separated seats for Walter and myself. We spent a miserable day, having already seen Fatehpur Sikri with its officious guides ("Come. Come. No, Madam, out of sun. Thirteen minutes to take picture.") and ubiquitous pedlars, but had forgotten doing so.

Watching the chained, long-haired bears with their trainers on the road back to Agra by bus and remembering a poem by Earle Birney returned me to reason. Hating the cruelty, Birney understood, when travelling the same route, that the men had no more choice than the bears: together they danced in the scorching heat for a few pennies tossed from windows:

> It is no more joyous for them
> in this hot dust to prance
> out of reach of the praying claws
> sharpened to paw for ants
> in the shadows of deodars
> It is not easy to free
> myth from reality
> or rear this fellow up
> to lurch   lurch with them
> in the tranced dancing of men.

⚜

Ever since I could remember, a replica of the Taj Mahal had sat on my mother's dressing table. She'd never seen it, but we were to do so. It's exactly as it appears in photographs. Despite having had its silver doors and gold sheathing stolen by vandals and being threatened by pollution, it still seems flawless. Built of blinding white marble, carved with irises and roses in bas-relief, inset with semi-precious stones in the shape of flowers—one may have up to 7080 different pieces—it shimmers in the heat. It took 20,000 men working around the clock for seventeen years to complete, and there's a story that after it was built Shah Jahan ordered the hands of his artists to be cut off so they might never repeat their feat. Our guide said this was not true, that the Shah had been a good and compassionate ruler (even though he'd had all his brothers and nephews killed on his accession), but that after some years the workmen's hands were wrecked: they were paid off and made to promise they would never teach others their skills.

The human story remains. Shah Jahan, who built the tomb for his adored wife when she died during delivery of her fourteenth child, was deposed by his son, Aurangzeb, identified as an "unworthy" ruler by some, as a Moslem saint by others. He imprisoned Jahan in Agra Fort, a magnificent structure across the Yamuna (Jumna) River from the Taj. There the prisoner waited for nine bitter years, looked after by a faithful daughter, never visited by his son. His room looked out on his masterpiece, and when he was dying he asked one of his wives to raise him up so he could see it. He died staring at the tomb of Mumtaz Mahal and was buried beside her.

We stood where he'd died, thinking of the great Mogul and the passionate love he nursed for his wife. Then the inevitable contrast occurred. When we left the compound, a taxi driver who insisted he'd been waiting for us all morning was determined to show us other sights. We said, "No shops. We don't want to buy anything."

"No, no, Sir. Where they make these things. You watch only. Brass, you understand."

It was, of course, a shop, and was owned by a smooth, chauvinistic man who sat us down, gave us cigarettes and beer, and started, in my view, playing Walter as if he were a fish on a line: friendly conversation only, he stated, men were buddies. He ignored me. My bad temper flared up, but Walter was ripe for consolation. This wretched man told us he'd not seen his wife before they were married and that now they lived separate lives: they only saw each other between nine and ten in the mornings. If it were five past nine, he wouldn't stay until five past ten. During that time, he would tell her if his love-making of the night before had been successful: "Very pretty, very nice."

I asked if she also had affairs and he said she was free to, a doubtful answer. At one point, Walter had the grace to tell him I was paying for our travelling. He was deprecating: "Oh, don't be silly, Sir. That's ridiculous." It wasn't worth arguing with him. Finally, to get out, I took two goblets. He waved airily to his attendant to wrap them up and said to Walter, "If she has what she wants, you must have what you want, is that not so? We men must stick together, isn't that the case, Sir?"

Male pride. Walter took two impressive mugs. I hated them. I hated this man. I hated Walter. And India. I thought gloomily of forts and palaces with their harems, of Emperor Akbar who is reputed to have had, in order of importance, one thousand elephants, thirty thousand horses, fourteen hundred tame deer, eight thousand concubines. His son, Jehangir, owned six thousand wives. If one were disobedient she was secretly hanged in the dungeons and her body thrown into the water below.

Of course, I was not being fair: in most accounts, women in kingly harems were well treated, well protected, and allowed some freedom and power, but even so they were pawns in alliances between their fathers and the current ruler. The Moguls connected with the Rajputs (Moslem with Hindu) and brought a measure of peace to India through their multiple marriages.

On the way back in the train, I sat, with Walter elsewhere, staring out into the darkness. The barred windows had no glass. Coal dust covered everything. Legless beggars crawled along the aisle, pulling themselves from seat to seat. Outside Delhi, we were delayed for a good hour. On the station platform a woman sat on the floor. She had three small children, one a babe in arms. Her little boy of four or five was flapping around in what appeared to be huge workman's gloves. They were his feet. As he lurched from one to the other, the swollen toes bent down under his soles. He hurried over to my window, staring up with a guileless smile. Sick at heart, I gave him five rupees, but he didn't know what to do with it. He flapped back to his mother and I hoped he gave it to her. A young man, a Westerner, horrified as I was, got out of the train and entertained him with a puppet he must have bought in Agra. Islanded on the bare boards of the dirty platform in the gloom, the small family laughed with joy.

When we arrived, more than one train disgorged at once. Walter and I found each other, clung together, were swept forward, realizing we could quite possibly be trampled to death. We had to go down a staircase. Someone had vomited on the steps. It was impossible to avoid it. We slithered in the pushing crowd, losing balance, gaining a foothold, dependent on each other's strength, our bad tempers forgotten.

⋖§§⋗

We had arranged to rendezvous with Jenny and to meet Mark Tully, the BBC correspondent for India, in New Delhi. Going to his house for lunch in a three-wheeler, we kept being held back and wondered why. Finally we reached a car directly in front of us holding four guards who were following a black limousine. At each stop, two of them jumped out and stood on either side of the car with machine guns at the ready. They wouldn't allow anything to approach. When the light changed, they jumped back in and continued to the next stop. Mark Tully later said the Minister of Justice must have been in the limousine.

We'd already noticed many armed police in New Delhi—guarding banks, the Parliament Buildings, the Embassies: the Canadian Embassy was almost impossible to get into. The city, with its wide streets, handsome architecture, cleanliness, sumptuous and expensive hotels, was a far cry from Calcutta and could, apart from a squalid tent town outside the Red Fort, have been a metropolis anywhere. There were beggars, of course, but they were not the cheerful, good-natured ones we'd encountered elsewhere: they were miserable, holding out filthy, sick babies for *baksheesh*. For us this whole tourist area couldn't compare with the east coast.

But Mark Tully saw it with different eyes. He'd been born in Calcutta and had lived there until he was ten, trapped, like Jenny, by the war, and like her grateful for it: "I couldn't be sent back to a 'nasty' school in England, although I was later and hated it. I didn't belong there. I didn't belong anywhere, I felt, until I came back here. Other people feel the way I do—it's important where you're born or where you spend your early life: the smells, the colours, the landscape. This is where my deep friendships are, as well as my memories. But I don't think I would have enjoyed it when our parents lived in an expatriate community. It's quite different now. I'm not an expatriate. At least, I don't feel like one."

We asked about the machine guns and riots. "The Indians are very volatile. You never know. My camera man was involved in a crossfire and was shot in the stomach by the police. I've tried to get a report on it—it happened two years ago—but still haven't succeeded."

Jenny said, "My father told me that during the riots after Partition, over a million people died in Calcutta, and the ships couldn't sail out of the Hooghly because their propellers were so fouled with dead bodies."

⋅§⋅

A bomb had gone off in a market in Delhi. One of the papers printed an agonized photograph of a woman whose mother, husband, and two small children had been blown to pieces: everywhere, scattered bodies and blood. It had not been set by terrorists, but by another family: the woman's husband had run a tiny kiosk which they had claimed.

A country of extremes: we drank beer at the five-star Imperial Hotel, carpeted in silks. In it, an art show stocked antique paintings on worm-eaten paper at huge cost for tourists; subsequently we met a dealer who told us the paper was indeed old, taken from ancient books, but the paintings had no doubt been done the week before. At the same show, young men were painting miniatures, copies, on ivory, using brushes with a single hair. I talked to a handsome fellow who became intensely passionate, asking if I believed in reincarnation: "Age makes no difference. Don't you think, met before, have we not?"

"I don't think so."

"Oh, yes, Madam, in a previous life. Please come back and have coffee with me. We will talk."

"But my husband is waiting for me."

"Your husband might like to do something else this evening. Lose you, I must not." He held my hand hungrily while I estimated how much he would make if I bought one of his intricate copies and how many Western women had already done so.

❧

In Delhi, we realized why potters are of such low caste. Our hotelier's daughter, Vinika Nath, who has business dealings with them, took us to their area: huge, purgatorial, covered by a dull grey sky. At least a hundred beehive-shaped kilns, about ten to twelve feet high and ten feet wide, belch black smoke into the air. Ash settles everywhere. The potters live in tiny quarters. They, their wives, and children, are coated in soot. The men do the throwing, the skilful part of the operation, and the women do the heavy work, carrying huge baskets of bricks on their heads, kneading the clay. They also sit in front of the burning kilns, throwing handfuls of sawdust into the flames, for up to ten or twelve hours. Vinika said they are at the bottom of the scale with a pittance for a wage.

Vinika, a modern woman, a university graduate, wears miniskirts at home, drives her own car, but said she receives no respect from the potters; they will not take her or her mother seriously, but if she takes her boyfriend with her when she gives her orders, it is all quite different.

We also discovered another reason why it is so hard to get anything accomplished. We ran into a demonstration against the government by 300,000 farmers who had come from all parts of the country, many walking for days and even weeks to attend. They lose huge areas of topsoil a year due to deforestation and have to pay high prices for fertilizers and pesticides. Farm owners are in irredeemable debt; labourers starve on ten rupees a day and are often out of work altogether. But when the great day for the demonstration arrived, the farmers split into two groups: one party thought the speaker should have a dais shaded from the sun while the farmers stood in the heat; the other thought they should all stand in the heat. Their attempt to improve conditions was in tatters.

An editorial in *The Hindustan Times* quoted a man who said, "Bihar is burning." The editor's comment was "India is burning."

But this is one aspect. There are so many others: lively, moving, unexpected, entertaining. In Khajuraho, the primitive little town filled with astonishing erotic temples, the night air heavy with jasmine and frangipane, fireflies flickered about us as we sat in the garden outside our hotel. Inside, while we were reading in bed, the light exploded, shattering us with glass. Walter shut his book and made his way to our bathroom, for some obscure reason locking the door behind him. He couldn't unlock it.

I fetched the desk clerk, who was bewildered, saying this had never happened before. He also couldn't open it; neither could the various handymen he called in. Finally Walter struggled through a window onto a railing, then back through the bedroom window, and the clerk moved us to the next room with many apologies. But then Walter remembered he'd left the basin plug—ours, and an invaluable commodity since they're not supplied—behind. Absolutely unable to face all the palaver again, he climbed through our new window, balanced along the terrace railing to our old bathroom, climbed in, retrieved the plug, came back, saying he was finished with India forever while he combed glass out of his hair.

And in Shekhavati, an area in Rajasthan located on what was once the silk (also opium, cotton and indigo) trade route, we ended up unwittingly in the India which is romantic beyond expectation. We'd already had a taste of its delights in the exquisite pink city of Jaipur, when an ancient rickshaw-*wallah* peddled us through the wide streets at night. We shared the thoroughfare with yawning camels pulling small carts;

with elephants; with *tongas* pulled by horses and carts pulled by sleek bullocks; with donkeys; with gaily turbaned men and with women in lightweight red saris, their faces covered with fine veils. All were making their way sedately past the pink Palace of the Winds, built by an emperor, a musician who played there with his orchestra: its façade is filled with slim, arched windows through which the breezes once wafted music across the town.

When my great-grandparents were in India, Shekhavati was a district of rich merchants who decorated their *havelis* (mansions) with huge frescoes: prancing blue horses, caparisoned elephants, chariots, dancing girls, lovers, and minareted palaces. Many of these buildings are now falling to pieces, inhabited by squatters and goats. The camel caravans no longer exist.

The Rajputs, known as the fiercest fighting men in the world with their emphasis on the nobility of battle, still exist but are greatly diminished. Their leaders, the rajahs, lost their power and autonomy with Independence but were permitted to keep their titles until Indira Gandhi brought in the War Measures Act. One of them told us with amusement that, jealous of their power, she'd come down heavily on them. At that time, he said, one of his friends, a maharajah, decided to visit England. Just before he was to leave, his house was invaded and searched by police who discovered he had $50.00 in his pocket to spend on the way. It was illegal to possess foreign currency and instead of travelling he was thrown into jail for three months. He asked his mother, who was influential, to go to Madam Gandhi on his behalf, but she stalwartly refused: "Madam Gandhi is my enemy. I will not ask her for favours."

I remembered the respect my parents had for these rajahs and the one who had given me the wonderful doll. We were now to meet them, and to be treated as honoured guests (at a hefty price), as my parents had not been: they were not of sufficiently high caste.

Despite assurances by a tour operator to the contrary, our driver and his brother could not speak English. We had no real idea of what was going on as we were escorted through Shekhavati from one Rajput palace to the next—seven, in all—which were now being run, we finally gathered, as hotels. The rajahs had not only lost their titles but also their income.

By the time we reached our third or fourth palace hotel—all with great halls, inlaid work, carved ceilings, but no apparent guests—we were hot and bored, but our guides, not understanding a word we said, took us to another, Dunlody, where we were shown a large room that we realized must have been the original for the Brighton Pavilion— mustard yellow walls, gilt pillars, gilt and silk furniture. A dishevelled man, followed by two disgruntled women, came up the stairs and, assuming he was also a tourist, I warned him gloomily, "You're about to see another palace."

He was disarming: "A family responsibility."

He was Ranbir Sinh, a rajah without the title, an intellectual who was mad about the theatre and was trying to turn, most unsuccessfully, his white elephant into a paying proposition. He didn't live there, but had come for a couple of days because of a local festival and gave us tea while he talked about adapting European plays for the Hindu theatre; his audience, he said, loved Molière because he spoke to them of corruption which they understood only too well. Even so, they were proud of their own tradition. He was almost stoned during a lecture in which he claimed the Sanskrit plays were written during the Roman rather than the Greek period: "In India everything has to be the oldest."

Ranbir Sinh, who had a passion for libraries rather than armies, said he couldn't afford a word processor to help him with a world theatre compendium he had embarked on, and that even if he could, he didn't know how he could get it into the country: "God knows, I'd have to pay a tax. God knows, what would happen in any case. When last in England, I bought books on the theatre—traditional and alternate. One had a nude on the cover, and the customs' officials said the book was pornographic and confiscated it. They kept all my books. In the end, I only got them back by running after an important friend. Who would want to be doing that kind of thing again?

"Now tonight, five thousand people will be here in the courtyard in traditional dress. It is the festival of Shiva and Pavarti—they are there by the door, hidden under those cloth cones, incommunicado until the event. I myself have written a play which will be performed. You must stay with me and see everything."

We hesitated. I was feeling slightly queasy, no doubt from an appalling lunch in which a slice of tomato had been hidden in a sandwich. Was this or wasn't it a hotel? If it was, could we afford it?

We went on, only to discover that our tour operator had booked us into a far more elaborate and very expensive palace, Castle Mandawa. We had no choice but to stay; there was nowhere else. It was run successfully by Mr. Kesrisingh, Ranbir's cousin, son of the former Maharajah of Jaipur. Handsome, gregarious, amusing, articulate, our host loved his role and shook his head sympathetically but with some scorn over the intellectual in the family who preferred sitting in the British Museum library to running his palace.

Walter admitted he thoroughly enjoyed the luxury of the palace, while I fretted. We were given a sumptuous suite: drawing room, bedroom with enormous beds, and a huge marble bathroom with a sunken tub. This must have been how the rajah's titled guests were entertained, and to Mr. Kesrisingh, his brothers (four of them altogether, a pride of lions), and his father, ex-maharajah, all there for the festival, we were guests, not just travellers. Exquisitely mannered, each made a point of talking to us while their beautiful wives in expensive evening gowns chatted together and ignored us. The men snapped their fingers for orange-turbaned servants; told us we should always keep servants waiting, they expected it; told us of others they knew who were also returning to India: indeed, two women had been there recently and missed by twenty minutes an old friend, another rajah, with whom they used to play tennis before Independence.

Finishing our drinks together, Mr. Kesrisingh said, "Shall we?" and took us into his gardens. Long paths were lighted by bulbs hidden inside carved containers. A spotlight lit the palace, a pink glow. The evening was so still that silver candelabra lighted squares of intricate carpets set on the lawn without a flicker from the candles. The carpets were surrounded by bolsters, each square seating about fifteen people. Long tables, covered with damask, held flowers, delicate china, silver, and glass. Reclining against our bolsters with other guests, all French, we watched while a procession approached between the lights, over the flagged paths: men dressed in white-belted tunics and women in brilliant traditional clothes. They carried rushlights and salver after salver of food. One of the women perched a baby on her hip. They were led by dancing men with instruments playing plaintive music. All moved rhythmically, their hips swaying as they approached the table and put down their burdens.

All night — I was up with the tomato problem — a woman sang in the distance: unaccompanied, wild, plaintive, a voice from Xanadu wailing for her demon-lover.

Chapter
Twenty-One

*E*IGHTEEN MONTHS (SEPTEMBER, 1989) after the first journey, we were in New Delhi again, starting off this time with a new travelling companion: Dale, a man in his forties, dark, good-looking, a compulsive spender, a target for hard-luck stories. Never before off the North American continent, he prepared himself with an extraordinary number of shots, antibiotics, pills, and remedies for the bowels, as well as with several pairs of dark glasses, goggles and smoke masks in case of fire, a Swiss Army knife, a compass and reflector, a red bandanna for signalling, a snake-bite kit, a mosquito net with a hundred feet of nylon cord—used only once in an attempt to keep mice out of his bed. He was a contrast to Jenny with her iron constitution and trust in the mercy of strangers.

Dale had some justification. We'd been warned of the dire situation in Kashmir, where we planned to go first: terrorism, bombs, assassinations, polluted waters, crowded houseboats on the Dal Lake. The economy was said to be reeling because tourists were avoiding the state, claimed to be the most beautiful in India, the "happy valley" of the Moguls. My aunts said, forgetting I'd left India as a small child, why not remember it the way it was and avoid disappointment?

The change had started after Partition. Kashmir-Jammu had been a princely state, ruled by one of the Hindu maharajahs, but the vast majority of the population was and still is Moslem. After some shilly-shallying, the ruler threw in his lot with India, even though Vallabhai Patel, India's powerful home minister, had insisted Kashmir should go to Pakistan, saying it would be a fishbone, which could neither be swallowed nor removed, lodged in India's gullet.

It's still lodged there. The referendum India promised never materialized. India and Pakistan have fought two wars over the territory, and while we were there a third threatened. Since then, the situation has grown much worse and the Kashmiris, who depend on the tourist trade ("If tourists don't come, we don't eat"), are bereft.

This time we were flying, a concession to Walter, and we found that everywhere we went, not just to Kashmir, the planes were several hours late and the security intense: suitcases were checked again and again, batteries were removed from cameras and tape recorders, light body-searches were conducted at each stop. The internal flights were chiefly made by old propeller planes. Many had been bought secondhand from countries which considered them too old to fly. Several had crashed. Others were grounded with cracks in fuselages. On one flight, Walter noticed the cabin was crumbling away, the panels pulling apart. He said he could see the battered engines on the wings and if we ever returned to India, we'd take the trains, which I'd wanted to do in the first place. But I didn't care. We were there. I simply didn't wear my glasses. Even the armed guards on the airstrips had to be pointed out to me.

On the plane to Srinagar, capital of Kashmir, where my sister, Dawn, had been born, we noticed a man sitting between two Western women and were fascinated because he held both of them so firmly by the hand, the three of them scrunched together. The women were young, pretty, well-dressed, wearing jewellery and beautiful shoes. On arrival in the airport, he still held them tightly—emotionally as well as physically they appeared a single unit—while a tall man in a well-cut grey suit wheeled their luggage behind them. One of the women had the worst black eye we'd ever seen: a large pouch of blood hanging beneath it. We assumed the man was a Muslim, and they were his wives. We assumed he'd battered her. The man looking after their cart was an enigma.

In Delhi, we had met a smooth travel agent, Nazir, who'd pressured us into spending far more money than we'd intended, but it was too late to do anything about it: he already had the bulk as down payment. Probably it was just as well. When we arrived we were scrutinized so severely we wondered if we'd be allowed into Kashmir at all. His agent met us, vouched for us, drove us to our houseboat, the White Horse, and said Nazir had returned to Srinagar and would meet us the next day. He did, only to tell us we couldn't fulfil our plans to go into Leh, capital of the Ladakh area, which was closed to tourists because of violence, but that he'd arranged a jeep safari to Zanskar instead. We'd never heard of Zanskar, and I desperately wanted to go to Leh to visit monasteries.

In support of Nazir, we were later told by our guide, Rasool, that on his last trip into Leh he and his party had had to leave in the middle of the night and walk three days and nights with little food and water. He claimed they'd been attacked by Buddhist monks who wanted to form an independent state so tourists would go directly to them rather than going through Srinagar. Buddhists are pacifists, we pointed out. It made no difference; they were armed, he said, and had killed tourists: three Japanese women as well as a taxi driver with his passengers: "When we get back safely and my party, French people, it gets to Delhi, they go to the ministry and say, 'If you want to kill your tourists, send them to Leh.' Now all tourist shops closed. No sleeping bags, no tents, no food."

On our own expedition, we found Rasool, a heavy man, was lazy and in poor shape: we wondered how he'd managed to walk for three days and nights without food. We would have thought the whole story concocted, except that large numbers of militia guarded any possible entrance to Leh.

There was a huge force—the Indian Army—occupying Kashmir. Ostensibly it's there to guard the Chinese and Pakistan borders, but in fact keeps close watch on the local population. The soldiers carry rifles—many from the First World War, according to Dale—and sten guns. Their lorries rumble through the streets, gun barrels poking out. The Kashmiris hate them, always speaking of India and the Indian Army as something quite separate from themselves. They say they also dislike Indian tourists, but need them to survive.

However, if we were sitting in a cauldron of discontent, we had little indication of it. The men who ran our houseboat, Gulam, the "captain," a worried introvert, and Abdul, the bearer, a cheerful extrovert, were young and engaging. They desperately wanted us to be happy and wouldn't let us alone, even sitting with us anxiously while we ate our meals, a thing that would never have happened when my family was there. They had a *shikara*, operated by a beautiful boy, to take us wherever we wanted to go. They insisted India was jealous of Kashmir and spread false rumours about bombs and riots to hurt their tourist trade. Like Rasool and others, they said they had been far better off under the British: the Dal Lake wasn't crowded, there was no pollution, the standard of living was higher, there was no inflation: "My father, my grandfather has told me."

I don't think there were any soldiers in Kashmir when I was a child. Srinagar had been a retreat, an oasis for women and children, to which husbands who were on duty could escape, chiefly from the North-West Frontier, on short leaves: the place where my mother and aunts, all so incredibly young at the time, had had some freedom to be more themselves.

There, romances, short for the most part, with unattached officers on leave had flourished, had probably seldom been consummated, had petered out: it was simply not done to break up a marriage. Irene, Enid and Gwen had lived on "The Lotus Eater," had gone swimming with Dawn and me. I had wandered into the living area—rich, red seat-covers—one day and found my mother crying. Long afterwards, I knew she had fallen in love with an officer—a pilot, motorcyclist, big-game hunter—who turns up constantly in the family photograph album. No doubt, that was why she was weeping silently, afraid of being heard. I remembered riding behind him on his motorbike: the exhilaration, the excitement. But he hadn't liked me; he thought I was too much like my father. And I think I hadn't liked him: he blew smoke in my face, close-up, as a joke. But I didn't dislike him. He flew his single-engined plane over us, dipping his wings in salute. This affair had actually gone on for some years, and Enid's sisters and friends knew about it. She was not criticised, the man she had married was sixteen years older than she was, she had not destroyed her family. Like others, she was given a great deal of freedom, but the code had held: "Well, you know, we just didn't."

My mother must have been twenty-three or four when she wiped the sympathetic tears off my face and laughed.

❧❦❧

The houseboats—ours was "super deluxe"—are far larger than I re-membered: outer porch, living room, dining room, three bedrooms with their own bathrooms. The furnishings are not the red and gold I recalled, but are upholstered in flowered cotton and, like the ceilings and walls, built of pale, carved cedar. Hand-woven carpets cover the floors. In Indian terms, they are enormously expensive and mortgage rates are outrageous, but even so their luxury is combined with the usual, rather charming discomfort. It would have been easy to do without the elaborate carving in exchange for toilets that worked, showers that dribbled reasonably temperate, rather than boiling or freezing water (we couldn't combine them), and reliable lights. During the day, the boats are dim; at night, we had to feel our way around. This is not the fault of the owners, but of the power company which keeps the electricity low because many Kashmiris, in cahoots with company men in return for a rake-off, steal it. Power cuts are endemic: "Oh, Madam, it is gone again."

Sixty years before, the rajah had owned the electricity and turned it on and off at will. One day my mother had decided to have a perm, given by a penurious Englishwoman on another boat. This was then an elaborate affair. Her hair in rollers, she'd been hooked up by multiple wires to an overhead contraption when the power had evaporated. Rather than take the rollers out and miss an ounce of curl (she's even more miserable over money than I am), she'd got into her *shikara* and returned to her own boat, still attached to the wires which, like a kitsch lampshade, fell over her head, face and body. The Indians, no doubt, thought she was crazy.

Despite dire stories, the Vale of Kashmir is just as beautiful as my parents had always insisted: sheltered, lush, with a string of connecting lakes and rivers surrounded by snow- and mist-covered mountains. And Srinagar, built along the Dal Lake, going back over 2000 years to the Buddhist Emperor, Ashoka, is a town with meandering streets holding stone, brick, and wooden three-storey, helter-skelter buildings; with men in bright shirts and shawls, women in black or earth-brown *burqqas*, looking like huge beetles, and others, unveiled, trotting under storage jars or enormous loads of wood; with laden donkeys, flowers, and mosques. Seven ancient bridges built over tributaries connecting the chain of lakes serve as extensions of the town. Formal, terraced Mogul gardens, planted beyond the small city, look down on still lakes with mountains behind them. None of this has changed in hundreds of years.

Our houseboat didn't have the diving boards and water shoots I recalled. None of them did. The water was too polluted in the area. Instead, a "swimming boat" was anchored some way off. Abdul accompanied me to it in the *shikara* while Walter and Dale went off on an expedition I happily missed: they returned in a rage, having suffered through a taxi with broken seats, a dog fight, and a wretched guide. In any case, they thought the water would be filthy. Abdul played cards while I sat with my legs over the side of the swimming deck. Thousands of tiny fishes nibbled and tickled my skin: they must have been descendants of the ones I'd fished for as a child, dehooking and putting them in a water bucket before throwing them back into the lake. It was growing cool—the end of the season—but the water was soft and warm. I swam out to the lilies, a few still in flower, and remembered being held up by the enormous leaves when I was small and unknowing. Around me, those who were still small and unknowing paddled their more primitive *shikaras*—hollowed-out logs, without the canopies on *pukka* ones for tourists—hawking lotus blooms. Large-eyed, neatly made, shy, small, the water was their natural habitat.

The houseboats, originally built by the enterprising British who were not permitted to buy land in Kashmir, have romantically deceptive names—Mona Lisa, Kashmir Hilton, House of Lords, Heavenly Flower, Happy Love Nest, Cautious Amorist. They have an upper deck for sunbathing and sitting in deck chairs drinking sundowners, and a lower porch where one is a part of all the coming and going—a dangerous place: all day merchants paddle up with their wares. The Kashmiris have a reputation for being the most charming and guileful traders in the world. They are also the most tenacious, each with his own territory; they were paying a fee, we discovered, to be allowed to approach their victims.

Dale was particularly gullible. We saw a whole new side of him. He and I egged each other on so effectively he had to leave India six weeks early. We bought hand-woven shawls, among them a true antique and another of cashmere that would slide through my wedding ring—the old test. Our shawl seller—amused at the game—returned with bedspreads, tablecloths, dressing gowns, shirts. When we teased him about constantly coming back, he shrugged, smiling, "I have to try, have I not?" Others came by with *tankas* (chiefly hideous, modern renditions for tourists), wonderfully crafted hunting knives, carvings, flowers, flower seeds, cigarettes, films, soft drinks. We were taken to a carpet "factory" and bought carpets—still egging each other on. Walter, not to be outdone, had a suit, which he's never worn, tailored for him. We were going quite mad.

The Kashmiris started watching Dale thoughtfully. He obviously appeared to be rich (quite untrue) and competent (true). A house designer, he could discuss building with them, give them advice. He was single. He started being invited into "special" ("not for tourist, for friend") shops and having long meetings with people. Invited out to dinner by Rasool and our safari cook, Sultan, he was approached about marrying Sultan's pretty sixteen-year-old daughter and going into business: he could buy property in one of their names and settle down to a prosperous married life. He replied, Kashmiri fashion, "God willing, it will happen; if not, it won't."

He was enchanted with the proposition; he also felt great affection for Sultan, who was gentle, troubled, with dangerous eye trouble, and looked sixty rather than forty. But during the long pre-dinner conversation, when these proposals were made, it was his bowels, despite all his potions, that concerned him most. Sultan's tiny house was built on stilts (he'd been flooded out); his mother, wife, and daughters were behind the flimsy partition. Everything could be heard. An embarrassed Westerner, Dale couldn't consider squatting over a hole and having everyone listen to the plops. Added to his problems, he'd had a huge lunch. Dinner was even huger: Sultan's wife served the men with mountains of rice, meats—including lamb, as a treat for Dale—cooked in various ways, an enormously long, very hot pepperoni, again especially for him ("Thank God, it was hollow"), vegetables, salt coffee which made him want to vomit, and as a final offering four bananas for himself alone. It was insurmountable, he said later, sighing.

On another of his pilgrimages, he was invited into one of the "special" shops and asked if there were any way in which one could send an eighteen-month-old child by itself on a plane from one place to another? His questioner claimed he was the child's grandfather. He said the baby, which kept him awake at night—he was getting no sleep—was his son's, but its mother was in New Zealand and he, as he was very tired, would like to return it to her. The baby had a passport. Dale said if they gave him a copy, he would enquire when we returned to New Delhi. When he went back to get the copy, the grandfather, sleepless nights or not, had changed his mind. This was obviously not what he'd been hoping for. Dale can't wait to get back to India. He'd found himself living in a Rushdie novel.

❦

Neither he nor Walter wanted to go to Padum, our destination in Zanskar. They were angry at the cost and in no mood to go after the disastrous excursion I'd missed—we were supposed to leave the next morning. On their return, Walter had collapsed on the bed, saying furiously, "I won't go."

We discussed it with Dale who mournfully backed me up, chiefly because there appeared to be no way to get our money back. When we went outside, still arguing, pedlars swarmed to the boat. I bargained for an old and expensive *tanka*, the last straw for Walter, and Abdul, sensing trouble, rushed to give him a chair which shattered under him. He lay, astonished, on the jetty. The Kashmiris were horrified, but Dale and I burst out laughing. Then everyone laughed, including Walter, and, good humour restored, we agreed to take our jeep safari, which Dale later called a hell of a euphemism.

I don't know what safaris are supposed to be like, so don't know if this was a euphemism or not. Dale was crammed into the back with Rasool and Sultan and all our baggage. I, with a bar to cling to, was placed beside the driver, Abasa, with Walter beside me next to a door that had to be held shut with string. Tents, sleeping bags, cooking gear, and a cage with white chickens in it, sat on the roof. Each morning, there was one less chicken, but it must have been a relief to them to be eaten: the heat when the sun was up was unbearable and they had no shelter from it. We drove ten hours a day with such excruciating difficulty that when we examined our itinerary we were only faintly surprised to see that on one particular day we were to make only ten kilometres. It was a misprint, but could have been possible: we were actually doing seventy kilometres in the ten hours. I said, in the early stages, "Oh, God, it would be easier to walk," but then took a second look at the road.

We drove through rivers, inched over bridges with signs saying "Caution: weak bridge": under them, vast drops ended in rushing waters. The road itself was constructed of helter-skelter stone blocks, twice the size of large kleenex boxes. In some places, we struggled over boulders, in others over rocks being broken up by men and boys sitting by the roadside using chisels and hammers. These road builders wrapped their hands in rags, wore thongs for shoes. They built the road as we used it. Siliceous dust hung, a heavy cloud, over them. Rasool said, "Very difficult road. Zanskar means dust." It was only later we discovered this was a joke—it actually means copper valley. Even so, when we stopped for a break the men in the back were so coated with gold-brown particles we didn't know at first which of them was Dale, who'd tied his red bandanna over his mouth.

Walter, who felt guilty over his front seat but also had a self-serving motive due to a bruised coccyx, said generously, "I'll change places with you. I wouldn't mind stretching out."

Dale, through his mask, was incredulous: "Christ, I was bent like a pretzel and I'm a foot shorter than you are."

I also felt I should do my part, particularly since the two of them were blaming me for the whole episode. "I'll sit at the back, Dale." But of course there was no way in which he could fit himself into my tiny area.

He said bitterly "I've lost $800.00—no offence, Rona—for seven days of misery."

Abasa, our driver, had put money into a shrine outside Srinagar and said a prayer. I'd given money to a beggar woman, but he'd snatched it from her and put it also in the box. Dale, who'd been impressed with this, said, "That may save us." Perhaps it did, but in any case Abasa felt safe ("I don't drive; God does") and his adrenalin flowed fast. At Drass, a checkpoint where a road forked off to Leh, we had to start travelling in convoy—cars were not supposed to pass each other. There the army, complete with field pieces, took particulars. We had to wait for the incoming convoy—a slow business. I went to sleep, sitting bolt upright, relieved I didn't have to hang on to my bar. Through a dream, I heard Dale say, "I don't believe this" and woke up to find we were off to the races with taxis, cars, jeeps, buses, trucks fighting to be first. On one side of the single-lane road (if you could call it that) a cliff reared up; on the other, there was a three-hundred-foot drop. Abasa won, leading the convoy, which meant the dust was not quite so bad, but he was stopped again later, and we ended up at the back of the line.

The whole way to Padum, three days' driving, there were yellow patches with messages in black painted on rockface: "Please bare with us"; "Woman tell man, wake for my sake"; "Drive like Hell, you will be there"; "Go, man, go, but drive slow"; "Be cautious, avoid pregnancy and widowhood"; "I want you darling, but not too fast"; "My curves are lovely, but Drive over them slowly"; "Better driver late than a late driver." And all the way memorial stones, it seemed not more than a hundred or so yards apart, commemorated people who had gone over the edge. Some had been in buses: their names made a long list.

I didn't dare look at Walter, who told me later he was himself driving the entire way. I clutched a bracelet I'd bought with the great Tibetan *mantra* on it and silently repeated another, to be used in extreme danger. It invoked three horrific demons—Vagrapani, Hiergriva and Garuda—who would get us through. After several hours, I realized I simply didn't believe in them at all.

And I learned something else. On one of our lunch stops in this valley of stones—most of the time there was no vegetation whatsoever—I climbed a hill looking for a rock high enough to squat behind. Seeing one in the distance, I rounded it and found, growing with no apparent soil, the most exquisite plant I'd ever seen: about eighteen inches high, the stem bore several delicate blue flowers with yellow stamens and pistil. I knew instantly it must be a *meconopsis aculeata*, the blue poppy my father had talked about. He'd said the hills and valleys were covered with them. They bloom in August. This one was very late.

It invoked his ghost, and I thought, standing there with my jeans unzipped, what a little prig I'd been with my anti-colonialism and self-righteousness. My ancestors were among the many who had managed to live in and administer this country for three hundred years. I'd assumed it had been an easy sit with multiple servants and lordly status. I'd been brainwashed by current attitudes. None of my relatives had wanted to return once they left. My father had talked of dirt and flies and heat and crowds. After he retired, he never complained about anything. He thought Canada the most wonderful country in the world, and was happiest reading *The Rubayat* until he knew it by heart, or limping down to the sea in the summer in his ancient khaki shorts with a thermometer so he could take the sea's temperature before he went swimming. At the time, this had seemed a perfectly normal procedure to us. I thought of my Aunt Irene, whose pleasure it was to water the flowers in her Worthing rest home until she finally discovered they were plastic; of my Aunt Gwen who gave all her antique Tibetan teapots and her silver to an animal rights' group and would, had she been younger, have stormed laboratories; of my Uncle Eric who once shouted at me nervously because he thought I was about to step on the only vegetable—a radish—he'd managed to grow on several acres of land; of my mother who toiled away with single-minded enthusiasm at a business, Scottish hand-weaving, when even the Scots had given up on it. Eccentrics, all of them, but never power-hungry or money-grubbing, never arrogant.

The first night out I was furious. According to our itinerary— hopelessly outdated—we were supposed to spend the first stop in a hotel in Kargil. But not at all. The men found a suitable place, got out of the jeep, and started setting up tents; Sultan, who turned out to be an excellent cook but took at least two hours to prepare a meal, was lighting his fires. It was growing dark while Walter and I argued, sitting in the jeep, and Dale, willing as ever, tried to help the crew but only got in the way. They knew exactly what they were doing. Finally, he came over to us and said, "Why won't you guys get out of the fucking jeep?"

"We're supposed to be at a hotel. It's on the itinerary. We could at least wash."

But in fact there was no choice. The camp was set up by a small stream. The sun was going down, and we were cold. We had no lights of any kind. We were apparently to sit outside on small stools to eat.

Meantime, the cosy cook tent glowed with warmth and light and bustle. I went into our tent to try to clean up in the gloom—my hair was so filthy I couldn't get a comb through it. In the middle of peeling dirt off with wipe-ettes and wishing we'd brought more than the half bottle of whisky we had with us (the area was Suni Moslem: no liquor), I looked up to find half a dozen silent children peering through the tent flap.

I needed to find a private place—we'd been promised some kind of toilet tent but nothing had materialized and everything appeared to be unpacked. The children followed me everywhere. Finally I said to Walter, "I do wish they'd leave me alone. I can't even pee."

With no sympathy, he answered, "But you like children."

We'd given some of them pens—a great mistake: there were soon half a dozen of them following while I tried to find a rock with Walter standing guard. By the following night, I'd become reasonably adjusted, learning the first thing to go is vanity, the next modesty, and finally cleanliness. However, I never got used to trying to clean my teeth, with their two removable partial dentures (necessary after a riding accident), while children stared in astonishment when I took them out of my head and scrubbed ferociously.

It was pitch dark when we ate. We wouldn't have been able to see anything if we hadn't sat fairly close to the glowing cook tent which spilled out a modicum of light. Dale looked dreadful. He and Walter had both developed diarrhoea. I was constipated—no doubt for psychological reasons. Our conversation had become boring beyond belief, centred as it was on the state of our bowels.

It was not until various names of villages—particularly Sonamarg and Drass—and valleys cropped up that I realized I was in exactly the right place for my quest: we were driving through the Sindh Valley, along the Sindh River. Old black and white photos in my father's album bore these names. I asked Masool if the white men had hunted and trekked there and he said, "Yes, great hunting area for British. Lions, tigers, deers, pheasants, bears. Few left now."

A photograph of a man standing in front of an enormous hanging bear skin, rifle in hand, and another of my Uncle Eric with various trophies enlivened my parents' album. My father had given up hunting, preferring to look for blue poppies. There was no road into the area in those days—it was first built in the early eighties, but was washed away and was still being rebuilt. The hunters must have trekked in with guides and porters to carry their gear.

On the second day, we were headed towards Rangdum,[21] nine hours away, our first Buddhist monastery. I was delighted; we were going to see monasteries after all. Dramatic changes were occurring. We were in Little Tibet. In this sparsely inhabited area, white *stupas* with flying flags replace mosques; the occasional man with a yak wears an earth-red jacket and skirt, a warm hat; the few women, heads covered, swathe themselves in dark woollen garments; small nomadic boys herd goats and sheep; tiny wild horses, no larger than great danes, scrabble for weeds among the stones. In the valley below us, we came across the occasional little village of mud huts with clay bricks for their second storeys and the odd stone hut with fodder stored on its sod-and-stick roof. One, apparently with a single room on each of two floors, crumbling to pieces, its first level the same height as Walter, had a sign on top: "Glacier View Hotel and Restaurant." Not surprisingly, it appeared deserted.

Rasool told us that when the snows melt, water rushes down the slopes and washes the huts away: each spring they have to be rebuilt. Pathetic trees, no more than sprigs, planted by the government, are encased in cages so they won't be eaten. Marmots, magpies, hawks provide flashes of life.

Above all, we were stunned by the colours: green glaciers; sharp white mountain peaks (Nun and Kun, both over 23,000 feet); moss-green, rosy-red, and yellow rock face flecked with silver and gold—quartz and iron pyrite—glittering in the sun; the bluest sky we had ever seen; and below us aquamarine streams. Zanskar is a valley of minerals, of clean, bright air once the road dust is left behind.

Dale, wedged in the back, claimed he couldn't see any of it but didn't care at all, he was so grateful that he couldn't watch the road or what the jeep was doing. He insisted he felt desperately sorry for us.

When we reached Rangdum Gompa, built two hundred and fifty years ago high up on a hill overlooking the valley, the yellow-capped monks were eating, sitting cross-legged on the stone floor. Our crew had refused to walk up with us: Rasool said they had no interest in that religion and the monks didn't like them, which may or may not have been true. They were charming to us, showed us around, and pointed out an enormous pile of large, flat, carved stones, which they said was "money." In fact, they were offerings and later we found many more—

---

[21] Also spelled Ringdom.

entire walls of them, one stacked on top of the other. Exquisitely worked, they depicted *mandalas, chortens,* figures of the Buddha, and the *mantra* which we were to find everywhere: *om mani padma hum.* I lusted to take one, but they were heavy and no doubt not for sale. It seemed sacrilegious even to ask, although they simply sat there through rain, winter ice, burning sun.

Pensi La Pass, our next stop, was fourteen and a half thousand feet. We arrived late; it was already dark and freezing. Rasool said we would only go on the next day if it weren't snowing. We hoped it would be. Sultan prepared his chicken soup—it took three hours to make. Dale offered to share his tent with Abasa, who slept, God knows how, in the jeep, but his offer was refused. The crew never ate with us, but since conditions were so extreme, they did allow us that night to eat first in their warm tent. We slept in every item of clothing we possessed and still froze. Sultan gave us hot-water bottles, but they didn't help. In the morning, Dale, sleepless, got up early and smacked our tent. It was white with frost and frost covered the ground.

We finally reached Padum, capital of Zanskar: a tiny village on a flat plain surrounded by mountains. Trekkers' tents were scattered across the scrub. These nature lovers had littered the plain with tinfoil, plastic, paper, cigarette packages, empty tins. Liquor bottles, which we thought might be useful, were left where they'd been abandoned: the monks wouldn't touch them for fear of contamination. Rasool told us German trekkers left nothing, but others didn't care.

In the distance the Karsha Gompa dominated the valley. Dogs barked continuously. Boys and young men, all monks and all hoping for pens, visited us. There was not an inch of privacy. I finally faced Rasool: "We were told we'd have some kind of toilet."

Very unwillingly, he erected a canvas outhouse (where had it been all this time?) and dug a shallow hole. The comfort was astonishing. I became unconstipated. Dale and Walter were ecstatic. To Rasool's extreme annoyance, other campers rushed to use it: a small thing, this smelly canvas cube, but of infinite satisfaction.

We asked Sultan about the cheerful boy monks, who appeared to be nine or ten years old. He said that at puberty they are given a "medicine" to dampen their sexual drive but if the desire for the world gets the better of them, they can leave the monastery. They are selected for their intelligence, sometimes by the monks, sometimes by their parents. It is a great honour.

Stone walls meandered everywhere, generally for no apparent reason, but some had been constructed in an attempt to cultivate tiny patches of soil on which to grow vegetables and wheat. Men and women carried enormous bundles of saplings collected from great distances. If we gave the children candies, one would carefully dole them out to others: happy, smiling, tough, handsome boys and girls, often with school satchels, who spoke, they said, Urdu, and learned a sketchy English at school.

We were undeservedly lucky in that we'd arrived at Karsha Gompa on a special occasion. The brother of the Dalai Lama, Dargon Rimpoche, in whose territory it was located, was preaching. We didn't know this when we climbed up to the monastery, thinking we'd die on the way. To the children it was nothing, but even our guide book for intrepid trekkers told us it was "sweat raising."

First we had to traverse a suspension bridge and then walk a couple of miles to the foot of the mountain. It was very hot. Snaking paths and vertical steps led up to the monastery so steeply that at one point I had to sit with my head between my knees, thinking I might faint and fall over the edge. I vowed (temporarily) to give up smoking. Patient Walter—it's time I paid tribute to his constancy even if it was tempered by his own exhaustion—kept me company but Dale strode off. We met a crazy Westerner who, for some mad reason, was carrying his pack up with him: young, angry, muscular, he'd fallen by the wayside and was so furious he would barely speak to us.

The Tibetan *gompas* are white and sprawling, built like eyries: remote, untroubled, above the whims of men, conclaves for *puja*, meditation, chanting. The air is thin and clear at 12,000 feet, the sky a vibrant blue.

First we found a lower chapel with its plain, whitewashed exterior and was told by a friendly monk who spoke a little English that there was to be a *puja* there at two o'clock. We climbed further to a second: its exterior and interior painted with enormous guardian demons; its benches covered with hand-woven, earth-coloured blankets; its flag-like *tankas* hanging free; its altar with the usual Buddhist paraphernalia, possibly including bone relics of Dorje Rinchen.

The *gompa* library was filled with long, board-covered books, written on loose leaves of hand-made paper. They were wrapped in silk. The librarian put one—a hundred and one years old, he told us—across his knees and chanted a long invocation from it for us.

Fortunately, since by one o'clock people were already arriving, we decided to go down to the other *puja* room early. Sitting quietly against a wall, where a few trekkers later joined us, we were ignored. Monks filed in and sat on embroidered cloths in a circle around a desk-table covered with beautiful silk materials, topped with gold in a diamond configuration and holding a microphone run off batteries. They were robed in dark red, some with a gold, silk shawl over the right shoulder. While they chanted, villagers entered with their children, the women wearing heavy headdresses made of wood and leather inset with turquoise and coral.

Despite the heat outside, it was cool and dim, but even so the crowd which crammed every inch of the small room, grew restive and chattered: there was none of the solemnity of Western churches. Finally Dargon Rimpoche came in, wearing the gold shawl over his left shoulder and a gold cap. He sat at the table, in front of a figure of Lhaso Cho Rimpoche with its gold crown inset with carnelian and turquoise, and chanted deep from his diaphragm. Then he started to speak, never hesitating, without notes, but of course we couldn't understand a word.

After about two hours, we decided to try to get out. A Western girl who seemed nervous asked Walter if she could follow him but was not aggressive enough and was left behind. As it was, while he tried to step between the sitting people, a woman beat on his legs. When we did reach the door—only about twelve feet away—we found a crowd outside stretching far down the entrance steps. Fortunately, because we'd never have found them, we had carried our shoes in with us.

Abasa had been waiting for us with his jeep for three hours on the other side of the suspension bridge.

Dale missed Dargon Rimpoche but found his own entertainment. On his way back to the village, he was appalled to find a large dump of trekkers' first-aid drugs stashed behind a wall. A half-hearted attempt had been made to burn them, but the foil packages had refused to light; syringes and pills were scattered across the ground. He thought of the children who might pick them up.

Going on, he climbed the mountain above the camp and, high up, found grazing fields and cattle which partially explained how these people survive. Night was coming on, when it would be pitch dark, before he realized he'd lost his way. Luckily, he came across a young herder who brought him back to the village. Dale, being Dale, gave the boy his watch and then demolished our bottled water.

On our way back to Srinagar, the road didn't worry me at all. The whole expedition had already become a fatalistic dream, but I did notice a new sign: "I once loved speed. She ditched me."

Dale and Walter were still capable of being concerned, especially when the jeep, in need of repairs, came to a halt. Instantly other drivers with spare parts stopped to help us: we had a broken spring bracket, stripped bolts, and, we discovered when Abasa tried to start up again, a non-functioning starter. Even the string holding the door shut had frayed away, and when he finally managed to move forward after more tinkering the door flew open. Walter hung on to the window frame—there was no window—from then on or we would probably have lost the door altogether. The jeep was only three years old, but the roads had already destroyed it.

Perhaps Abasa knew the state it was in. Stopped again by the army in its usual convoy of trucks, he was asked for his papers. He didn't want to show them and hugged the small package to his chest, supplicating his questioner, who became very angry. Apparently all vehicles were supposed to be checked regularly, and although he'd applied, he said, to have his examined, he hadn't been able to wait to do so.

We gathered most of this from Rasool, who was unsympathetic. He told us Abasa would merely have to go before a judge and pay a fine but that since he'd refused to show the papers the fine had already doubled. We were so sorry for him—he would lose anything he might have made—that when we arrived we gave him a tip large enough to cover the fine. He was ecstatic, but Rasool was gruff, feeling he should have had the major amount.

After that, we were stopped constantly and checked. As it turned out, Abasa had returned on an unpropitious day. A bomb had exploded in the Old Market and all vehicles were being searched. We never found out how large it was or how many people were killed. Tourists were not to be informed. When we mentioned it to a taxi driver later, he looked surprised and said, "What bomb?"

About thirty miles before Srinagar, a road branched off to Manasbal Lake, which we'd arranged to see on the way back. This was the secret area, I'd been told, reached only by *shikara* through reedy waterways, where my parents had spent their honeymoon. They'd slept on the bank, and one night my father had whispered to my mother, "Don't move. There's a leopard walking around us."

There are no leopards now. The road has been constructed, land has been cleared and fenced, hotels built. *Shikaras* sit in a row along a grassy bank. The shallow lake has become an ordinary place for tourists, nothing more.

By the time we approached Srinagar, it was dark. Abasa had learned little from his recent encounter. To save a few rupees, he drove the final miles to the town and then through it in pitch blackness, without lights. He felt his way.

A concerned Abdul, delighted to see us back, was waiting with his usual patience at the dock with the houseboat's *shikara.* When we reached the White Horse, Dale breathed a huge sigh of relief: "Finally, finally, some peace." He and Walter muttered about the comforts of home. Even so, they both long to go back.

Abdul and Gulam were full of stories. With winter approaching, Gulam recalled being a little boy and working on his father's boat. To keep warm in freezing weather, he had held a pot of coals, a normal procedure, beneath his "upper garment." One of the men in a French family staying with them late in the year had been charmed with the child. Playing with him, he had suddenly picked him up and held him upside-down. All the coals had tipped out of the pot, giving the boy terrible burns down his chest and neck. Gulam smiled gently, "Nice man. Very worried."

I remembered the child, so badly burned my parents wondered if she would survive, brought to them on their honeymoon. My father had often talked about the danger of these fire-pots, which are still used.

Walter and I went with the agent's agent, the man who had met us at the airport, to Gulmarg, a high peak outside Srinagar, to see if I could find the hotel where I'd eaten a plateful of spinach to please my nanny. I also wanted to visit my father's favourite golf course, which had been one of the reasons for our spending the summers in Srinagar.

There were two hotels, the Touristi and the Neros, both of which had been there in the early thirties and long before. They were ghostly shades of the Raj. In its reception area, the bedraggled Touristi had a cheap reproduction of the Mona Lisa, ancient hunting prints, and a series of slightly risque lithographs, which might have come out of *Punch,* on its walls. It also had a scenic water colour painted by a British woman who had undoubtedly painted others, it was so similar to them, in my mother's possession. Yellowed, fly-spotted, forgotten, no one had taken it down.

We walked through a rising rain storm to the Neros and were invited into an empty room where the head waiter, an old man, gave us coffee out of an elaborate silver service, and we both became excited when he heard I'd been there as a child; there was no doubt this was the place I was looking for. He himself had been there—as sheepherder, golf caddy, waiter, headwaiter—all his life, and he rolled off a string of British names. I thought one of them might have referred to my godfather, but when we worked dates out realized this was impossible. Despite his ancient appearance, he was not yet fifty.

Gulmarg is the highest golf course, and reputedly the most difficult, in the world. We saw no one actually playing. Sheep grazed across it (everywhere small brown pellets, excellent fertilizer), deodars surrounded it, and groups of children wearing school uniforms and speaking excellent English ran over the grass. They were friendly, wanted photographs of us, wanted to exchange addresses. With the sweeping rain coming down from the mountains, it was all fresh and lovely, probably little changed since my father played there, even though the old waiter insisted it had been better before, when the British rode up or were carried in *dooleys* and there had been no dust or exhaust from cars. I had ridden up then and had sat watching idly while my father killed a snake with his riding crop and Luke, my sausage dog, eagerly looked for more in the shrub beside the stony road.

❦

In Srinagar, we had a reasonably intimate view of family life. Nazir, the travel agent, invited us to dinner in his palatial house with its stiff furniture, never used by the family, in the front room. We ate dinner off a stained cloth spread on the floor in another room—an enormous vegetarian meal. Nazir claimed the women generally ate with the men ("We eat together and pray together") in his extended family, but he alone ate with us. We talked about arranged marriages, which he considered far preferable to love matches, and how great an affair a Moslem marriage is with hundreds of guests as witnesses and many written contracts (including a financial settlement for the bride, non-existent in Hindu unions), which made divorce extremely difficult. He and his two brothers with their wives, children, and their old mother live together, the men bringing in the money while the wives do the housework, clean the enormous bins of beans and vats of rice, and take turns with the cooking. He said the whole arrangement works out well, with no quarrelling, but he joked about his own liberated wife being off with her boy-friend. We doubted him.

Despite the splendour of the house, when he showed us the kitchen, complete with shining brass utensils on the wall, we found a couple of the wives sitting on the floor washing dishes in a shallow basin and cooking on a primitive two-burner, also on the floor. His mother, who he claimed to be a young woman, sat smoking a hubble-bubble. She was so enormous, we wondered if she could get up. These women were not veiled, but apparently get little exercise. They were shy and unwilling to speak to us, although he had told us women have the same education as men. Whatever the truth of the matter, Nazir held his parents in esteem and affection—his dead father's portrait was draped in wreaths, and his mother, to him, was still lovely.

His attitude towards India was the same as that of others, with their hatred of the Indian Army, in truth an occupying force, and contempt for the people. For example, he insisted that in India 55,000 babies are born every minute (actually, the population swells by about 50,000 a day) and implied that this unlikely procreation is due simply to lack of control. When we mentioned Rushdie, he said, as others did, "Why should he mock what we believe in? They'll get him. Thousands of men are after him. He'll die."

We saw one of the wedding parties just before we left. The celebration took place at night. Three brilliantly lighted houseboats crossed the Dal Lake, with the first holding musicians playing drums and what sounded like bagpipes. Gulam told us these are like bagpipes, but are begpipes: he didn't explain the difference. An army could have been sailing towards us.

The temperature had dropped dramatically and it was cold. Few tourists would now come and the houseboat people would settle down into a long, icy winter. On the final evening, Gulam invited us to a feast in his tiny, separate house on stilts, where we again sat on the floor, but this time wrapped in quilts. The hut was single-walled, without insulation; Abdul said they would keep themselves warm with the traditional fire-pots and ponchos. The wives didn't join us, but Gulam's mother sat silently with a child in her arms: as far as we could make out, she had the money for their venture. Afterwards they set off fireworks. Rockets and catherine wheels and stars shot out over the water. This was the leave taking, cheered by our promises to return, but at the moment that is politically impossible. Kashmir-Jammu is in turmoil, its tourist trade in shambles, its inhabitants under threat of torture and death. Recently *The Washington Post* (May 1993) published an article claiming that in Kashmir soldiers are setting fire to houses and shooting unarmed residents trying to escape and that civilians are tortured, raped, and shot. The violence is growing at least partly out of strained India-Pakistan relations. We wonder what has happened to our gentle house-boat people, to Abasa, Rasool, Sultan.

Chapter
Twenty-Two

*P*ESHAWAR WOULD BE THE END
of a journey into the past. I still didn't know what I was looking for, but
had nowhere else to search. The long tunnel back into a dimly remembered childhood had come to its end. Only the briefest fragments,
recalled under hypnotism, went further into the darkness.

I'd had vague concepts and desires: the wish for some kind of
illumination, the possibility of a spiritual enlargement, a coming to
terms with myself. I'd found what many others have found: a tempered
respect for the British in India; a love for the country and people; the
possibility of regarding life, no matter how frustrating or appalling, with
humour; the knowledge that the consumerism of the West makes people
no happier than, and perhaps not as happy as, the poverty-stricken life
of the East. Even so, a part of me hungered for some further resolution
—some kind of individual reconciliation.

❧

Peshawar is no longer in India, but in Pakistan. We were not able to take
the excellent road connecting Srinagar to Islamabad, a mere couple of
hours drive away: the road, as far as I knew, the one my father had
described. Lined with tall poplars, it took my family into the lush valley
of Kashmir out of the heat and turmoil of the North-West Frontier
Province. Now it's barricaded. Islamabad, capital of Pakistan, is located
in the Punjab state with its territory split between the two countries.
Limited trains from India, and those booked at least three weeks in
advance, cross the border, so we had to return to Delhi and fly, realizing once again how extreme the tension is between India and her
neighbours.

We arrived (as usual) some five hours late to find a dignified Pakistani,
Rashid, holding up a large sign with our names on it, at the barrier. He
was chauffeur to our friends, Peter and Erica Dodd, and had been sent to
meet us, carrying a letter from them: the *mashaira* at which I'd been

invited to read poetry, was being held that evening, they had waited until the last moment, but now, if we arrived in time at all, would we like to join them? Rashid would drive us to the home of the American Cultural Attaché, where the event was taking place.

Rashid took us to our hotel (the Dodds were de-mothing their house and all was disorganized) to change rapidly, and we went on. By the time we arrived, the reading was over: held in a large room with poets, chiefly reading in Urdu, and guests sitting on luxurious cushions in a large circle, it had been a great affair. Afterwards, at candlelit tables set out of doors under arching vines, they had been eating and drinking: in this Moslem area, we discovered then and later, there was little difficulty in obtaining alcohol as long as one wasn't of the Faith — even if one was of the Faith, one could obtain it on the black market. This was another of those romantic occasions — beautifully dressed people discussing the arts, gentle servants, excellent food, warm enthusiasm. We met poets famous in their own country and beyond. One, Ahmed Farez, we were told, drew tens of thousands of people when he read.

A radical, political poet, an affable man, Ahmed is well looked after by his admirers, one of whom is Kwalid, who'd made a fortune in Toronto, to which he'd gone when he was nineteen, by inventing a machine to make pita bread swiftly. He'd taken his entire family to Canada — mother, father, brothers and sisters, who were still there — but had himself recently returned to Pakistan, where he was building a splendid house: he wanted his children to know something of their native culture.

Kwalid invited us to lunch the next day with Ahmed Farez, Ahmed's girlfriend, an outspoken, entertaining woman, angry because he'd not taken her to the *mashaira*, and a Canadian journalist, Cathy Gannon, from a small town in northern Ontario. She covered Afghanistan and told us she'd gone in and out easily despite the war, sometimes by wearing the all-encompassing veil. Like Tom, the American, and a young Danish woman we'd met in New Delhi — in love with the Afghan people and their unspoiled tribal life — she took all this casually. Perhaps it's only from a distance that crossing war-torn borders appears harrowing.

The day drifted on with libations and good talk. Lunch — served by Kwalid's gentle wife, who didn't eat with us although he said "She and I are partners in all things" — didn't arrive until well on in the afternoon. We met the children, and Kwalid's son told us how much he hated his boarding school, run by the military at fees of 4000 rupees a month — a fortune. After a Canadian school, the shock was insufferable. He had to get up at five in the morning, exercise for two hours, and then study intensively for eight. Kwalid told us there is no free schooling in Pakistan: people are more amenable without education. Later we met an American teacher who said the government spends two per cent of its income on education.

Kwalid drove us to see the new house, not yet completed, and on the way we passed thin woods filled with marijuana plants, a weed impossible to control so simply accepted. He took us in his Japanese car, telling us there are no Indian cars in Pakistan. In fact, there's no trade between the two countries.

At the building site, looking over a valley, the six-bedroom house sat above a squalid tent which housed those doing the construction. A small girl squatted in the dirt, washing cooking utensils in a wretched basin of dirty water and trying to light a cooking fire with a few sticks of wood. She was also looking after a baby. Inside the tent someone was asleep. It was hot and dusty, but we were happy with good food, drink, amusing conversation, and a splendid view. Poverty goes unnoticed by those who live with it. Our people's poet joked about building himself a hut on "the leftover land." No one appeared to notice the pathetic child not twenty feet from us.

It was night by the time Kwalid returned us to our hotel—a sweet, warm darkness with a rising moon, a single bright star off its tip. Warm, generous, he expected no return for his hospitality. He missed Canada and admired poets, that was all.

⋘ ۽ ⋙

Pakistan is unexpectedly different from India. Particularly in Islamabad, built in 1961, we noticed the wide, handsome streets; the shops filled with luxury goods from the U.S. (good soap, Elizabeth Arden cosmetics, kleenex, toilet paper); the proliferation of mosques, especially the enormous modern and controversial—because of its design—Shah Faisal Masjid, a gift from Saudi Arabia, with its eternal flame burning at the shrine of Zia; the freedom from beggars and hawkers; the lack of *tongas* and bullock carts as well as of sleek cows and other animals; the magnificent houses built chiefly by Zia's former administrative staff. But the corruption, we were told, is not different from that of India. Money intended for the best of purposes is syphoned off by middlemen so it's almost impossible to get anything accomplished, particularly with regard to education. Property owners who have grown out of the Zamindar system pay no land tax: the burden falls, as always, on the poor. Money is printed as it's needed so is worthless outside the country. Any political party knows it will not be in power long and therefore makes the most of the trough while it's able to do so. We were told Benezir Bhutto—in office at the time—was, as a woman, almost powerless, but was kept in her position because the West had fallen in love with her. Her husband, on the other hand, wielded power so successfully that every time he signed a document, he demanded one million rupees.

Rashid drove us, with Erica Dodd, to nearby Rawalpindi, once home to a British cantonment, with its spacious gardens still flowering, where my father had once been stationed. The new military area boasts aircraft hangars, barracks, wide streets. The old town is a warren of lanes— bazaars with silver, silks from China, jewellery from Afghan refugees, copper utensils, leather—no doubt unchanged for centuries. Erica suggested I buy a *shameez* and *shalwar*: to show one's ankles in Pakistan is considered very immodest.

In this part of the world there are real differences between the time of the Raj and the present. Not only is the area no longer a part of India and is an Islamic rather than a Hindu state, but it has also suffered from one repressive government after another. In addition, the Americans have taken over the British role. The U.S. pours money into Pakistan, builds dams and bridges, supplies educational and cultural officers, encourages trade, and feeds the military. While we were there, Bush put through Congress an enormous loan, based on the premise, verified by Benezir Bhutto, that Pakistan did not have, and was not working towards, the atomic bomb.[22] The area forms a buffer state, a former defence against Russia, which was at the time pouring money into Afghanistan. Peter and Erica Dodd, both highly educated, concerned, incorruptible people are now, like their friends, sahib and memsahib and are called such. They look after the visiting dignitaries, contend with varieties of insects, attempt to teach servants to soak vegetables and fruit in chlorinated

---

[22] In March, 1991, the U.S. announced that in accordance with the Pell Amendment it would no longer give aid to Pakistan, which has, unhappily, built the atomic bomb. Most U.S. personnel will be withdrawn. The Pakistan government is defiant over the issue.

water, live in an exile which is by any account luxurious but which entails hard work and denial of those things we take for granted: films, theatres, dances, and other entertainments contrary to Moslem faith. The U.S. is not an openly imperialistic country, as Britain was, but in fact is, with its hegemony based on money rather than on patent occupation.

❧❧

We took a small "tour" up to Peshawar. This entailed a car, driver, and night at a magnificent hotel for a fraction of its usual charge. Erica had talked about the terrors of the drive, saying that every year many people are killed because the drivers love to play "chicken," but the car was comfortable, the country lovely, and nothing could faze us after Zanskar. Contrary to experiences in India, our driver, Zuheir Ahmad could speak some English although we'd been told he couldn't, which meant we were doubly fortunate in that we weren't paying for a guide.

We drove along an arrow-straight section of the Grand Trunk Road (shades of Kipling's *Kim*) linking Delhi to Kabul, with our splendid driver stopping to show us a portion of the original, built of flat stones at the turn of the fifteenth century by the Mogul Emperor, Babur, and later used for raids into India. After the Marghalla ("Place to plunder cara-vans") Pass, we had crossed the boundary between the sub-continent and Central Asia.

Taxila (3000 BC), once known as the "Holy Land" of the Buddhists and centre of the ancient Gandhara Culture, lay on our route. Before the Buddhist era, Alexander the Great had interrupted his endless conquests to stop and discuss philosophy in what was even then a highly cultured university town. He left a garrison behind, with its descendants, known as the Bactrian Greeks, recalled by stone sculptures with Mediterranean features and flowing robes.

The ruins of Buddhist monasteries scatter the area. One, the Jaulian, filled with votive *stupas* and headless sculptures—disfigured by various invaders—was sacked by the White Huns in 455 AD. It had once included a school with individual cubicles, each for a boy monk and his tutor: a dispensation our society cannot afford. One or two clay pots for water remained, shelves for oil lamps. Fifteen hundred years later, our place in history shrank to the size of a farthing.

The last invaders were, of course, the British: trading invaders, but that makes little difference. When we reached the Indus River at Attock, we also reached the new bridge and the ancient fort built by Akbar, its crenellated, twenty-foot walls overlooking the water. It's still a military installation, off-limits, guarded by Pakistani soldiers.

We asked Zuheir Ahmad to take us to the old rail and road bridge, built, I'd been told, by my great-grandfather, Micah Gregory. I'd wondered if it actually exists. It does. With huge cement buttresses and iron trusses it spans the Indus boiling and whirlpooling beneath it. The rail line, still in use, stretches over the passage for cars, no longer permitted on it. Pedestrians are, provided they have passes. Guards with guns stand at the entrance. We could take photographs nowhere in the area, but the guards, interested when they heard my story, allowed Walter and me to walk over it.

The bridge was so long, we went only halfway, two solitary figures walking back in time. Midway, we found a plaque stating it had been built by Westwood, Bailey, and Co., Engineers and Contractors, London, 1880. I was disappointed not to have found the name "Gregory" on the brass, but was satisfied because the date coincided. Micah, who was fortunate in that he went to India shortly after Lord Dalhousie (appointed Governor-General in 1848) created the Public Works Department to build railroads and bridges, must have worked for this firm. I had no doubt, when Walter and I hung over the side, looking far down into the swift currents beneath us, that the family story claiming the task had been considered impossible was true: it was awe inspiring to imagine how it had been built at all with the equipment of the time. Micah had been the first of my mother's family to go to India: I had a calm, restful sense of having come home.

We went on to the junction of the Kabul and Indus rivers: mauve-brown into brilliant blue with a long line of demarcation between them. While we stared down at it, Zuheir said unexpectedly that if we gave him some extra money for time and gas he would drive us into the tribal territories, but that it was absolutely prohibited to go to Landi Kotel, closed through U.S. pressure in an attempt to control drug smuggling, or the Khyber Pass, equally out of bounds because of the Afghan War. Both these names were part of my childhood; my father had served at the Pass, restricted even then, when we'd lived in Peshawar. For millennia, it had been the gateway for marauding forces until the British had finally taken it from the Pathans and Afghans. Now, Zuheir said, there were tribal problems and shots over the border. I'd known we were not permitted to go there, but had still hoped for some unlikely possibility:

so often one may be told one thing and find another. As it was, according to our guidebook the tribal lands were off limits, and people we later spoke to were astonished we'd managed to get into them at all.

Ridiculously, we hesitated because of the money, but in the end overcame our tendency to think of a rupee as worth a dollar. Zuheir drove through Peshawar, almost on the Afghan border and capital of the North-West Frontier Province, and went on for twenty-five miles. He drove fast and wouldn't stop to let us out to take photographs although he slowed occasionally so we could do so through the window.

In explanation, he told us the road alone belongs to the government and that up until very recently the Pathans were so angry with the administration, they would shoot out the tires of any car that went onto the verge. They are fiercely independent, he said, with their own laws, and permit no police into their lands. There is, however, an administrative officer who is more or less responsible for the territory.

Everything he said reinforced the stories my father had told me about these Pathan marksmen, whom he'd admired, and who were now still as fierce and proud as when he was in the country. He had written a description of what it was like to serve there in the heat of the summer when the rest of the family had been in the exquisite coolness of Srinagar, swimming in the Dal Lake:

> Ponk [obviously a fictitious name] was the last place the Almighty made after he had run out of ideas. It is hidden in a baking valley in the N.W. Frontier. It consists of hard mud: a military outpost surrounded by barbed-wire. There is nothing green in sight, and the glare is such that everyone goes around in dark glasses. The water is piped into the garrison from a permanent piquet mounted over a spring. The pipe runs over naked rock and reaches a point close to boiling. The evening bath must be poured out several hours before it is required, and left to cool off sufficiently to become supportable. The officers' cook-house in this delectable spot is a sheet of tin, whereunder is a mud oven. The place is fly-ridden, except for two months when the heat gets so intense it kills the housefly but simultaneously gives birth to the sandfly whose bite injects and passes around a maddening species of virulent fever. Every year some of the garrison commit suicide. . . .

My uncle, Eric Gregory, had also been stationed on the North-West Frontier. A highly-strung, eccentric individual, I never knew whether or not to believe his stories, so far-fetched, they might have come out of *The Boys' Own Annual.* He was a colonel in the Intelligence Service and certainly did roam the bazaars to pick up information dressed as a

Pathan—we still have the clothes he wore. Apparently he darkened his face with walnut juice (he was a fair man) and probably used henna, a common adjunct, in his hair.

Interested in photography, he processed his own prints, keeping a giant enlarger in his office: "Those fellows were terrified. Always gave in. Never had to threaten them twice. I'd just turn the light on—show them how it worked—and tell them I'd put their heads under it and fry their brains if they didn't tell me what I wanted to know." He had a sudden laugh, a snort, and while he showed a photograph of some unfortunate man who was about to be interrogated, he would give this snorting laugh, indicating what energetic entertainment it had all been. It must actually have been a splendid idea since it did not involve any physical torture.

He told a story about being trapped on a hill on the Afghan border with his men during some troubles. They were outnumbered and surrounded by belligerent tribesmen. He claimed that if one of his men were killed, others instantly lopped off his head, put a red hot metal disc on his neck, and positioned his body downhill. With the nerves still working, the dead man would run towards their enemies who naturally thought the forces they were tackling were far larger than they'd supposed.

Eric, generous, hooting with laughter, drinking a *chota peg* while telling his outrageous stories, had remained in India until Partition when he'd driven around in a jeep trying to break up bloody confrontations. He was the last of a family to leave the country in which it had spent over a hundred years.

We passed long compounds, the same colour as the arid land, with high mud walls, some with beautiful gateways. Walter asked if the walls and the houses inside them are damaged in the monsoons. Zuheir said that yes, they're washed away, but are rebuilt. He told us twenty or thirty families, all related, live in each compound and that a man with a gun is on guard in each one night and day; there are constant skirmishes between extended families. The women and children seldom come out, and if a woman does she's heavily veiled. We asked him if his own wife was in *purdah* and his reply was typical: "It is the custom of our country."

We also drove by Afghan refugee compounds, which are identical to the others. Close to two million refugees had at one time or another

285

crossed a border which is so in name only: the Pathan tribes stretch over it. Zuheir told us the Afghans in these areas had brought wealth with them and purchased much land. As a result, Pakistan is suffering from inflation. He had no liking for them, saying they were crazy men, and wouldn't pause near their compounds. He also had no liking for India, which he claimed had trapped 100,000 Pakistani prisoners of war in Bangladesh during the last conflagration and had given them ground glass in their food.

We passed the odd man standing in a gateway. There and later, in Darra, inhabited by men and growing boys, I noticed the loose trousers and *kurtas*, like Eric's, but saw no pillbox hats, like his, although we did later find these in Peshawar. Here, they wore soft white caps. But we did occasionally come across men in decorated waistcoats, some sporting bright-orange hair.

We saw no women on the entire excursion into the tribal lands. Later, when we returned to New Delhi, we talked to a European who had worked with the Afghan refugees and was familiar with the Pathan compounds. He told us that after one particularly bloody feud, police and doctors had gone in to rescue badly injured, and in some cases dying, women and children. There had been a tremendous outcry, less because police had invaded the territory than because doctors had seen the faces of the women they'd taken to hospital.

We passed graveyards, some with brilliantly coloured tombs; the Moslems—and these are rigid fundamentalists—do not, of course, burn their dead. Apart from Christian plots, chiefly for the British, we'd come across none in India. These, as well as beef for sale and occasional thin, sway-backed brown cows rather than sleek white ones, along with elaborately painted trucks, buses, and even cars, were further differences.

Darra, the arms capital of the Province, to which we headed, is quite small: one long street with booths on either side, almost all manufacturing guns inside and selling them at open counters. A lively town, loud with gunfire as weapons are tested, it was established late in the last century under the aegis of the British with the odd notion that it would be better if the tribesmen made their own weapons rather than buy more accurate commercially manufactured ones. The canny British had asked for a return boon, which was granted: safe conduct along the frontier roads.

286

The weapons are still hand-made, skilfully crafted with pride in each step of the process, and—ironically—admired for their accuracy. Zuheir claimed that a Pathan craftsman has only to see a gun once to copy it in every respect and that men come from all over the world to buy these weapons. They are not sold to armies, he said, because there are not enough of them, but the tribesmen do well since there are constant skirmishes of one kind or another. Without being constricted by regulations, they also sell hashish and hard drugs—by the tonne to dealers, in manageable amounts to individuals. While we were watching a gunsmith turn metal on a lathe, a man across the narrow street beckoned Walter over in an attempt to sell him hashish. The vendor's stall was open—he could have been trading in vegetables—but Walter didn't buy any, rather thinking, apart from other considerations, our driver might not approve. However, when we questioned Zuheir later, he simply said, "What else can they do? These people have to make a living."

They appeared to make a good living—all were in spotless white clothes—and were handsome, cheerful, proud. Men on the street carried guns and some wore bandoliers filled with cartridges across their shoulders. They are exceptionally attractive. Even the air felt unencumbered: open prairie land stretching into the distance, no crowding, no beggars, no cripples, no police, simply men and their craft. Inside a shop, a young boy showed us various weapons, including a "pen gun": it was a replica of a pen made to be clipped to a breast pocket. To shoot it, one merely raised the clip. We were later amused to see a notice in the airport when we left Pakistan stating that pen guns were not permitted in hand luggage. We'd been told they kill people quite successfully.

The shop owner asked us if we'd like to try shooting: it would cost us ten rupees a bullet. Given a copy of a Russian Kalashnikoff, we went outside and first Walter aimed it at a stony hill behind the town. The explosion was very loud. I wanted to try, and the man who'd come with us looked surprised; in fact, I flattered myself with the possibility that he glanced at me with admiration: a woman and (no doubt) old? Fortunately, he and Walter adjusted the heavy weapon on my shoulder or I should certainly have dislocated it. The kick was tremendous and the noise deafening. Men are, without doubt, imbeciles.

❧

We'd been told by the Danish woman at the Naths in New Delhi that Peshawar, meaning "City of the Pathans," is filled with secret agents from all over the world; she said she could smell them. Even our guidebook recorded the same thing in less dramatic terms. It's little wonder, with its close proximity to Afghanistan (then backed by Russia), to China, to India, and with its subjection to the U.S. sphere of influence. This is the area where the Great Game was played (in part, of course, by Eric) and is no doubt still being played, if under a less romantic name.

We'd been booked into the Pearl Continental—the only large hotel I've ever yearned to return to. After huge baths, we enjoyed a bar for those without the Faith and an excellent smorgasbord. The most entertaining part of the evening and the next morning lay in trying to decide who were spies and who weren't. None of the guests—chiefly men in well-cut suits—spoke to us. But we did observe several young Americans and Germans who appeared to be in small national groups and who hobnobbed only within that group. The Germans swam and played in the pool: cocky, casual, used to the environment. We saw only two women, both English, unfriendly, middle-aged, conservatively dressed, and attached. Perhaps these various men were there merely on business or holiday, but they didn't give that impression: our noses twitched as we tried to emulate our Danish informant.

The next day Zuheir took us to the old city and the bazaar: crowded streets filled with smuggled goods coming from Russia by way of Afghanistan, silks from China, copper, brassware, exotic hand-made shoes, and jewellery, including rare lapis lazuli and silver ornaments sold by Afghan refugees.

He drove us to the museum containing Greek and Roman coins, Corinthian capitals, and a "Fasting Buddha" in stone, carved with wisps of material exposing each bone and ligament, a skeleton in the lotus position, hair knotted on top of the head, face calm and entranced. Certainly, this is how he must have appeared during seven years under the Bo tree, more like a starving mendicant than like the serene, well-fed figures found all over the world. The image delineated man's suffering as nakedly as his salvation.

We didn't see the Anglican church, another monument to British imperialism and probably one I'd gone to as a child, but we did go through the former cantonments with their tree-lined streets, where my family had lived so long ago and where much of what I remembered of my life in India had taken place. I knew this for certain later, when I checked with my mother. After some thought, she said that yes, we'd lived in Peshawar with summers in Srinagar the whole time Nana had been with us. Two years. It was where she had died. I hadn't connected this bleak period in my childhood with Dehra Dun, and I was correct.

It was dusk by the time we reached the huge graveyard, apparently attached to the church by another entrance, and looked at some of the grave markers. We happened to come in by a gate close to an area where many British children had been buried. Not far away, there were also adult graves. The ground was hard packed, not cared for, with fallen markers left where they had collapsed. Only one monument was recent —that of a woman of eighty-five who'd died in England and whose ashes had been sent out for burial beside her husband, interred forty years before. Several young soldiers, twenty-one and twenty-two years old, probably killed in skirmishes, had been buried by their comrades. One stone signified a medical officer, Master of the Vale Hunt, who'd been thrown from his horse into a river and drowned while hunting in 1931. My father no doubt knew him. Another, much earlier stone, had an unfortunate inscription: "Captain Ernest Bloomfield, accidently shot by his orderly, March 2, 1879. Well done good and faithful servant."

By chance, in the children's area the time stretched from 1922 to 1929, which included the years we were there. The crosses were pathetic. Most of the children—and there were many—had died before they were five years old, some when they were only a few days. One inscription commemorated Mavis, beloved only child of her parents. Most crosses —a faint breath of hope—were engraved with: "He [She] is not dead, but sleepeth." All these graves, except for the one containing ashes, dated before the 1940s. They were a testament to the approaching end of the British Empire.

Dawn, my sister, had been dangerously ill with dysentery in Peshawar and had been tirelessly nursed by Nana. My parents had said, more than once, if it hadn't been for that devotion she would have died. She would have been buried in this graveyard. I also was constantly ill, and could have all too easily been buried among those whose remains, if any, lay at our feet.

Reading headstones in this silent, neglected place, I knew with absolute and unexpected certainty that my search was over. I knew, even before I recognized that this must be where Nana had been buried. Here, so remote from my later life, the pain of childhood was finally confronted and quietly laid to rest: pain engendered less by an individual than by a tradition.

I also knew that I wouldn't need to return to India again. If I did, it would be merely as a tourist. I'd not found a metaphysical enlightenment, but I had been enlightened and I had learned what I needed to learn.

The graveyard was huge and night was falling. It would be impossible to find Nana's grave. In any case, she'd always been Nana, and although I'd found that single letter from her to my mother, I had not particularly noted her name. Even my mother had forgotten it.[23]

---

[23] After returning from Pakistan, I read *To the Frontier* by Geoffrey Moorhouse. He also visited the graveyard and found the same area as the one I mention although his markers vary in some respects from mine. He states that he couldn't find the amusing inscription about the "good and faithful servant" mentioned in his guidebook. It was not referred to in mine, but certainly exists.

Glossary

Aditi: mother of all the gods.

Akond: title formerly given to rulers of Swat.

Anna: small currency, one sixteenth of a rupee; no longer used.

Ashram: a secluded place for a community of Hindus.

Atman: the universal soul.

Ayah: child's nurse; also ladies' maid.

Babu: Indian clerk: lit. honorific "father," but also derogatory.

Baksheesh: alms; led to buckshee, meaning "free."

Bangla: intoxicant.

Banya: moneylender.

Bearer: *Sahib's* valet.

Bhagavad Gita: "Celestial Song"; section of the *Mahabharata* in which Krishna reveals himself as god incarnate.

Bhakta: worshipper.

Bhakti: to worship; thus *bhakti* poetry.

Bhangi: an untouchable.

Bhisthi: Anglo-India variation *bheesti*; water carrier.

Biga: an acre.

Box-wallah: a European businessman, generally derogatory, derived from an Indian door-to-door salesman.

Brahma: var. Brahman; supreme God in some traditions, maker of the universe.

Brahman: var. brahmin; one belonging to the priestly or educated caste, now considered, particularly by Westerners, to be the highest caste but in historical terms the system was not hierarchical: the three upper castes could wear the sacred thread and each had specific, differing duties. According to Bharati, in northern and central India a *banya* (a merchant, member of the *vaisya* caste) may be considered to belong to the highest and richest caste. Gandhi was a *banya*.

Obviously this is too complex a matter for a non-Indologist like myself.

Brata: vow, small instructional prayer, generally in rhyme.

Bundobust: var. *bandobast*; arrangements; lit. "tie up loose ends."

Burqqa: var. *burka*; garment worn by Moslem women which covers the entire body.

Chappals: sandals.

Charpoi: var. *charpoy*; wooden frame bed with webbing; lit. "four legs."

Chatti: clay container, especially cup for tea.

Chee-chee: derogatory adjective, chiefly for Eurasians, derived from rhythms in speech.

Chorten: Tibetan word for *stupa*.

Chota: small

Chota hazri: breakfast.

Chota peg: single whisky.

Chaukidar: Anglo-Indian var. *chokidar*; watchman; in Hindi—*jo admi ghar ke sanhne sota hai*—"the guy who sleeps in front of the house." Not intended facetiously, but apparently all too often true.

Chela: disciple.

Dal: var. *dhal*; lentils.

Dandy: open litter, much used in the Himalayas, carried by four *dandy-wallahs*.

Darzi: Anglo-Indian var. *derzi*; dressmaker, tailor.

Deha-shuddhi: a strict course of discipline entailing complex religious demands and taboos.

Devadasis: var. *devadassis*: hand-maidens to the god; perhaps temple prostitutes.

Dharma: the path, the Sacred Law, class and stage of life.

Dhobi: washerman.

Dhoti: loincloth. In caste Hindus the cloth is pulled up between the legs.

Dooli: var. *dooley*. Covered litter.

Durbar: court, levee.

Durga: Goddess Parvati, consort of Shiva, in her terrifying aspect; lit. "difficult to penetrate."

Durrie: coarse cotton or wool rug woven in India.

Galla Walla: a British recruiter.

Gecko: small lizard.

Gali: to abuse, harass.

Ganja: hashish.

Gaushalas: old cow asylums; also called *pinjrapoles*.

Ghat: steps or landing on a river; area for ritual bathing or for burning corpses.

Ghee: clarified butter.

Godown: warehouse, storage space.

Gompa: Tibetan Buddhist monastery.

Gopuram: pyramidal gateway tower of Dravidian temple.

Gopi: milkmaid; Radha, beloved of Krishna, is a *gopi*.

Gussal-khana: bathroom.

Guru: master, teacher, holy man.

Harijans: "Children of God," Gandhi's gentle name for untouchables. These people are now referred to as the "scheduled castes."

Haveli: mansion with an interior courtyard.

Hijra: one who is neither man nor woman; a man whose outer sexual organs have been removed. His/her function is to go through certain rituals at the baptism of an infant.

Hindustani: dialect combining Hindi and Urdu, once *lingua franca* of almost all India.

Holi: An Indian spring festival, claimed by some British to be a fertility festival.

ICS: Indian Civil Service.

IMS: Indian Medical Service.

Kali: the black goddess of death and destruction; an aspect of Parvati in the Shakti pantheon.

Kama: desire, physical passion; Kama is the god of love; hence *Kama Sutra*, a treatise on positions for love-making. See Manmata.

Kamiz: long shirt.

Karma: effect of former deeds, performed in this life and in previous ones, on one's present and future condition.

Khansaman: cook; lit. "he who is in charge of the utensils."

Khidmatgar: Anglo-Indian var. *khitmagar*, which in actual fact, according to Bharati but unknown to the British, means "a crocodile wallowing in human feces." A servant who waits at table, etc.

Khush: happy; persons are *kush*; n. *khushi,* happiness.

Krishna: Pastoral hero and amorous lover of Radha; as supreme lord he is an incarnation of Vishnu.

Kshatriya: warrior caste of the Hindus; warrior aristocracy.

Kukri: short Gurkha weapon with curved blade.

Kurta: man's shirt with long tails.

Lathi: a long stick used as staff or weapon.

Lakh: Anglo-Indian var. *lac*; a hundred thousand.

Lakshmi: goddess of the lotus, good luck, prosperity; consort of Vishnu.

Lassi: a delicious milk drink.

Lingam: var. *linga*; phallus; the symbol of Shiva with numinous connotation.

Machan: shooting platform.

Mahabharata: epic poem telling of the civil war in the kingdom of the Kurus.

Mahant: A wealthy Hindu office-holder.

Mahout: elephant rider, master.

Maidan: open place, public land.

Mali: gardener.

Mandala: visual representation containing the archetypal keys and symbols necessary for spiritual understanding and growth. Principal function is to aid in meditation.

Mani stone: stone carved with Tibetan-Buddhist chant, *om mani padme hum*—"Hail to the jewel in the lotus"—and with other significant religious depictions.

Manmata: also known as Kama. The god of love, equipped with a bow of sugar cane, bowstring of murmuring bees, and shafts of fragrant flowers.

Mantra: Magical verbal formula used in meditation.

Masalchee: scullion, lower servant.

Mashaira: poetry reading.

Masjid: mosque.

Maya: illusion, dream; interpretation of the whole phenomenal universe, including the gods themselves, as illusionary.

Memsahib: lady; from "madam-sahib."

Mogul: var. Mughal, Moghul;. Moslem dynasty that ruled large parts of north-western India from early sixteenth century to mid-eighteenth century.

Mulligatawny: Anglo-Indian for *mulakka tanni*, meaning "pepper water," comes from Tamil.

Muri: fried snack-food.

Nandin: mount of Shiva; a bull.

Nirvana: In Buddhism, the complete extinction of all ties to the phenomenal world of *maya*.

Paisa: var. pice; small coin, one hundredth of a rupee.

Pandit: teacher or wise man.

Pardah: var. *purdah*: seclusion once expected of high-class Indian women; lit. screen or veil; for Hindu women it means distance from male affiliative relatives. Still in use among Moslems.

Parvati: "Daughter of the Mountains"; consort of Shiva; embodiment of peace and beauty.

Phuka: unhappy practice of irritating a cow's vagina to make it produce more milk. Outlawed by British.

Pi dog: mongrel. *Pi* dogs are found all over India; term originates with "pariah."

Pice: var. paisa.

Puja: worship, prayer.

Pukka: var. *Pukkah*; proper. A Raj term; e.g., *pukka* sahib, meaning "real gentleman."

Pagri: Anglo-Indian var. *puggaree*. Turban.

Radha: Consort of Krishna; his favourite *gopi*; in some traditions, she embodies *shakti*, the female energy of the gods, the active, energetic aspect of a god personified as his wife.

Rajput: Hindu rulers of Rajasthan and the Punjab hills. No longer titled.

Rama: hero of the *Ramayana*.

Ramayana: great epic poem to do with the abduction of Sita, Rama's wife, by the demon king Ravana.

Rath: enormous carved chariot used for transporting the gods.

Rickshaw: two-wheeled vehicle, generally pulled by a man on a bicycle; originally pulled by a man on foot, many are now motorized.

Rupee: chief Indian currency. In the late nineteen-eighties, the Indian rupee varied in value from ten to sixteen rupees to one U.S. dollar. In Pakistan, the rupee levelled at twenty-three to the U.S. dollar. In about 1930, there were three rupees to the dollar.

Sahib: sir, lord.

Salaam: salutation, ceremonial greeting.

Samadhi: ecstatic state; union with God.

Samosa: curried vegetable snacks wrapped in a pastry triangle.

Sannyasin: Hindu ascetic, often devoted to Shiva.

Sanskrit: classical language of ancient India.

Sarasvati: river goddess identified with wisdom and music; depicted with the swan; sometimes daughter and consort of Brahma.

Sari: Indian woman's costume.

Sati: good wife; a virtuous woman, especially a widow immolating herself on her husband's funeral pyre. In some traditions, Sati, a goddess, is an aspect of Parvati, consort of Shiva.

Ser: a weight slightly above a kilogram.

Shalwar: pantaloons.

Shameez: female version of *kurta*, the knee-length shirt.

Shamiana: canopy, awning.

Shikar: hunting expedition.

Shikara: gondola-like boat used on the Dal Lake.

Shikari: big-game hunter; used here in sense of expedition.

Shirley Temple: a non-alcoholic drink.

Shiva: var. Siva; great Hindu god characterized by his cosmic energy; "Lord of the Dance"; like Kali, he is both creative and destructive.

Shoe-trees: a device inserted in a shoe to maintain its shape.

Siddhartha: name of the Buddha.

Sircar: government in complimentary sense.

Sita: virtuous wife of Rama.

Stupa: Hemispherical mound associated with Buddhism and Jainism, symbolizing the universe itself; originally intended to contain relics.

Sudra: lowest of the four castes; not to be mistaken for untouchables which in a true sense have no caste.

Surya: sun god.

Swami: title given to initiated monks; means "Lord of the Self."

Syce: groom.

Tanka: var. *thanka*; Tibetan painting on cloth scroll, generally depicting the lineage of a teaching, used as a visualization for meditation.

Tantra: A Hindu religious order marked by mysticism, magic, and the belief that informed sexual union may lead to illumination; hence tantric.

Thuggee: religiously inspired assassins, devotees of Kali.

Tiffin: snack, particularly at lunch time. Raj term.

Tikka: a dab of generally dark red ointment placed by a priest over the "third" eye in the forehead. It signifies a blessing.

Tonga: a two-wheeled horse or pony carriage.

Topee: var. *topi*; a light-weight hat or helmet made of cork.

Tulsi: household tree (basil), sacred to Vishnu/Krishna; tended by women.

Vaisyas: members of merchant caste.

Varaha: boar; third incarnation of Vishnu.

Virasaivas: saints; those people who sing hymns to Lord Shiva.

Vishnu: Hindu god associated with creation and preservation myths; his various incarnations restore the balance of the cosmos.

Wallah: person, fellow.

Yoga: school of philosophy and psycho-physical discipline.

Yogi: one who practises yoga.

Yuga: one of the four vast measures of time which in aggregate form a time-cycle (*mahayuga*), at the end of which the world is purified through total destruction; after destruction, a new cycle begins.

Yoni: female genitalia; a pedestal encircling the *lingam.*

Select Bibliography

Allen, Charles, ed. *Plain Tales from the Raj.* Futura Publications Limited, London, 1975.

Basham, A. L. *The Wonder that was India.* Grove Press, New York, 1959.

Blaise, Clark and Mukherjee, Bharati. *Days and Nights in Calcutta.* Doubleday, New York, 1977.

India, a travel survival kit. Lonely Planet, U.S.A., 1984.

Isherwood, Christopher and Prabhavananda (Swami). *The Bhagavad Gita.* Penguin, London.

Kashmir, Ladakh and Zanskar, a travel survival kit. Lonely Planet, U.S.A., 1985.

Lal, P., trans. *The Mahabharata.* Tarang Paperbacks, Vicas, New Delhi, 1989.

———. *The Ramayana.* Tarang Paperbacks, Vicas, New Delhi, 1989.

LaPierre, Dominique (trans. Kathryn Spink). *The City of Joy.* Century, U.S.A., 1985.

Matthiessen, Peter. *The Snow Leopard.* Viking Penguin, N.Y., 1984.

Mayo, Katherine. *Mother India.* Harcourt, Brace, and Co., U.S.A., 1927.

Moorhouse, Geoffrey. *India Britannica.* Paladin Books, London, 1984.

Narayan, R. K. *Gods, Demons, and Others.* Bantam, U.S.A., 1964.

Radhakrishnan, S. *The Bhagavadgita.* Blackie and Son, Bombay, 1982.

Ramanujan, A. K., trans. *Speaking of Siva.* Penguin, 1973.

Romain, Rolland (trans. E. F. Malcolm-Smith). *The Life of Vivekanada and the Universal Gospel.* Advaita Ashrama, Calcutta, tenth impression, 1984.

Tucci, Sandro. *Gurkhas.* Hamish Hamilton, London, 1985.

Wiser, William and Charlotte. *Behind Mud Walls 1930-1960.* University of California, U.S.A., 1967.

Index

First Journey

BEGINS AT CALCUTTA
ENDS AT NEW DELHI

1 **Calcutta** via plane to . . .
2 **Madras** via motor rickshaw to . . .
3 **Mahabalipuram** . . .
4 **Chidambaram** . . .
5 **Tanjore** and finally . . .
6 **Madurai** via plane to . . .
7 **Hyderabad**, another plane to . . .
8 **Bhubaneshwar** via train to . . .
9 **Puri**, 9A **Konarak** via train back to . . .
1 **Calcutta**, then train to . . .
10 **Varanasi** (Benares), by bus to . . .
11 **Sarnath** and back; train to . . .
12 **Bareilly**, then by rail and bus to . . .
13 **Nainital** via buses to . . .
14 **Jim Corbet National Park** . . .
15 **Ramnigar**, 16 **Hardwar** . . .
17 **Dehra Dun**, still on buses to . . .
18 **Rishikesh**, 19 **Mussoorie**, train to . . .
20 **New Delhi** via trains and bus to . . .
21 **Agra**, 22 **Fatehpur Sikri** and . . .
23 **Jaipur**, auto trip; then rail to . . .
24 **Shekhavati**, back to 20 **New Delhi**.

Second Journey

BEGINS AT NEW DELHI
AND RETURNS

20 **New Delhi** via plane to . . .
25 **Srinagar**, 4-wheel drive to . . .
26 **Drass**, 27 **Kargil**, and 28 **Padum** . . .
25 **Srinagar** via plane to . . .
20 **New Delhi**, another plane to . . .
29 **Islamabad**, by car to 30 **Rawalpindi** . . .
31 **Attock**, 32 **Darra**, 33 **Peshawar**
29 **Islamabad** via plane to . . .
20 **New Delhi**, 34 **Khajuraho**, a side trip.

AFGHANISTAN

IRAN

PAKISTAN

Arabian Sea

✹ CITIES WITH AIRPORTS